HOME &
SCHOOL

Royal
Geographical
Society
with IBG

David & Jill Wright

CHILDREN'S SCHOOL ATLAS

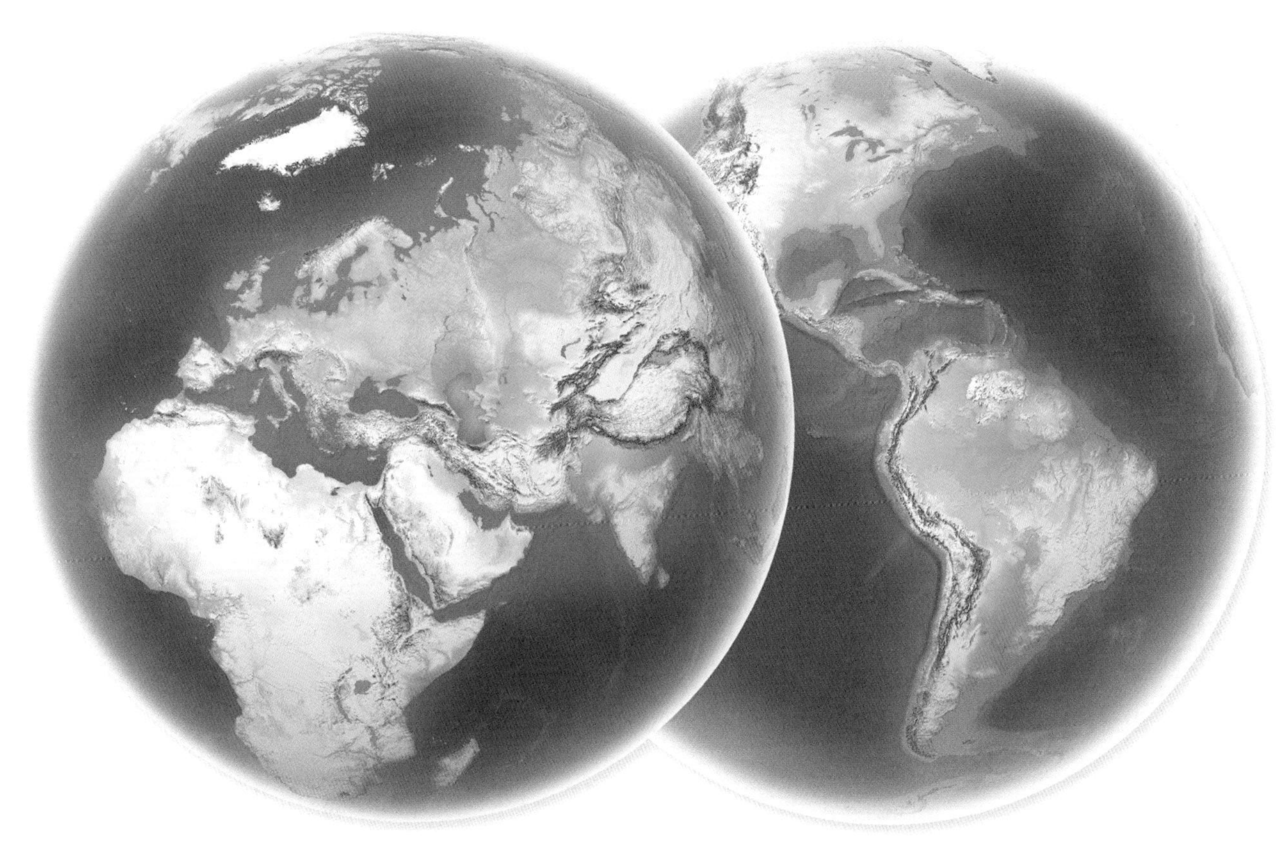

CONTENTS

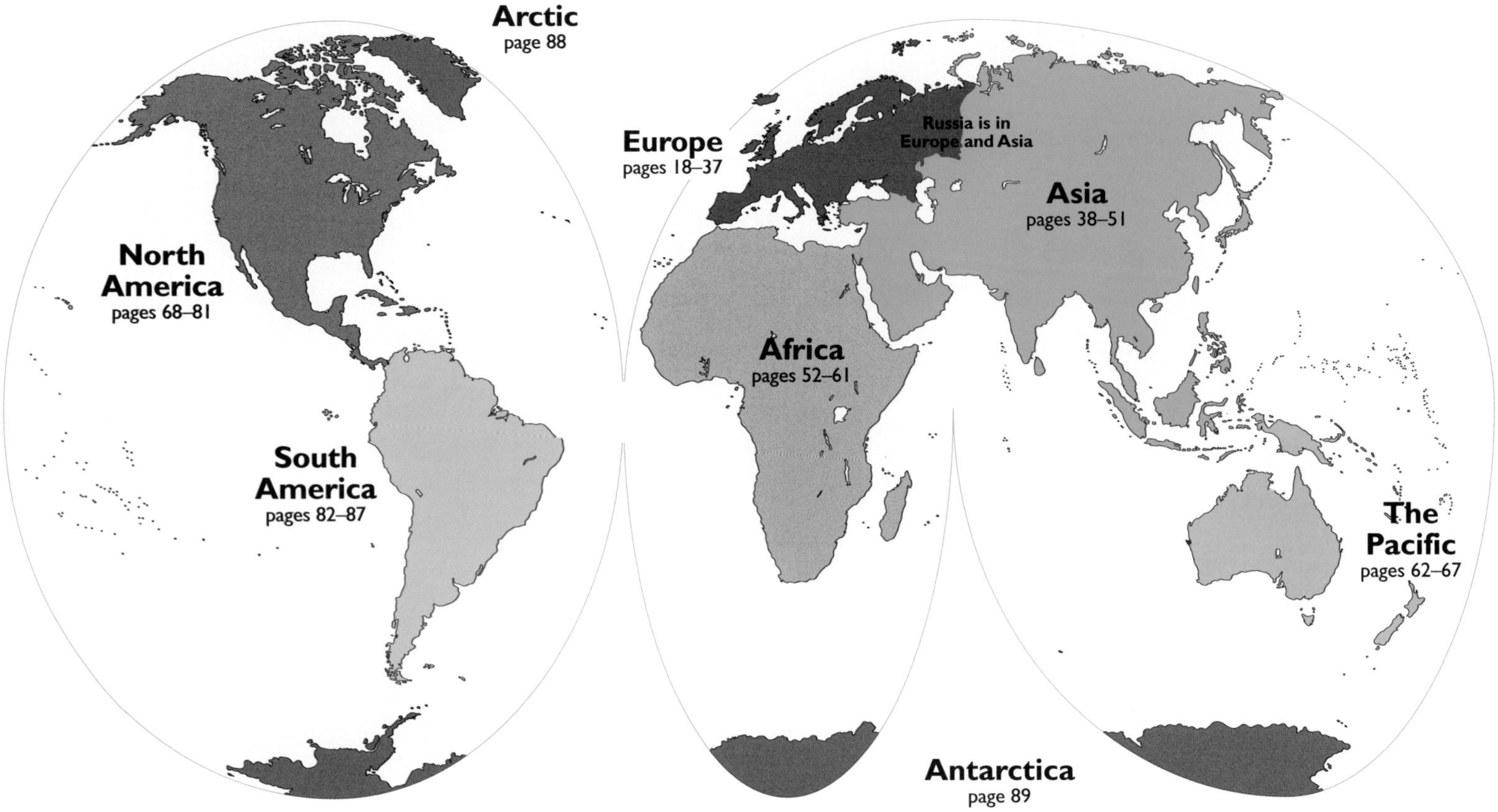

Arctic page 88

Europe pages 18–37

Russia is in Europe and Asia

Asia pages 38–51

North America pages 68–81

Africa pages 52–61

South America pages 82–87

The Pacific pages 62–67

Antarctica page 89

TO HELP YOU FIND YOUR WAY ....

Each continent is COLOUR-CODED on this map
AND on the contents page (opposite) AND on the heading of each atlas page.

ABOUT THIS ATLAS

Philip's Children's Atlas is written by people who enjoy learning about our wonderful world and want others to enjoy it, too. David and Jill Wright have taught geography in schools and colleges. We have visited more than a hundred countries to understand the scenery and people better and to take photographs. Some of these visits have been made with our own children or with student groups. This has helped us to see the world through children's eyes.

There is so much we want to tell you about, and so little space. We have had to choose what to write about and what to leave out – very hard! The world is always changing too, and this new edition has the very latest facts and figures. So we hope this atlas will help YOU, the reader, to begin a lifelong exploration of the world, to notice all the links we have with all parts of the world, and to find out more from other books and websites.

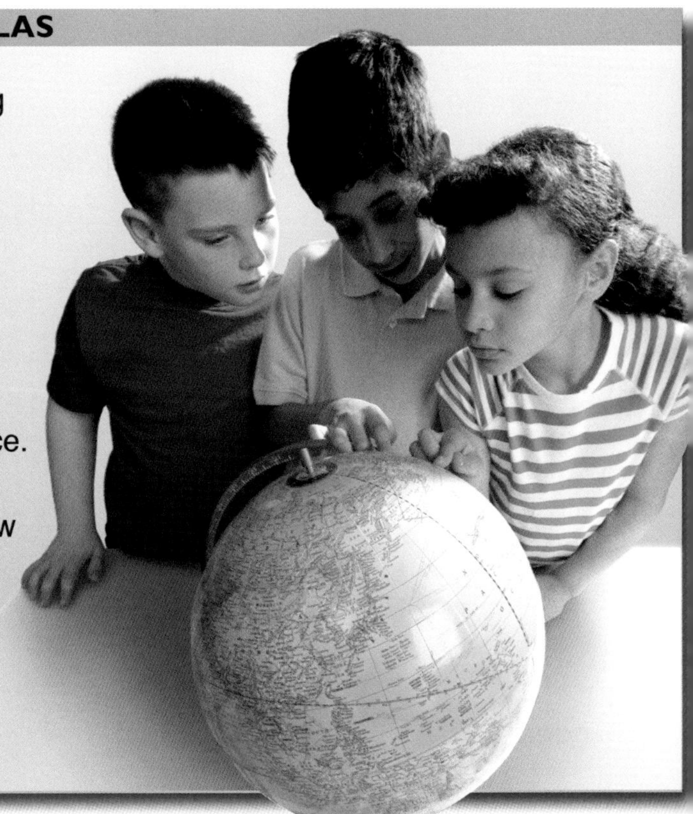

OUR PLANET EARTH

Our Planet Earth 4–5
Mountains, Plains and Seas 6–7
The Countries of the World 8–9
People of the World 10–11
Cold and Hot Lands 12–13
Wet and Dry Lands 14–15
Enjoying Maps 16–17

EUROPE

Europe 18–19
Scandinavia 20–21
The UK and Ireland 22–23
Benelux 24–25
France 26–27
Germany and Austria 28–29
Spain and Portugal 30–31
Switzerland and Italy 32–33
South-east Europe 34–35
Eastern Europe 36–37

ASIA

Asia 38–39
Russia and Neighbours 40–41
Middle East 42–43
South Asia 44–45
South-east Asia 46–47
China and Mongolia 48–49
Japan and Korea 50–51

AFRICA

Africa 52–53
North Africa 54–55
West Africa 56–57
Central and East Africa 58–59
Southern Africa 60–61

THE PACIFIC

The Pacific 62–63
Australia 64–65
New Zealand 66–67

NORTH AMERICA

North America 68–69
Canada 70–71
United States of America 72–73
Eastern USA 74–75
Western USA 76–77
Central America 78–79
West Indies 80–81

SOUTH AMERICA

South America 82–83
Tropical South America 84–85
Temperate South America 86–87

THE ARCTIC AND ANTARCTICA

The Arctic 88
Antarctica 89

QUIZ QUESTIONS AND INDEX

Quiz Questions 90–91
Index 92–95
Glossary 96–97
Answers to Questions 97

OUR PLANET EARTH

OUR Earth is made of layers of rock. The diagram below shows the Earth with a slice cut out. The hottest part is the core, at the centre. Around the core is the mantle, which is probably slightly liquid and moves very slowly. The outer layer, the crust, is quite thin under the oceans, but it is thicker under the continents.

Scientists now know that the Earth's crust is cracked, like the shell of a hard-boiled egg that has been dropped. The cracks are called faults. The huge sections of crust divided by the faults are called plates and they are moving very, very slowly. The continents have gradually moved across the Earth's surface as the crustal plates have moved. Sudden movements near the faults cause volcanic eruptions or earthquakes. Undersea earthquakes cause huge waves called tsunamis.

▲ ***The Earth from space:*** *this satellite image shows Africa, Arabia, the Mediterranean Sea and Europe. The Sahara Desert has no cloud and is all sunny. Some of the white clouds near the Equator show where there are thunderstorms.*

Can you name the oceans to the west (left) and to the east (right) of Africa? And can you name the continent – and the country – on the far west (left) of this image? (The maps on pages 7 and 8 will help you. Answers on page 97.)

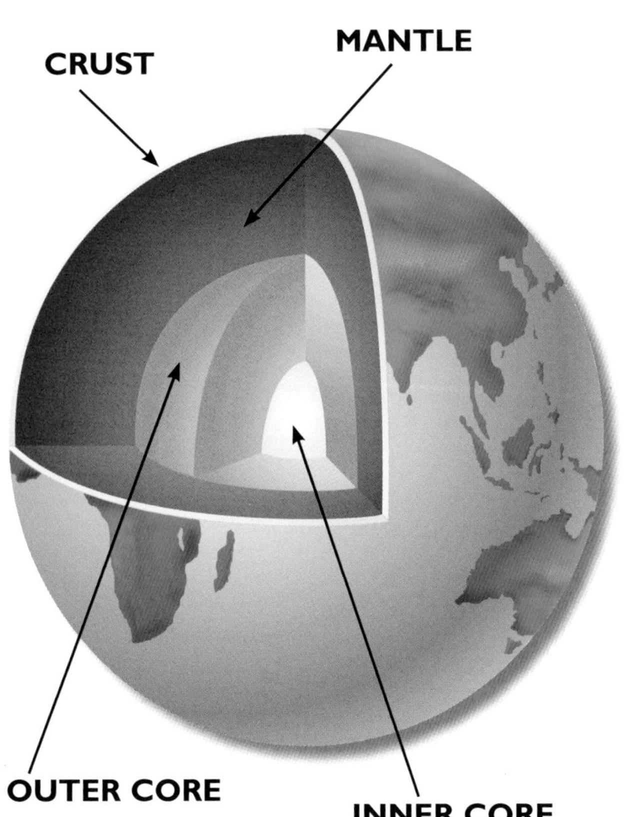

FASCINATING FACTS ABOUT THE EARTH

DISTANCE AROUND THE EQUATOR 40,075 kilometres
DISTANCE AROUND THE POLES 40,007 kilometres
DISTANCE TO THE CENTRE OF THE EARTH 6370 kilometres
SURFACE AREA OF THE EARTH 510,065,600 square kilometres
PROPORTIONS OF SEA AND LAND 71% sea; 29% land
DISTANCE FROM THE EARTH TO THE SUN 150,000,000 kilometres
(It takes 8½ minutes for the Sun's light to reach the Earth.)
DISTANCE FROM THE EARTH TO THE MOON 384,400 kilometres
THE EARTH TRAVELS AROUND THE SUN at 107,000 kilometres per hour, or nearly 30 kilometres per second
THE EARTH'S ATMOSPHERE is about 175 kilometres high
CHIEF GASES IN THE ATMOSPHERE Nitrogen 78%; oxygen 21%
AVERAGE DEPTH OF SEA 3900 metres
AVERAGE HEIGHT OF LAND 880 metres

The Earth travels round the Sun in 365¼ days, which we call a year. Every four years we add an extra day to February to use up the ¼ days. This is called a Leap Year. The Earth travels at a speed of over 107,000 kilometres an hour. (You have travelled 600 kilometres through space while reading this!)

The Earth also spins round and round as it travels through space. It spins round once in 24 hours, which we call a day. Places on the Equator are spinning at 1660 kilometres an hour. Because of the way the Earth moves, we experience day and night, and different seasons during a year (see page 13). No part of our planet is too hot or too cold for life to survive. Yet the Earth is 150 million kilometres from the Sun.

The Moon is our nearest neighbour in space. It is 384,400 kilometres away. The first men to reach the Moon took four days to travel there in 1969. On the way, they took many photos of the Earth, such as the one on the left. The Earth looks very blue from space because of all the sea. It is the only planet in the Solar System with sea. Look at the swirls of cloud. These show that the Earth has an atmosphere. Our atmosphere contains oxygen and water vapour, and it keeps all living things alive.

The diagram below shows all the planets in our Solar System. The Earth is the third planet from the Sun.

THE SOLAR SYSTEM – RELATIVE SIZES OF THE PLANETS

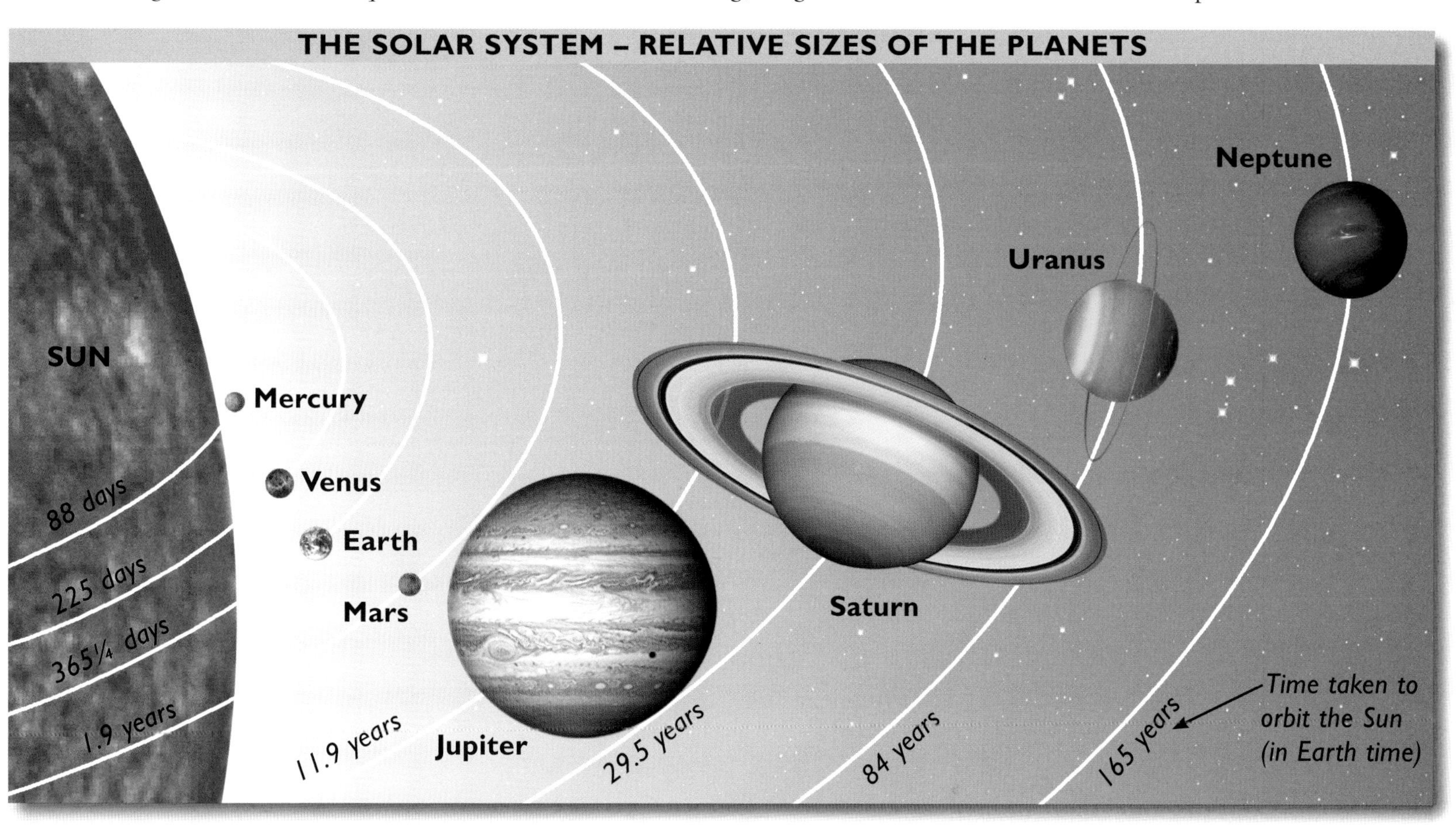

OUR WONDERFUL WORLD

Earth is the only planet in the Solar System – and might be the only one in the whole Universe – to have life.

Our atmosphere keeps temperatures exactly right for all the different species. And the dominant species is us – human beings. There are lots of us (page 10) and most of what we produce depends on burning oil, gas or coal. This produces Carbon Dioxide (CO_2). Although CO_2 makes up a very small part of the atmosphere it has a very big effect. For the past 200 years richer countries have put more and more CO_2 and other gases into the atmosphere. These change the balance of the atmosphere, which acts like a blanket trapping the sun's heat so that the earth is getting warmer – like being in a greenhouse.

As more people understand Global warming and notice how the climate is changing (page 15) they are asking governments to act to stop pollution and to produce 'clean energy' by using the sun and wind to make electricity. Trees absorb CO_2 and there are campaigns to stop more forest being cut down (for example, in the Amazon, page 84) and to plant more trees where they can help prevent floods or stop deserts spreading.

MOUNTAINS, PLAINS AND SEAS

THE map shows that there is much more sea than land in the world. Over two-thirds of the Earth's surface is covered with water or ice. The Pacific is by far the biggest ocean; the map splits it in two.

The mountains are shown with shadows on this map. Look for the world's highest mountain range – the Himalayas, in Asia. There are high mountains on the western side of both American continents. Most of the world's great mountain ranges have been made by folding in the Earth's crust.

The green expanse across northern Europe and northern Asia is the world's biggest plain.

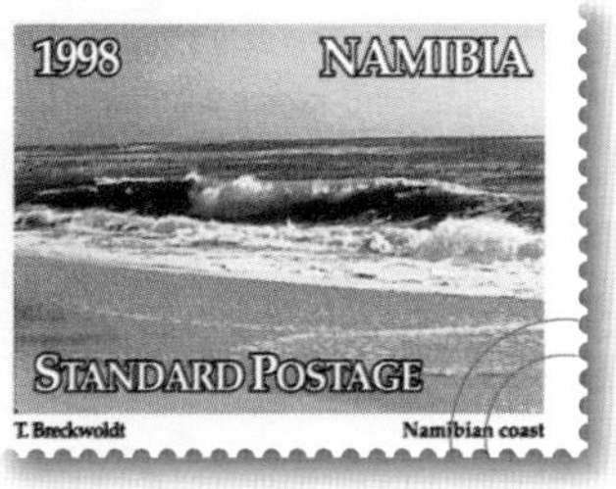

▲ ***The Atlantic Ocean** washes the desert shore of Namibia, in southern Africa.*

MOUNTAINS AND PLAINS

In which country does this animal live? (***Answer on page 97.***)

▲ ***Farming the Great Plains of North America.** The Plains cover large areas of the USA and Canada. This land in Alberta, Canada, has just been harvested. The almost flat land of the Great Plains ends where the Rocky Mountains begin.*

*To see all of **Antarctica** turn to page 89.*

WORLD RECORDS: LARGEST • LONGEST • HIGHEST • DEEPEST

LARGEST OCEAN Pacific, 155,557,000 sq km
DEEPEST PART OF OCEANS Mariana Trench, 11,022 metres (Pacific)
LARGEST LAKE Caspian Sea, 371,000 sq km (Europe and Asia)
DEEPEST LAKE Lake Baikal, 1620 metres (Russia)

LONGEST RIVERS Nile, 6695 km (Africa); Amazon, 6450 km (South America); Yangtze, 6380 km (Asia)
LARGEST ISLANDS Australia, 7,690,000 sq km; Greenland, 2,175,600 sq km
LARGEST DESERT Sahara, 9,100,000 sq km (Africa)

HIGHEST MOUNTAIN Everest, 8849 m (Asia)
LONGEST MOUNTAIN RANGE Andes, 7200 km (South America)
LONGEST GORGE Grand Canyon, 446 km (North America)
HIGHEST WATERFALL Angel Falls, 979 metres (Venezuela, South America)

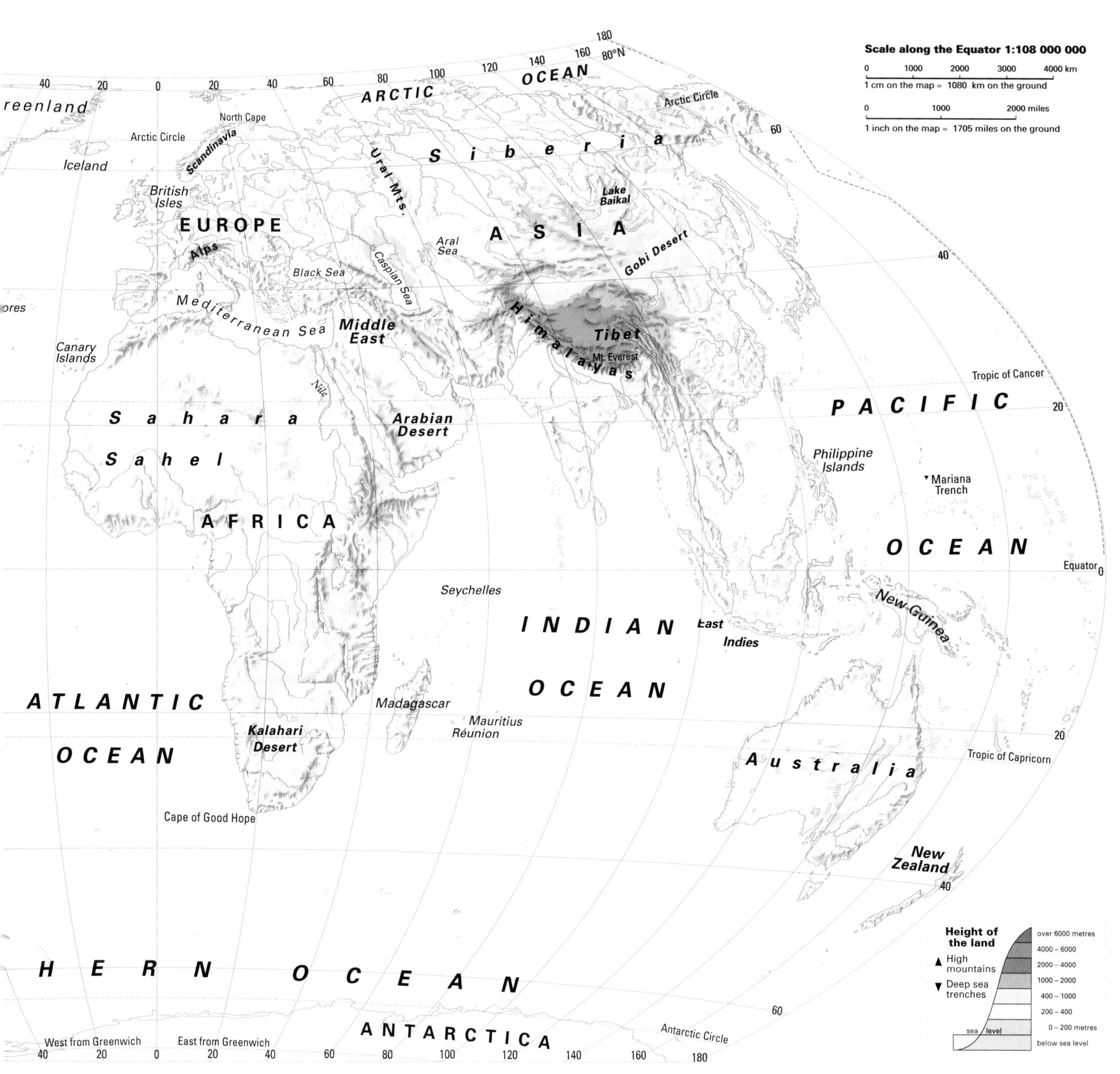

THE COUNTRIES OF THE WORLD

FIVE of the continents of the world are divided into countries.

Look at the borders between countries: they have all been decided by people. Some follow natural features, such as rivers or mountain ranges. But some borders separate people of the same language, and this can cause problems.

This map has been drawn to show each country at the correct size. So you can see which countries are big, which are middle-sized and which are small. But because the sizes are correct, some of the shapes are not quite right. To see **both** correct size **and** correct shape we all need to look at a globe.

▲ ***The United Nations flag*** *with an unusual map of the world surrounded by olive branches for peace.*

A D-I-Y QUIZ

On this map, some small countries are labelled with only the first few letters of their name. Try to guess the whole name. Then check your answers on the continent maps: *Europe page 19; Asia page 39; Africa page 53; Pacific pages 62–63; West Indies page 81; South America page 83.*

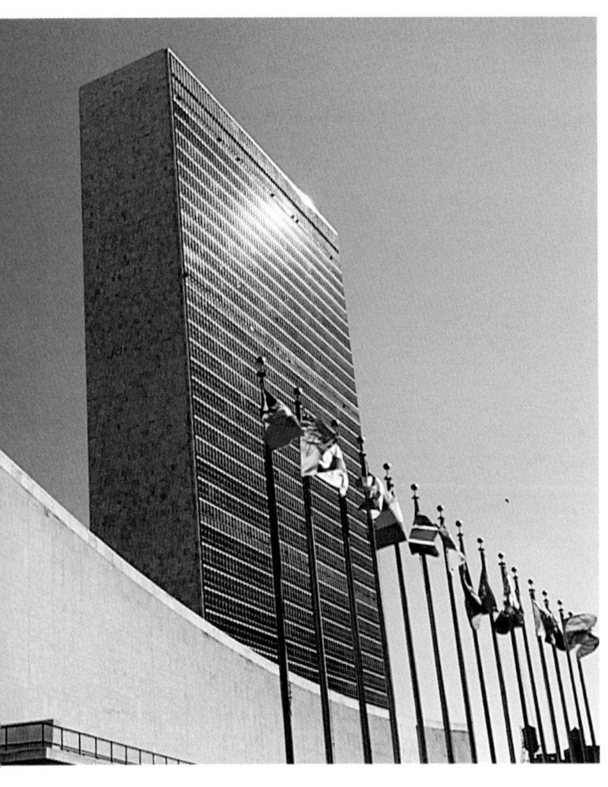

▲ ***The United Nations building,*** *in New York City, USA. The world's problems are discussed here – and sometimes solved.*

180 160 140 120 100 80
80°N
Arctic Circle
Alaska (U.S.A.)
60
CANADA
40
UNITED STATES
ATLANTI
Tropic of Cancer
BAHAMAS
OCEAN
MEXICO
CUBA
20
Hawaiian Islands (U.S.A.)
JAMAICA
HAITI
DOM. REP.
ANTIGUA & B.
DOMINICA
BELIZE
ST. KITTS & N.
ST. LUCIA
GUATEMALA
HONDURAS
EL SALVADOR
ST.VINCENT
BARBADOS
GRENADA
TRINIDAD & TOBAGO
NICARAGUA
International Date Line
COSTA RICA
VENEZUELA
PANAMA
GUYANA
PACIFIC
SURINAME
French Guiana
COLOMBIA
0
Equator
Galapagos Islands (Ecuador)
ECUADOR
KIRIBATI
PERU
BRAZIL
SAMOA
AMERICAN SAMOA
OCEAN
BOLIVIA
TONGA
20
PARAGUAY
Tropic of Capricorn
URUGUAY
CHILE
ARGENTINA
40
Falkland Islands (U.K.)
SO
60
Antarctic Circle
180 160 140 120 100 80

WHICH ARE THE WORLD'S BIGGEST COUNTRIES?

Only five of the 'top ten' countries with large populations are also among the 'top ten' biggest countries.

TOP TEN COUNTRIES BY SIZE (SQUARE KILOMETRES)

1.	Russia	17,075,400	6.	Australia	7,741,220
2.	Canada	9,970,610	7.	India	3,287,263
3.	USA	9,629,091	8.	Argentina	2,780,400
4.	China	9,596,961	9.	Kazakhstan	2,724,900
5.	Brazil	8,514,215	10.	Algeria	2,381,741

TOP TEN COUNTRIES BY POPULATION

1.	China	1398 million	6.	Nigeria	220 million
2.	India	1339 million	7.	Brazil	213 million
3.	USA	335 million	8.	Bangladesh	164 million
4.	Indonesia	275 million	9.	Russia	142 million
5.	Pakistan	238 million	10.	Mexico	130 million

PEOPLE OF THE WORLD

THERE is *one* race of people: the human race. In Latin, we are all known as *Homo sapiens* – 'wise person'. The differences between people, such as dark or light skin, hair and eyes, are small.

The smaller map (below) shows the rich and the poor countries of the world. In any one country there are rich and poor people, but the difference between countries is even greater.

The map shows that the richest countries are in North America, Europe, Japan and Australia. Here most people usually have plenty to eat. They can buy many kinds of food; they can go to a doctor or hospital when they need to, and the children can go to school.

The richest countries are the ones that control most of the world's trade and make decisions about international rules. But they also give aid to help the poorer countries.

The poorest countries (shown in dark green) are in the tropics – mostly in Africa. Life in these countries is very different from life in the rich world. Many people struggle to grow enough food, and they are often hungry.

People who do not have enough to eat find it difficult to work hard and they get ill more easily. They do not have enough money to pay for medicines or to send their children to school to learn to read and write. Some of the poorest people live in shanty towns in or near large cities.

But many people in the tropics do manage to break out of this 'cycle of poverty'. They now have a better diet, and more and more people can obtain clean water. Primary schools now teach most children to read and write and do simple arithmetic – though there are few books and classes may be very large. In many places, village health workers are taught to recognize and treat the common diseases.

▲ ***Crowded and poor:*** *a shanty town in Brazil. These shanties on a steep hillside in Rio de Janeiro were built by people who have nowhere else to live. Some of them have low-paid jobs, but others have to beg to get enough to eat.*

THIRD WORLD AID

This young boy is collecting water from a tap in his village in Uganda. Now he and his family have clean, safe water to drink and wash in. They no longer have to walk far for water. Many schemes like this are helped by money given by the rich countries of the world.

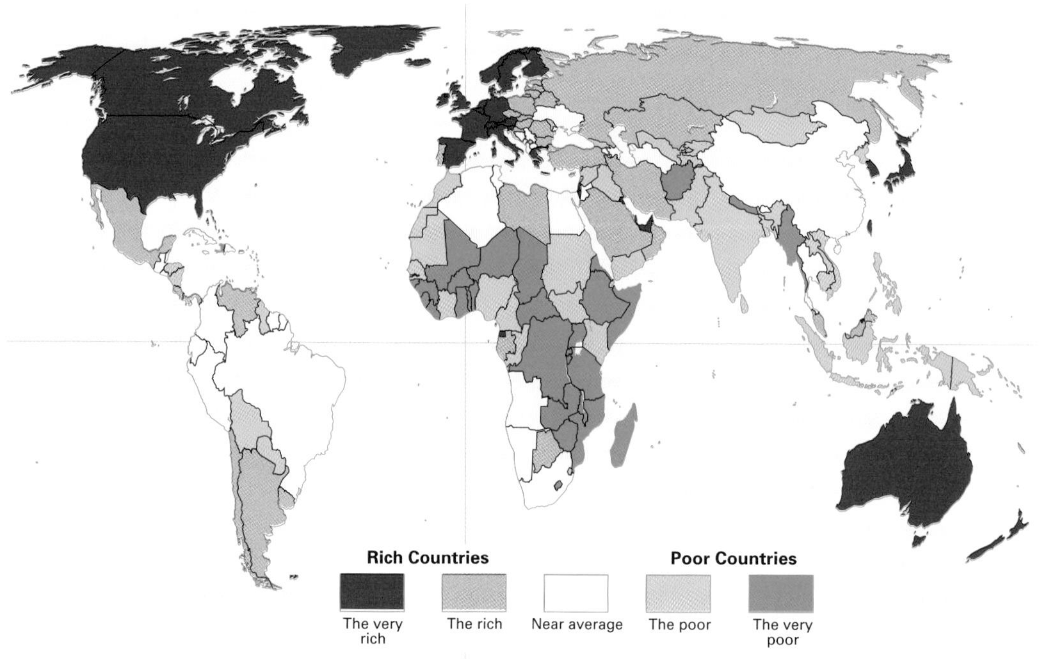

The map below shows where the world's people live. The darker the colour, the more people there are. Most of the world has very few people: the cream or yellow areas.

The areas with few people are mostly desert, or high mountains, or dense forests, or very cold. Over half the world's people live in the lowlands of south and east Asia.

Other crowded areas are parts of Europe and the Nile Valley. The most crowded places of all are the big cities. Find the cities with more than 10 million people on the map.

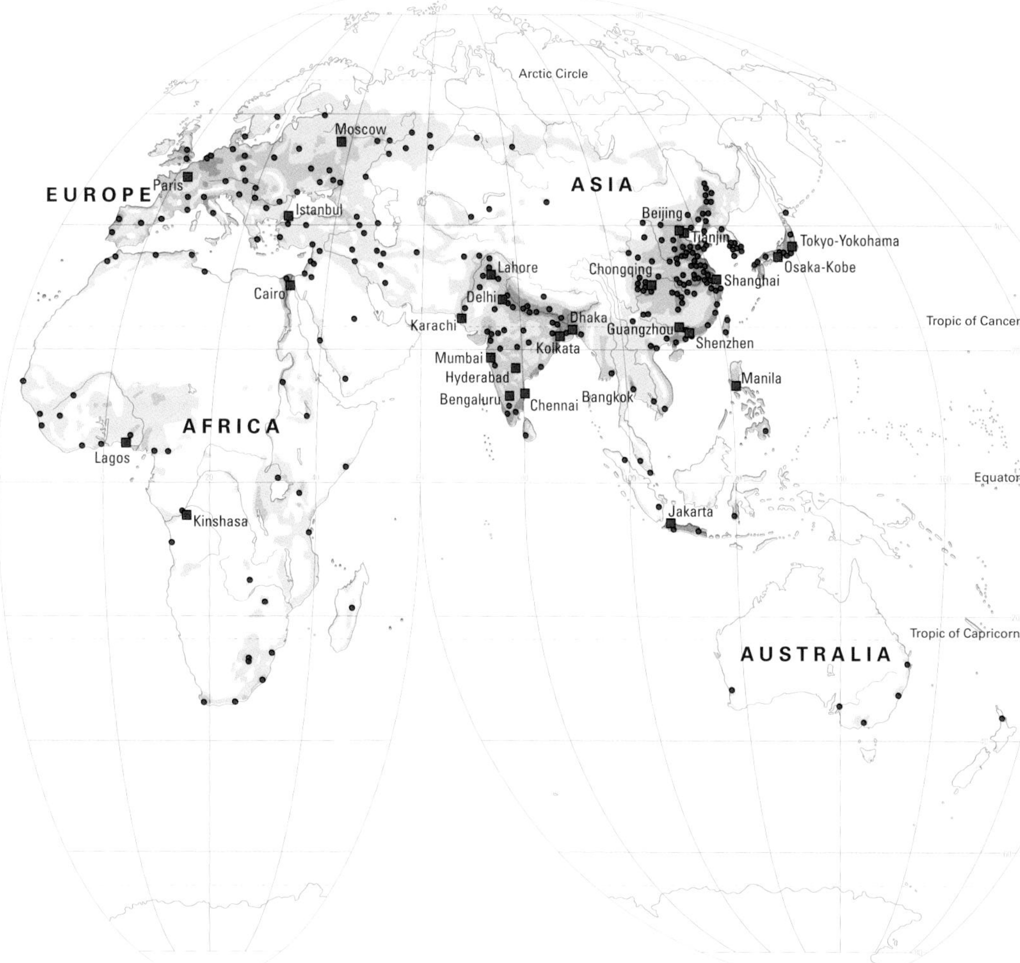

▲ ***Empty and poor:*** *a Tuareg nomad living in the Sahara desert, in Mali. It is hot and dusty and life is hard. The nomads move around with their animals.*

▲ ***Crowded and rich:*** *the skyscrapers of San Francisco seen from the bay. San Francisco is a city in California, on the west coast of the USA. Only the richest people can afford the apartments with the best views. The USA is the world's richest country, but there are poor people living in some areas of the cities.*

COLD AND HOT LANDS

▲ ***Arctic winter.*** *Winter begins early in Greenland. This fishing boat is frozen in the harbour at Angmagssalik, near the Arctic Circle. There are 24 hours of dark and cold at Christmas. Yet by June, the ice will have melted, and there will be 24 hours of daylight.*

FIVE important lines are drawn across these maps of the world: the Arctic and Antarctic Circles; the Tropics of Cancer and Capricorn; and the Equator. They divide the world roughly into *polar*, *temperate* and *tropical* zones.

The *polar* lands remain cold all through the year, even though the summer days are long and some snow melts.

The *temperate* lands have four seasons: summer and winter, with spring and autumn in between. But these seasons come at different times of the year north and south of the Equator. June is midwinter in southern lands.

The *tropical* lands are always hot, except where mountains or plateaus reach high above sea level. For some of the year the sun is directly overhead at noon (local time). Look at the **red** area on the maps.

The map on **this** page shows the world in June. Hardly anywhere is very cold (except for Antarctica in midwinter, of course). Most of the very hot areas in June are **north** of the Equator.

The December map (opposite page) is very different. Both Canada and Russia are **very** cold. Most of the hottest areas in December are **south** of the Equator, near the Tropic of Capricorn, because December is midsummer.

DID YOU KNOW?

Children in New Zealand open their Christmas presents on 25th December which is in midsummer!

Hot and Cold in June

- Very hot
- Hot
- Warm
- Cool
- Cold
- Very cold
- Frozen seas

Greenland

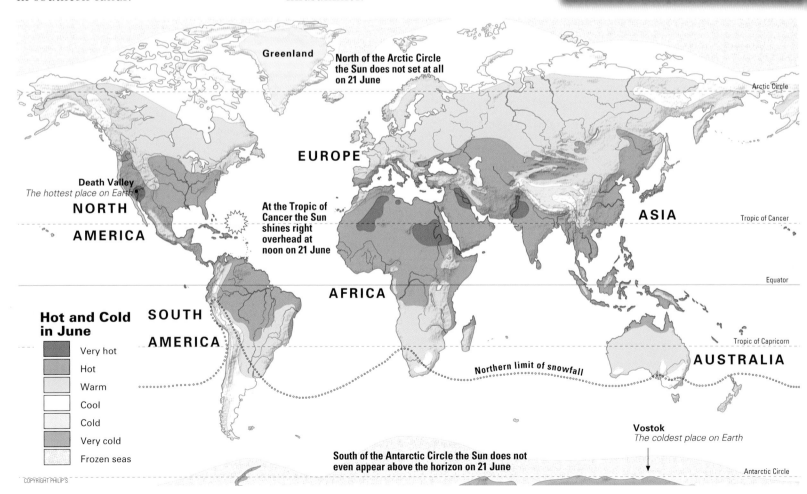

North of the Arctic Circle the Sun does not set at all on 21 June

Arctic Circle

EUROPE

Death Valley
The hottest place on Earth

NORTH AMERICA

At the Tropic of Cancer the Sun shines right overhead at noon on 21 June

ASIA

Tropic of Cancer

Equator

AFRICA

SOUTH AMERICA

Tropic of Capricorn

AUSTRALIA

Northern limit of snowfall

Vostok
The coldest place on Earth

South of the Antarctic Circle the Sun does not even appear above the horizon on 21 June

Antarctic Circle

COLD & HOT LANDS FACTS

HOTTEST RECORDED TEMPERATURE
57°C at Death Valley in USA

COLDEST RECORDED TEMPERATURE
–89.2°C at Vostok in Antarctica

GREATEST CHANGE OF TEMPERATURE AT ONE PLACE IN A YEAR
From –70°C to +36.7°C at Verkhoyansk in Siberia, Russia

▲ ***In the hot, wet tropics,*** *trees grow tall and ferns grow fast. It is all green – and quite dark – in this forest on the island of Tobago, in the West Indies* *(see page 81).*

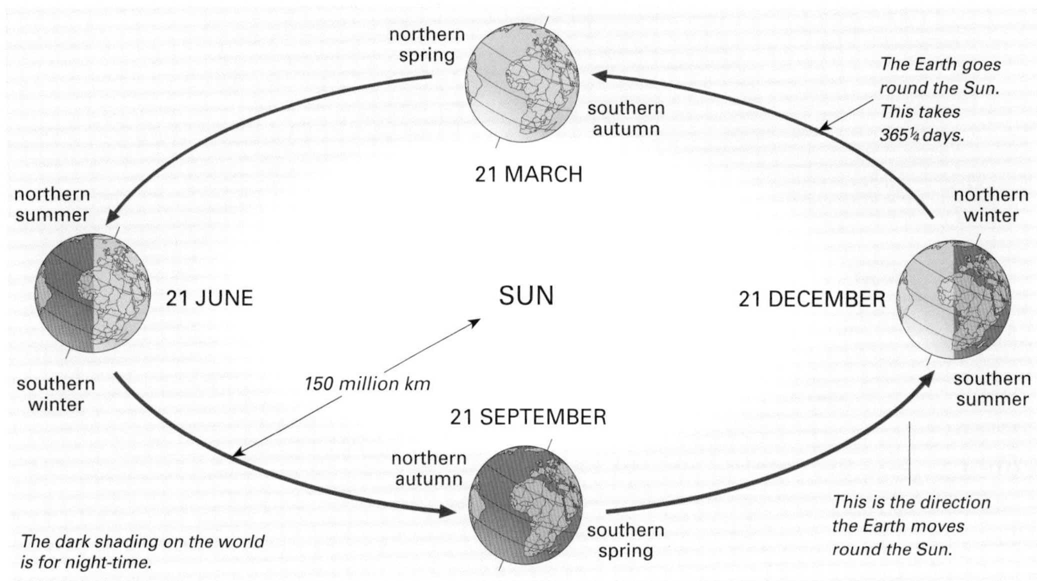

The seasons are different north and south of the Equator. In June it is summer in North America, Europe and Asia. The sun is overhead at the Tropic of Cancer. The North Pole is tilted towards the sun, and the Arctic enjoys 24 hours of daylight. Notice that Antarctica is in total darkness.

By December, the Earth has travelled halfway round the sun. The sun is overhead at the Tropic of Capricorn. The South Pole is tilted towards the sun. Antarctica now has 24 hours of daylight, and it is summer in South America, southern Africa and Australia. But the Arctic is in total darkness and the Arctic Ocean is frozen.

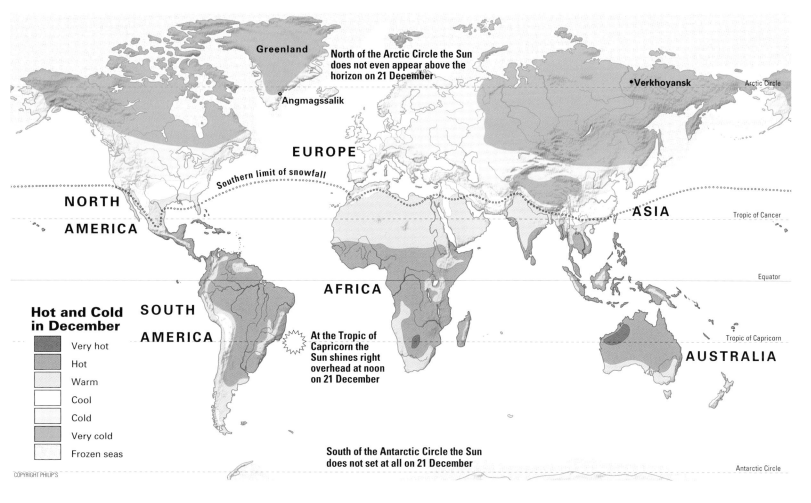

Greenland
North of the Arctic Circle the Sun does not even appear above the horizon on 21 December
Angmagssalik
Verkhoyansk
Arctic Circle
EUROPE
Southern limit of snowfall
NORTH AMERICA
ASIA
Tropic of Cancer
Equator
AFRICA
SOUTH AMERICA
At the Tropic of Capricorn the Sun shines right overhead at noon on 21 December
Tropic of Capricorn
AUSTRALIA
South of the Antarctic Circle the Sun does not set at all on 21 December
Antarctic Circle

Hot and Cold in December
- Very hot
- Hot
- Warm
- Cool
- Cold
- Very cold
- Frozen seas

WET AND DRY LANDS

WATER is needed by all living things. But different parts of the world receive different amounts of water.

Follow the Equator on these two maps: the dark blue colour (below) shows heavy rain. Thick tropical forest grows here (page 15).

Now find the Tropics of Cancer and Capricorn: many parts are dry all year, and there are big deserts. Between the tropical forests and the deserts, there are 'savanna' areas, with tall grass and bushes: these areas have a wet and a dry season.

North of the Sahara Desert, near the Mediterranean Sea, it rains in winter. Summers are hot and dry.

In temperate lands, places near the oceans receive rain from the damp winds that blow from the sea all year. Trees grow well here. Far inland, it is much drier and there are vast grasslands, like the prairies of North America and the Russian steppes. In the centre of Asia, there is a desert with very cold winters.

Further north, temperate forests of pines and firs stretch right across North America, Europe and Asia.

In the far north, there is 'tundra', with no trees. The land is snow-covered for many months in winter, and marshy in the short summer.

Finally, Greenland and Antarctica are mostly snow and ice: find them on pages 88 and 89.

▲ ***Forest and mountains in Alberta, Canada.*** *The coniferous trees can survive Canada's bitterly cold winters. In the high mountains, trees cannot grow: it is too cold and the soil is too thin. Can you see the forest across the lake?*

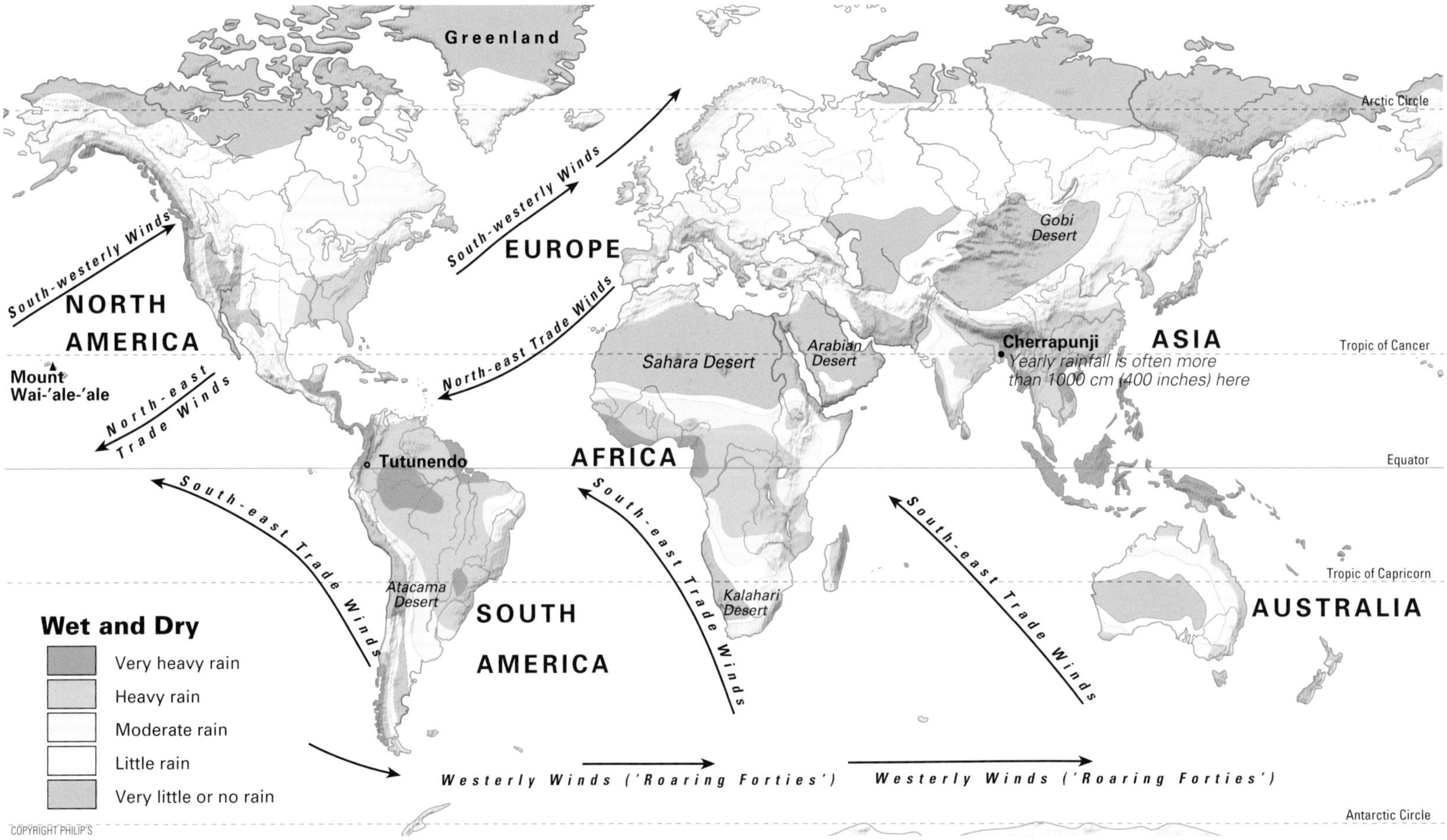

Wet and Dry

- Very heavy rain
- Heavy rain
- Moderate rain
- Little rain
- Very little or no rain

Greenland
Arctic Circle
Tropic of Cancer
Equator
Tropic of Capricorn
Antarctic Circle
NORTH AMERICA
EUROPE
ASIA
AFRICA
SOUTH AMERICA
AUSTRALIA
Gobi Desert
Sahara Desert
Arabian Desert
Atacama Desert
Kalahari Desert
Mount Wai-'ale-'ale
Tutunendo
Cherrapunji
Yearly rainfall is often more than 1000 cm (400 inches) here
South-westerly Winds
South-westerly Winds
North-east Trade Winds
North-east Trade Winds
South-east Trade Winds
South-east Trade Winds
South-east Trade Winds
Westerly Winds ('Roaring Forties')
Westerly Winds ('Roaring Forties')

WET & DRY LANDS FACTS

HIGHEST RAINFALL IN ONE MONTH
9299 mm in one month at Cherrapunji, India

HIGHEST RAINFALL IN ONE YEAR
26,461 mm in one year at Cherrapunji

MOST RAINY DAYS
350 days in a year at Mount Wai-'ale-'ale in Hawaii

WETTEST PLACE ON AVERAGE
Over 11 metres of rain a year at Tutunendo, Colombia

DRIEST PLACE In the Atacama Desert, northern Chile: no rain for 400 years!

This map shows NATURAL vegetation – but in many places people have cut down forests to make farmland and towns. Most scientists now believe that pollution is changing the climates of the world: we can expect more storms, more floods, more droughts and hotter temperatures. As sea level rises, the lowest land near the sea is at risk from floods.

▲ ***Burning the savanna, in northern Ghana, West Africa.*** *At the end of the long dry season, farmers burn the bush (long grass and small trees). The land will be ready for planting crops when it rains. Sometimes, lightning can cause fires.*

▲ ***Sand dunes in the desert in Namibia, southern Africa.*** *The Namib Desert has given its name to the country of Namibia. It is a very dry area, west of the Kalahari Desert. But most of the world's desert areas are rocky, not sandy.*

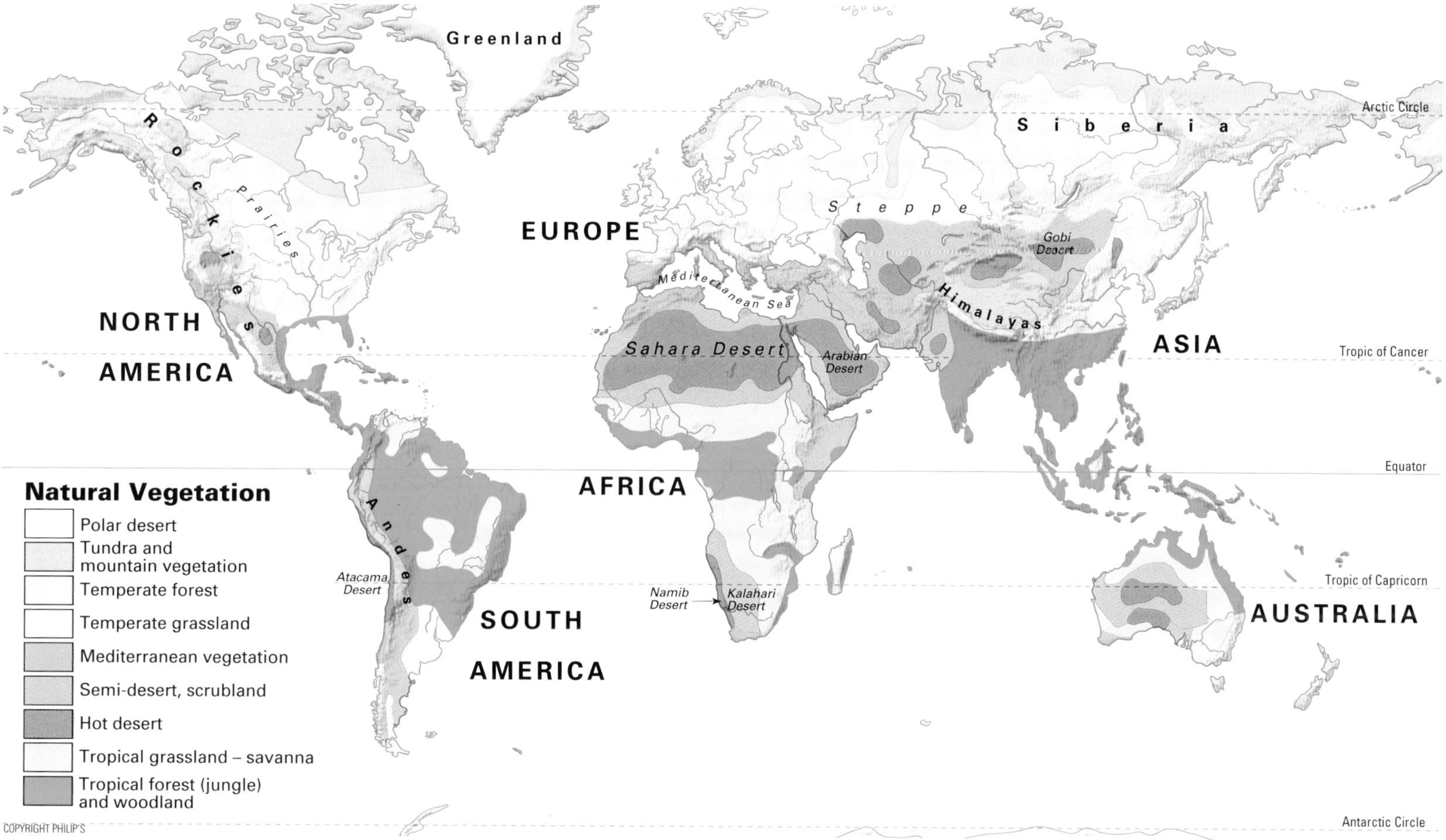

Greenland
Rockies
Prairies
NORTH AMERICA
Arctic Circle
Siberia
Steppe
EUROPE
Gobi Desert
Mediterranean Sea
Himalayas
Sahara Desert
Arabian Desert
ASIA
Tropic of Cancer
Equator
AFRICA
Andes
Atacama Desert
SOUTH AMERICA
Namib Desert
Kalahari Desert
Tropic of Capricorn
AUSTRALIA
Antarctic Circle

Natural Vegetation
- Polar desert
- Tundra and mountain vegetation
- Temperate forest
- Temperate grassland
- Mediterranean vegetation
- Semi-desert, scrubland
- Hot desert
- Tropical grassland – savanna
- Tropical forest (jungle) and woodland

ENJOYING MAPS

AN atlas is a book of maps. The maps in this book have been carefully drawn by cartographers (map-makers) to tell us about the countries of the world.

The maps on pages 6 to 15 show the whole world. Because the world is round, the best model is a globe. It is impossible to draw a really accurate map of the round world on a flat piece of paper. That is why the Pacific Ocean is cut in half, and Antarctica becomes a long thin strip. On pages 88 and 89 there are maps of parts of the world viewed from a different angle.

The maps on pages 18 to 89 show the continents and countries of the world. Each map has a key, with information that will help you 'read' the map. Use your imagination to 'see' what the land is like in each part of the world that you visit through these pages. The photos and text will make your picture clearer.

These two pages explain the key to all the maps. The country of GHANA is used as an example. Ghana is in square B2 of the map (right). Find Ⓑ at the top of the map with one finger, and ②➤ at the side of the map with another finger. Move each finger in the direction of the arrows; Ghana is where they meet.

The capital city of each country is underlined on the maps. The rulers of the country live in the capital city, and it is the biggest city in most countries. But not all capital cities are big. On this map, you can see three sizes of city. The biggest ones are marked by a square; they have the most people. Middle-sized cities have a big circle, and smaller cities have a small circle. Small towns and villages are not shown on maps of this scale, but some have been included in this atlas because they are mentioned in the text.

COINS OF THE WORLD

The Ghana coin (left) shows cocoa pods growing on the branches of a cocoa tree. Cocoa is a major export from Ghana. Another Ghana coin (right) shows traditional drums.

Other countries also picture familiar items on their coins. **Nigeria** has a palm tree on its coins; **The Gambia** has a sailing ship on one of its coins (see page 53).

But don't believe everything you find on coins: some UK coins have pictures of lions, yet there are no wild lions there.

POSTAGE STAMPS ... are on some pages of this atlas

You can learn so much from stamps! The map shows you that Ghana is a country; the stamps tell you the official language of Ghana, and show you Ghana's flag.

The map tells you that Ghana has a coastline; the 10Np stamp tells you the name of Ghana's main port, and shows you the big modern cranes there.

The map shows that this port is very near to Accra, which is the capital city of Ghana.

The map tells you the name of Ghana's biggest lake (man-made). The 6Np stamp shows you the dam and its name.

You can see that they chose the narrowest part of the valley to build the dam. On page 57, there is a picture of a ferry on the lake.

▲ ***The border between Ghana and Burkina Faso.*** *The red lines on the map show the borders between countries. When travelling from one country to another, you have to stop at the border. These children live in Ghana and their flag flies on their side of the border.*

'BYE-BYE SAFE JOURNEY' *is the message on the arch. In Ghana, most officials speak English. In Burkina Faso officials speak French.*

HEIGHT OF THE LAND

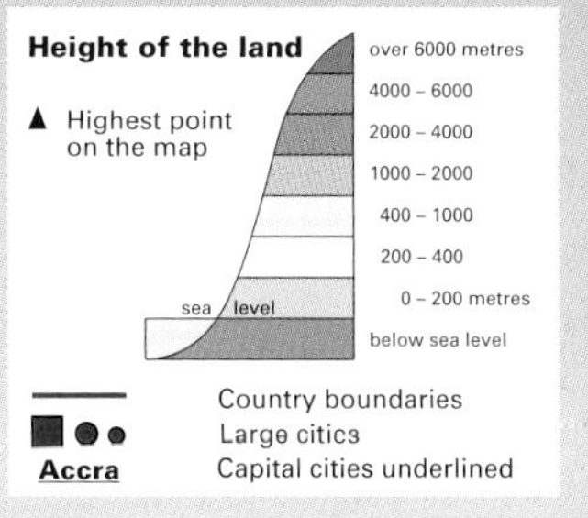

The countries of West Africa are coloured so that you can tell the height of the land. Green shows the lowest land. Often the real land will not look green – in the dry season the grass is brown. The higher land is coloured brown, even though some parts are covered with thick green forest!

The highest point in West Africa is shown with a small black triangle – find it in square C2. And to find land below sea level (dark green) try page 25. In West Africa, Cameroon has some dramatic mountains, but elsewhere the change from lowland to highland is often quite gentle. The 'shadows' on the map help you to see which mountains have steep slopes.

Blue means water: the oceans, big rivers and lakes. Their names are in *italic print*, such as *Lake Volta* (B2). Blue dashes show rivers which dry up in some years (B1).

Find Lake Chad in square D1. Its size depends on how much rain falls in the wet season.

SCALE

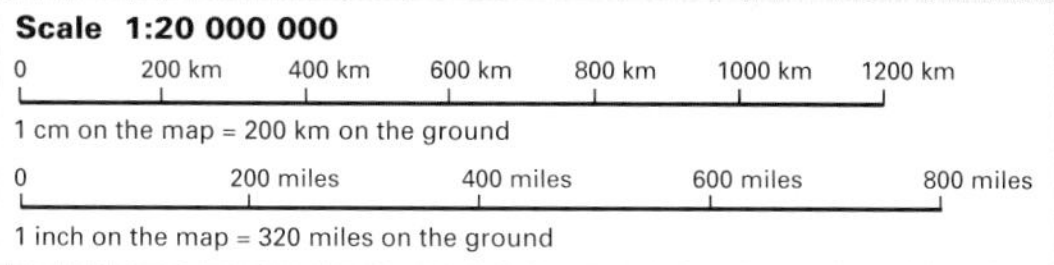

This box shows the scale of the map. The scale can be written in different ways.

Scale 1:20 000 000
0 — 200 km — 400 km — 600 km — 800 km — 1000 km — 1200 km
1 cm on the map = 200 km on the ground
0 — 200 miles — 400 miles — 600 miles — 800 miles
1 inch on the map = 320 miles on the ground

The map is drawn to a scale of 1:20,000,000, which means that the distance between two places on the ground is exactly 20 million times bigger than it is on this page! Other maps in this atlas are drawn to different scales: little Belgium (page 25) is drawn at a scale of 1:2 million, while the largest country in the world is drawn at a scale of 1:45 million (Russia, page 41). Another way of writing the scale of this map is to say that 1 centimetre on the map is equal to 200 kilometres on the ground in West Africa.

You can use the scale line to make your own scale ruler. Put the straight edge of a strip of paper against the scale line and mark the position of 0, 200, 400, 600 kilometres, etc. Carefully number each mark. Now move your scale ruler over the map to see how far it is between places. For example, Accra to Abidjan is 400 kilometres.

EUROPE

THE map shows the great North European Plain that stretches from the Atlantic Ocean to the Ural Mountains in Russia. This huge area of lowland has most of Europe's best farmland, and many of the biggest cities.

To the north of the plain are the snowy mountains of Scandinavia. To the south are even higher mountains: the Pyrenees, the Alps and Carpathians, and the Caucasus Mountains. Southern Europe has hills and mountains by the Mediterranean Sea. The areas of lowland are carefully farmed.

PUZZLE

The most important building in Europe?
• Where is it found?
(Answer on page 97.)

EUROPE FACTS

AREA 10,531,000 sq km (including European Russia)

HIGHEST POINT Mt Elbrus (Russia), 5642 metres

LOWEST POINT By Caspian Sea, minus 38 metres

LONGEST RIVER Volga (Russia), 3690 km

LARGEST LAKE Caspian Sea*, 371,000 sq km

BIGGEST COUNTRY Russia*, 17,075,400 sq km (total area – Europe and Asia)

BIGGEST ALL-EUROPEAN COUNTRY Ukraine, 603,700 sq km

SMALLEST COUNTRY Vatican City* (in Rome, Italy), less than half a square kilometre!

MOST CROWDED COUNTRY Malta

LEAST CROWDED COUNTRY Iceland

* A world record as well as a European record

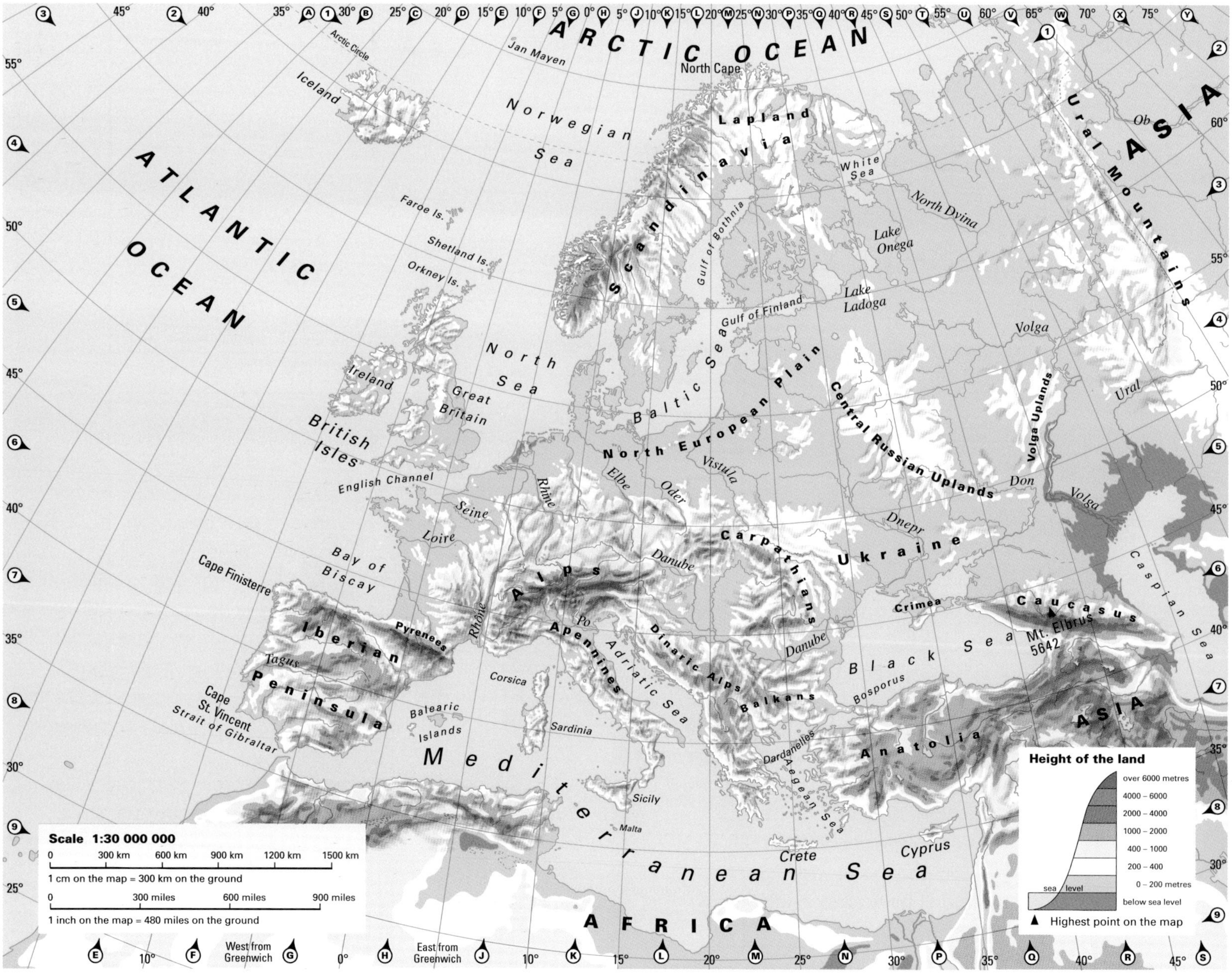

Scale 1:30 000 000

0 300 km 600 km 900 km 1200 km 1500 km

1 cm on the map = 300 km on the ground

0 300 miles 600 miles 900 miles

1 inch on the map = 480 miles on the ground

Height of the land

over 6000 metres
4000 – 6000
2000 – 4000
1000 – 2000
400 – 1000
200 – 400
0 – 200 metres
sea level
below sea level
▲ Highest point on the map

▲ ***Northern Europe: Iceland.*** *Lake Jokulsarlon has many small icebergs which break off the glacier that comes from the ice-cap. Ice melts to make the lake.*

▲ ***Central Europe: Austria.*** *These high mountains are called the Alps. In winter, there will be snow here. In summer, the grass is for the cows – can you see any?*

▲ ***Southern Europe: Sardinia.*** *The island of Sardinia is part of Italy and is in the Mediterranean. These children are enjoying their holiday in the hot sun.*

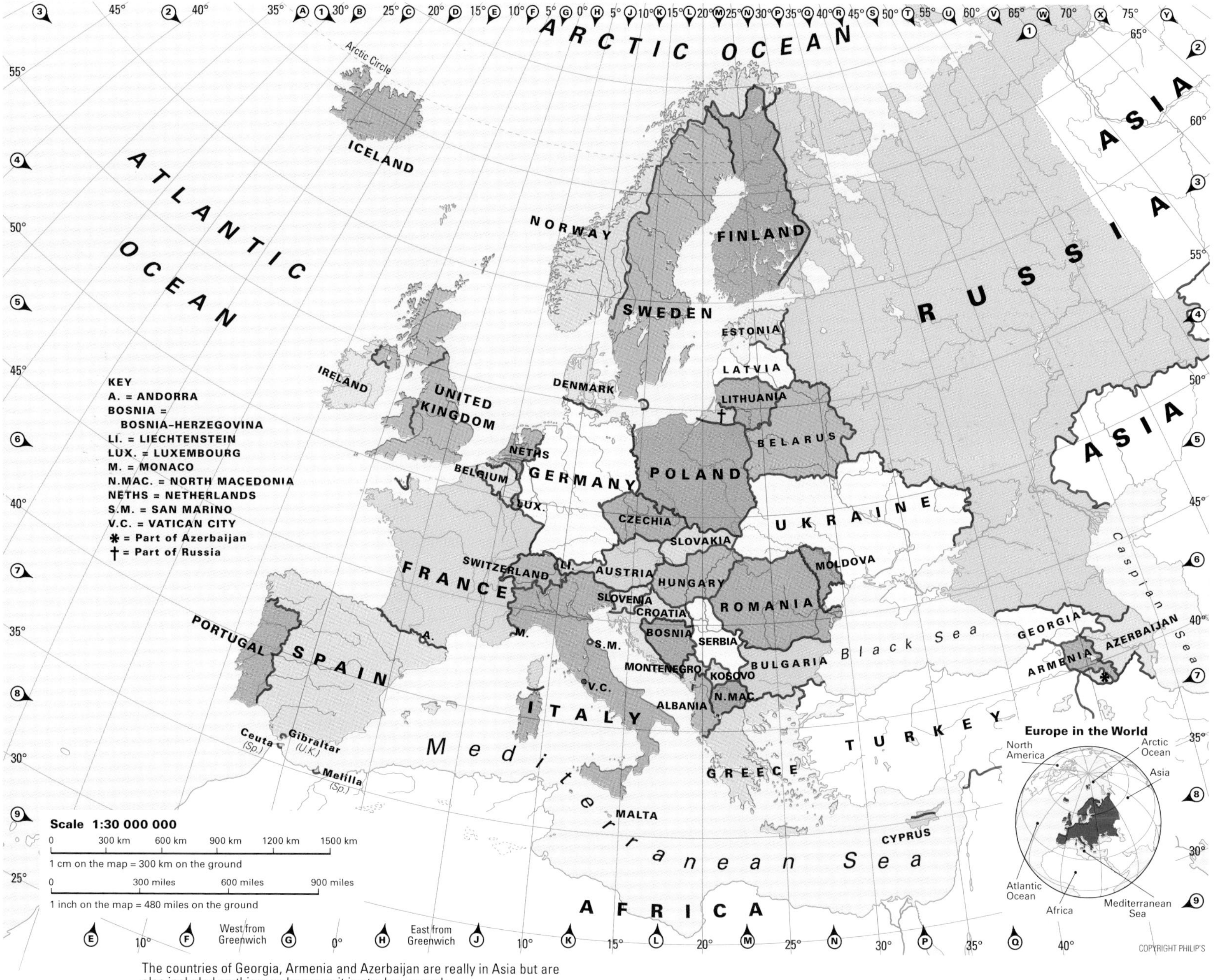

ARCTIC OCEAN

ATLANTIC OCEAN

ICELAND, NORWAY, SWEDEN, FINLAND, RUSSIA, ASIA, ESTONIA, LATVIA, LITHUANIA, DENMARK, IRELAND, UNITED KINGDOM, NETHS, BELGIUM, LUX., GERMANY, POLAND, BELARUS, UKRAINE, CZECHIA, SLOVAKIA, MOLDOVA, FRANCE, SWITZERLAND, LI., AUSTRIA, HUNGARY, ROMANIA, SLOVENIA, CROATIA, BOSNIA, SERBIA, S.M., M., A., PORTUGAL, SPAIN, ITALY, V.C., MONTENEGRO, KOSOVO, ALBANIA, N.MAC., BULGARIA, GREECE, TURKEY, GEORGIA, ARMENIA, AZERBAIJAN, CYPRUS, MALTA, AFRICA

Black Sea, Caspian Sea, Mediterranean Sea, Arctic Circle

Ceuta (Sp.), Gibraltar (U.K.), Melilla (Sp.)

KEY
A. = ANDORRA
BOSNIA = BOSNIA-HERZEGOVINA
LI. = LIECHTENSTEIN
LUX. = LUXEMBOURG
M. = MONACO
N.MAC. = NORTH MACEDONIA
NETHS = NETHERLANDS
S.M. = SAN MARINO
V.C. = VATICAN CITY
✱ = Part of Azerbaijan
† = Part of Russia

Scale 1:30 000 000

0 300 km 600 km 900 km 1200 km 1500 km

1 cm on the map = 300 km on the ground

0 300 miles 600 miles 900 miles

1 inch on the map = 480 miles on the ground

West from Greenwich | East from Greenwich

Europe in the World

North America, Arctic Ocean, Asia, Atlantic Ocean, Africa, Mediterranean Sea

The countries of Georgia, Armenia and Azerbaijan are really in Asia but are also included on this map because it is at a larger scale.

SCANDINAVIA

FINLAND

AREA 338,145 sq km
POPULATION 5,587,000
MONEY Euro

DENMARK

AREA 43,094 sq km
POPULATION 5,895,000
MONEY Danish krone

THE five countries that make up Scandinavia are rich and successful, yet the people live further north than in almost any other part of the world.

The total population of each of these countries is small, and very few people live in the far north. Most people live in towns and cities, with excellent central heating in their houses and flats.

Farming is difficult this far north because the winters are long and cold. Scandinavia has hardly any minerals except for iron ore in **Sweden** and oil under the North Sea.

The mountains of **Iceland** and **Norway** are high and rugged, making travel difficult. There are large ice-sheets and glaciers in the highest areas of both countries. Iceland has many volcanoes.

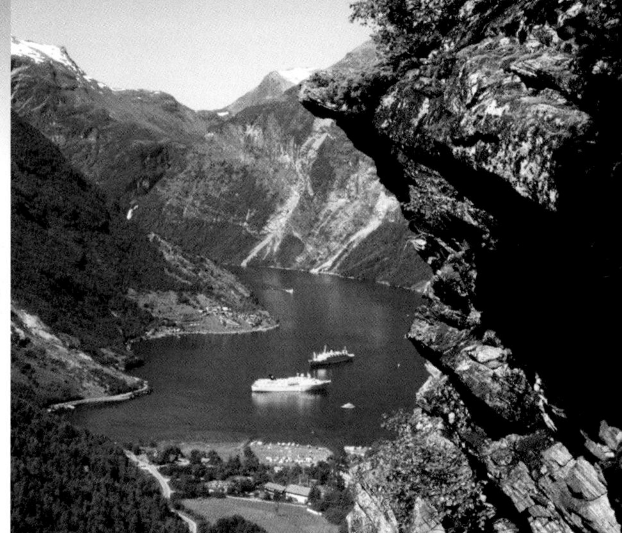

▲ ***Geiranger fjord, Norway,*** *is one of many long, narrow inlets of the sea along the Norwegian coast. Glaciers dug these deep, steep valleys. The village is on the flat land at the head of the fjord. The steep mountains mean that the best way to travel is often by boat.*

LEGOLAND MODEL VILLAGE

Lego was invented by a toymaker in Denmark. Legoland Denmark has a model Village near the factory. There are models of famous buildings as well as ordinary houses from different parts of the world. The photograph shows the model of a typical fishing village in the Lofoten Islands, which are off the northern coast of Norway. The Lego man and his friends can be found in shops all over the world!

▲ ***Reindeer in Lapland. Lapland*** *is the northern part of Norway, Sweden and Finland, where the Lapps (Saami) live. They keep reindeer for their milk, meat and leather, and to pull sledges. They search under the snow for lichen and other food. In winter, it is dark here even at midday, but in summer it is light at midnight.*

NORWAY

AREA 323,877 sq km
POPULATION 5,510,000
MONEY Norwegian krone

SWEDEN

AREA 449,964 sq km
POPULATION 10,262,000
MONEY Swedish krona

▲ ***Lake Saimaa, Finland,*** *is one of hundreds of lakes in the southern part of that country. Only the largest are shown on the map. During the Ice Age, ice-sheets scraped hollows in the rock which filled with water after the ice melted. Many families own a summer cottage among the trees beside a lake.*

Denmark, Finland and southern Sweden are low-lying. The soil is formed from sand, gravel and clay brought by ice-sheets in the Ice Age. There are large lakes in Sweden. Some people have holiday homes on their shores.

The islands of Denmark are now linked by big bridges. Since 2000, Denmark and Sweden have been connected by road and rail through a tunnel 4 km long and over a bridge nearly 8 km long.

Scale 1:10 000 000

0 – 100 km – 200 km – 300 km – 400 km

1 cm on the map = 100 km on the ground

0 – 100 miles – 200 miles

1 inch on the map = 160 miles on the ground

Height of the land

▲ Highest point on the map

over 6000 metres
4000 – 6000
2000 – 4000
1000 – 2000
400 – 1000
200 – 400
0 – 200 metres
sea level
below sea level

Icefield
Country boundaries
Large cities
Capital cities underlined

COPYRIGHT PHILIP'S

▲ ***Stockholm harbour, Sweden:*** *this fine nineteenth-century sailing ship is now a Youth Hostel for visitors to the capital city of Sweden. Stockholm is a seaport with a large harbour. It is built on lots of islands and the nearby mainland, so there are many bridges.*

LAND OF ICE AND FIRE

The volcanoes of Iceland are mostly quiet and peaceful (above left). But sometimes a great volcanic eruption lights up the night sky and the light is reflected in the sea (above right). Ash can shoot high in the sky.

Only 354,000 people live in Iceland. It is near the Arctic Circle and there is ice on the mountains, in glaciers and ice-sheets. A warm Atlantic current keeps the sea ice-free and it is full of fish. Iceland has an important fishing fleet.

THE UK AND IRELAND

UK

AREA 241,857 sq km
POPULATION 66,052,000
MONEY Pound sterling
CAPITAL London

THE United Kingdom (UK) is made up of Great Britain (England, Wales and Scotland) and Northern Ireland. The UK parliament meets in London, but Wales, Scotland and Northern Ireland have their own parliaments.

Look at the high land on the map: it is in the north and west of Great Britain, where the rocks are older and harder than in the south and east. Many old factories and mines were in the north and west on the coalfields and they have closed now. The higher land gets more rain, and has pasture for cattle and sheep. Most of the arable farming is in the lower, drier and flatter south and east of Britain.

▲ ***Windsor Castle*** *is the oldest and largest castle in the world that is still lived in. It is the official home of the Queen, although she also has palaces in London and Edinburgh. Windsor is a small town beside the River Thames, west of London. Tourists come from all over the world to visit historic places, and the 'tourist industry' is very important for the UK.*

▲ ***The city of Newcastle*** *has many bridges over the River Tyne. This steel arch is the same design as the Sydney Harbour bridge in Australia.*

IRELAND

AREA 70,273 sq km
POPULATION 5,225,000
MONEY Euro
CAPITAL Dublin

▲ ***A reservoir in Wales*** *where the River Elan is held back by the Craig Goch dam (Welsh for 'Red Rock'). The water is piped from Wales, in the wetter west, to Birmingham. It is also used to make electricity.*

LONDON

Can you spot 8 famous historic London landmarks? *(Answer on page 97.)*

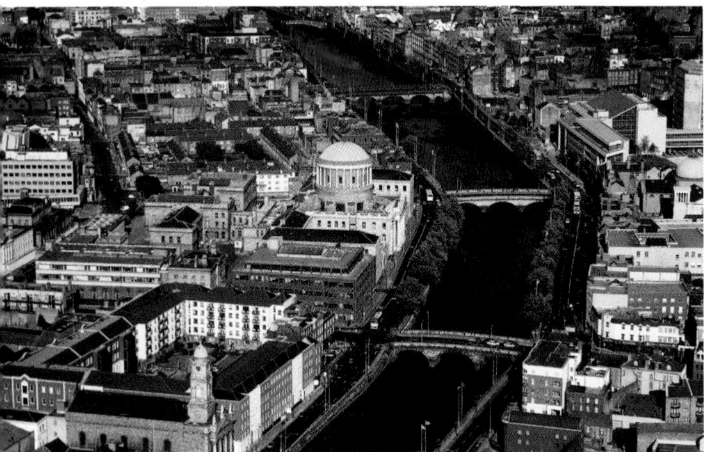

▲ ***Dublin, the capital of Ireland.*** *This air-photo shows us that Dublin is built on both sides of the River Liffey. How many bridges can you see? A quarter of Ireland's population lives in Dublin and its suburbs.*

▲ ***The Somerset Levels,*** *south of Bristol in south-west England. The foreground was marshland which has been drained – it is below the level of high tides.*

CAN YOU FIND THESE ON THE MAP?

Highest mountain – Ben Nevis
Longest river – Shannon
Largest lake – Lough Neagh
Greenwich Meridian – 0°

Ireland is a completely separate country from the UK although it was part of Britain until 1922. Its money is the Euro. It also has its own language, Irish, though everyone speaks English too. There were twice as many people in Ireland 180 years ago as there are today. Many Irish people emigrated to the UK or USA to find work. Farming is still important, but new factories have been built in many towns.

▲ ***The Highlands of Scotland*** *are very beautiful. The hard rocks are hundreds of millions of years old, and they were eroded by glaciers in the Ice Age.*

BENELUX

BELGIUM

AREA 30,528 sq km
POPULATION 11,779,000
MONEY Euro

NETHERLANDS

AREA 41,526 sq km
POPULATION 17,337,000
MONEY Euro

BENELUX is a word made up from BElgium, NEtherlands and LUXembourg. Fortunately, the first two letters of each name are the same in most languages, so everyone can understand the word. These three countries agreed to co-operate soon after World War 2. But they still have their very own Kings (of Belgium and of the Netherlands), and Grand Duke (of Luxembourg). Look at the coins below.

The Benelux countries are all small and are the most crowded in mainland Europe, but there is plenty of countryside too. Most of the land is low and flat, so they are sometimes called the Low Countries.

▲ ***Are these windmills?*** *Most Dutch 'windmills' are really wind-pumps. They were used to pump water up from the fields into rivers and canals. The river is higher than the land! These are at Kinderdijk, east of Rotterdam.*

GAINING LAND

The map shows that a large part of the Netherlands is below sea level. For over 1000 years, the Dutch have built dykes (embankments) to keep out the sea and rivers. Then the water is pumped out to create dry land called 'polders'. Once they used wind-pumps (see photo above); today they use diesel or electric pumps. The rich farmland grows vegetables and flowers.

▲ ***Bruges*** *is a historic town in Belgium. This horse-drawn carriage is taking tourists round the medieval market square. Look at the 'stepped' gables of the old buildings behind the market stalls.*

LUXEMBOURG

AREA 2,586 sq km
POPULATION 640,000
MONEY Euro

WHICH COUNTRY?

These Euro coins come from the Benelux countries – but which coin belongs to which country? The Dutch coin shows Queen Beatrix who reigned until 2013. (*Answers on page 97.*)

▲ ***Europort, Rotterdam****. Rotterdam is by far the biggest port in Europe. Ships come from all over the world, and barges travel along the River Rhine and the canals of Europe to reach the port. Containers unloaded from this ship may be taken to other ports around the North Sea.*

PUZZLE

A puzzle from the Netherlands:
What are these round yellow items for sale in a market? (Some have been cut and sliced.)

(*Answer on page 97.*)

Belgium is *one* country with *two* languages. South of Brussels most people speak French. In the north they speak Flemish (similar to Dutch). Road signs in Belgium are in both languages.

Brussels is an important city. It is the capital of Belgium and the headquarters of the whole European Union.

The eastern part of the **Netherlands** has large areas of heath and forest.

But the best-known Dutch landscape is the 'polders' of the west. Look at the map to see how much of the land is *below* sea level – and threatened with floods if the sea level rises. But this is the country's best farmland.

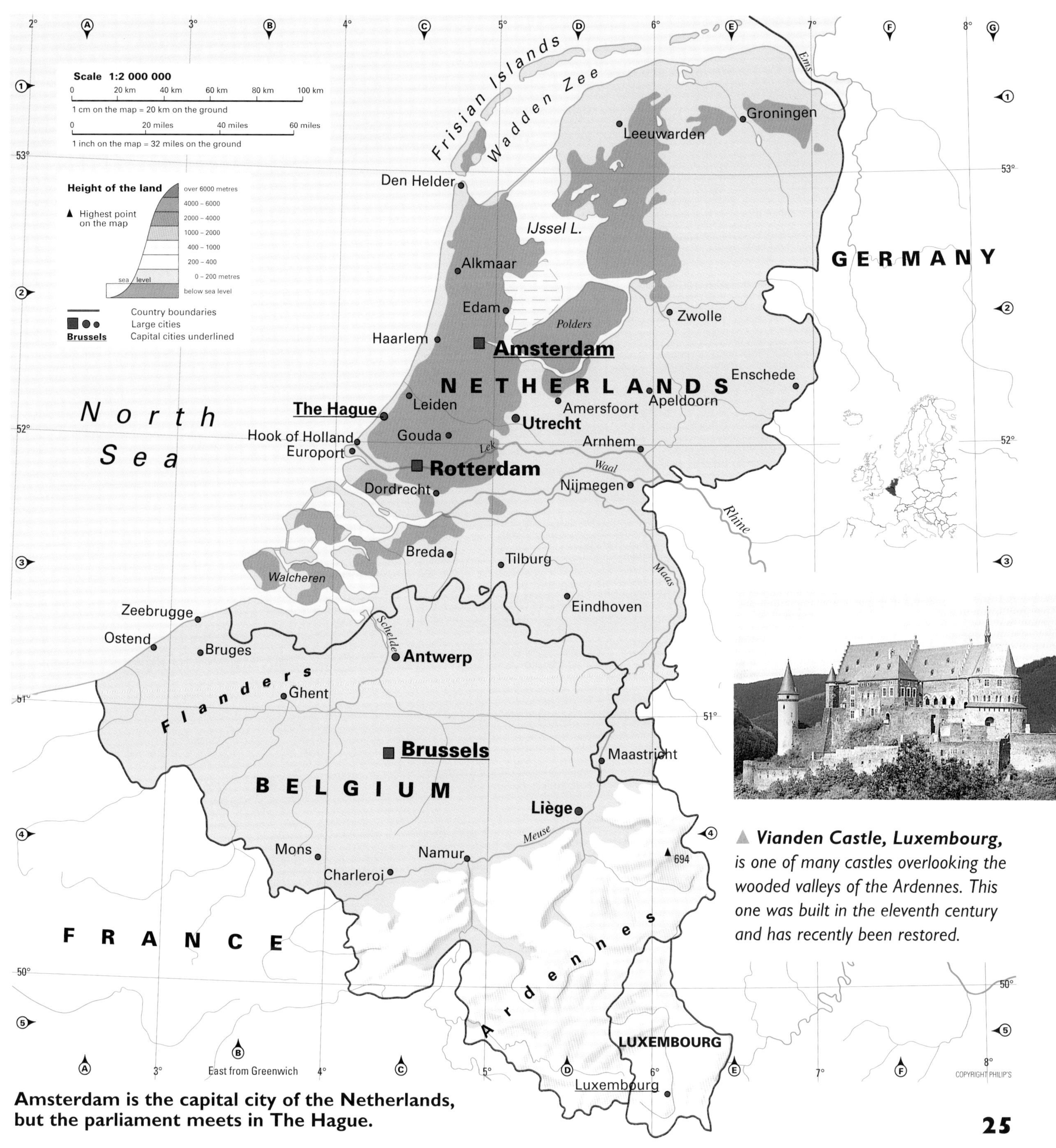

▲ ***Vianden Castle, Luxembourg,*** *is one of many castles overlooking the wooded valleys of the Ardennes. This one was built in the eleventh century and has recently been restored.*

Amsterdam is the capital city of the Netherlands, but the parliament meets in The Hague.

FRANCE

FRANCE

AREA 551,500 sq km
POPULATION 68,084,000
MONEY Euro

The French flag is called the 'tricolore'. It has been used since the French Revolution in 1789.

▲ ***The Eiffel Tower*** *was built in Paris in 1889. It was designed by Monsieur Eiffel, an engineer. It is 300 metres high and weighs 7000 tonnes! Lifts go to the top.*

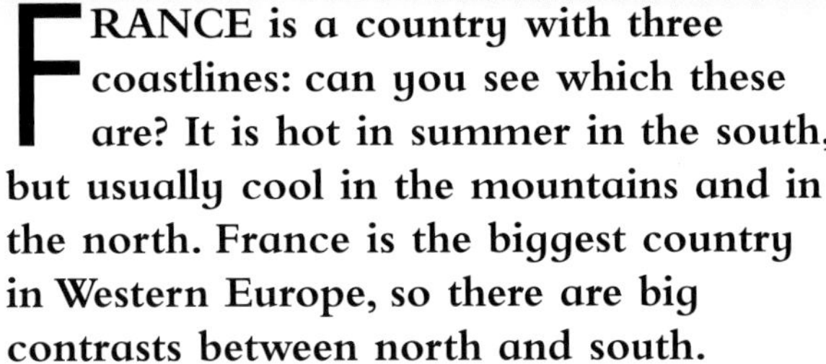

FRANCE is a country with three coastlines: can you see which these are? It is hot in summer in the south, but usually cool in the mountains and in the north. France is the biggest country in Western Europe, so there are big contrasts between north and south.

The highest mountains are the Alps in the south-east and the Pyrenees in the south-west. They are popular for skiing in winter and for summer holidays too.

More than half the country is lowland, with wide rivers. Farming is very important: besides fruit and vegetables, France is famous for its many different cheeses and wines, as well as delicious *cuisine* (cooking).

▲ ***Market at Grasse.*** *Some of this lovely fruit has been grown in the warm sunshine of the south of France. Every town in France has a good market selling fresh produce.*

▲ ***The Camargue*** *is a wetland area in the delta of the River Rhône. It is important for wildlife.*

▲ ***Mont Blanc.*** *The 'White Mountain' is the highest mountain in Western Europe. It is 4808 metres high. Even in summer (as here) it is covered in snow. Cable-cars take tourists and skiers up the mountain. There is a road tunnel through Mont Blanc to Italy.*

FRENCH WINE

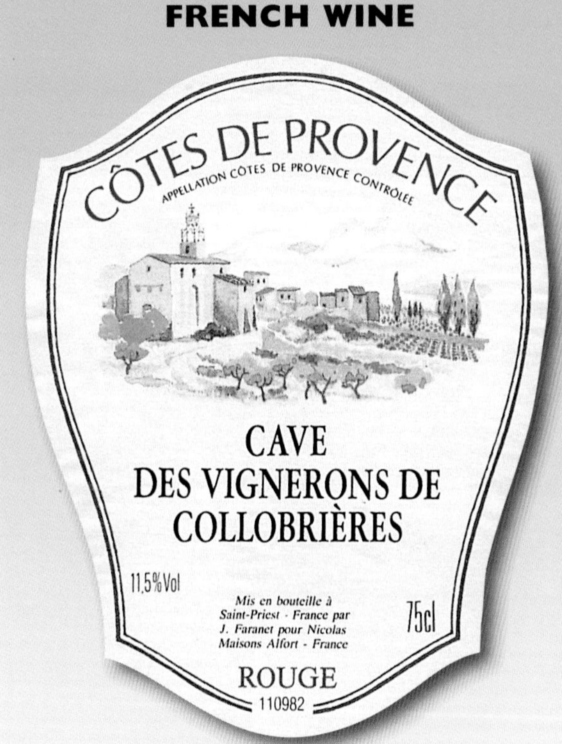

CÔTES DE PROVENCE
APPELLATION CÔTES DE PROVENCE CONTRÔLÉE
CAVE
DES VIGNERONS DE
COLLOBRIÈRES
11,5%Vol
Mis en bouteille à
Saint-Priest - France par
J. Faranet pour Nicolas
Maisons Alfort - France
75cl
ROUGE
110982

This label is from a bottle of red wine from Provence, in the south of France. It tells you where the grapes were grown and where the wine was bottled. Collobrières is a village east of the River Rhône. The houses have red tiled roofs. Around the village are fields of fruit trees and vines. Rows of tall trees have been planted to shelter the crops from cold winds. The red grapes are picked in the autumn.

The biggest city is Paris, which is also the capital and the official home of the French President. Ten million people live in the Paris region. Five big new towns have been built, linked to the city centre by fast trains.

Tourists come to Paris from all over the world. Here, you can enjoy a boat trip on the River Seine past Notre Dame Cathedral on the Ile de France, or travel east to the Disneyland Resort, Paris.

CAN YOU FIND...

the names of long rivers that flow from the...

- Alps to the Mediterranean
- Pyrenees to the Bay of Biscay
- hills of Burgundy to the Channel

See page 33 for Corsica

GERMANY AND AUSTRIA

GERMANY

AREA 357,022 sq km
POPULATION 79,903,000
MONEY Euro

AUSTRIA

AREA 83,859 sq km
POPULATION 8,885,000
MONEY Euro

GERMANY has more people than any other European country apart from Russia. Most of the 81 million Germans live in towns and cities. Several million people called 'guest workers' have come from southern Europe and Turkey to work in Germany's factories. But nowadays there is unemployment in Germany, as in other European countries, and many 'guest workers' have returned home. Among the many different goods made in Germany there are excellent cars: Audi, BMW, Mercedes, Opel, Porsche and Volkswagen.

There is also plenty of beautiful and uncrowded countryside. The north is mostly lowland. Parts of the south, such as the Black Forest, are mountainous and popular for holidays.

Germany was one country from 1870 to 1945. In 1990 it became one country again. From 1945 until 1990, it was divided into West Germany and East Germany, and there was a border fence between the two. In Berlin, the high wall that divided the city into east and west was knocked down in 1989. It became the capital city again in 2000.

▲ ***Berlin:*** *this ruined tower, next to the new tower of the Memorial Church, is left as a reminder of the destruction caused by war. It is in the city centre. Berlin is no longer divided and is once again the capital of a united Germany.*

▲ ***Edelweiss*** *are flowers that grow high in the Alps. They can survive in thin soil on steep slopes, and do not mind being buried by snow all winter. They are a national symbol in Austria.*

▲ ***The Rhine Gorge****, in western Germany. Castles once guarded this important river route. The River Rhine flows from Switzerland, through Germany to the Netherlands. Big barges travel between the ports and factories beside the river. Tourists travel along the river to enjoy the beautiful landscape.*

TRANSPORT

Germany has excellent roads and railways. The picture above shows an inter-city express (ICE) train passing on a bridge over an *autobahn* (motorway).

This cable-car (left) is in Austria. Tourists can ride high into the Alps to ski in winter and walk in summer. The Alps continue into Switzerland and Italy (p.33) and France (p.27).

AUSTRIA: Until 1918, Austria and Hungary were linked, and together ruled a great empire which included much of Central Europe and Slovenia, Croatia and Bosnia (see page 34). But now Austria is a small, peaceful country.

Most Austrians live in the lower eastern part of the country. The capital is Vienna, on the River Danube. Many famous composers have lived in this city. It was once at the centre of the Austrian Empire: now it is in a corner of the country.

In the west of Austria are the high Alps. Many tourists come to enjoy the beautiful scenery and winter sports. Busy motorways and electric railways cross the Austrian Alps to link Germany with Italy.

WHO ARE THE NEIGHBOURS?

Nine countries have borders with Germany – Austria is one of them. Try to name the others – then check your answer on the map on page 19.

▲ ***Hallstatt, Austria,*** *is built on steep slopes which are part of the Dachstein Mountains in the eastern Alps, south-east of Salzburg. It lies beside a deep blue lake with the same name. There is plenty of snow in winter.*

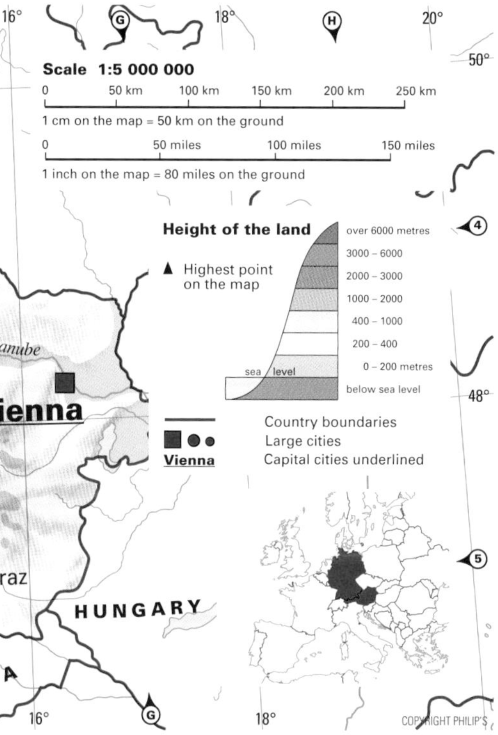

SPAIN AND PORTUGAL

SPAIN

AREA 497,548 sq km
POPULATION 47,261,000
MONEY Euro

PORTUGAL

AREA 88,797 sq km
POPULATION 10,264,000
MONEY Euro

SPAIN and Portugal are separated from the rest of Europe by the high Pyrenees Mountains. Most people travelling by land from the north reach Spain along the Atlantic or Mediterranean coasts.

The Meseta is the very high plateau of central Spain. Winters are very cold, and summers are very hot. The capital city, Madrid, is about 650 metres above sea level. Olives and grapes are the main crops, and both Spain and Portugal export famous wines such as sherry and port. Cars are a major export from Spain nowadays. Both Spain and Portugal have fine cities with great churches and cathedrals, built when they were the richest countries in the world.

▲ ***Benidorm on the Costa Blanca*** *('White Coast') is a famous tourist resort in Spain. Until the 1960s Benidorm was a quiet fishing village. Since then, all these skyscrapers have been built as hotels and apartments for tourists who come by aeroplane to enjoy the sun, sea and sand.*

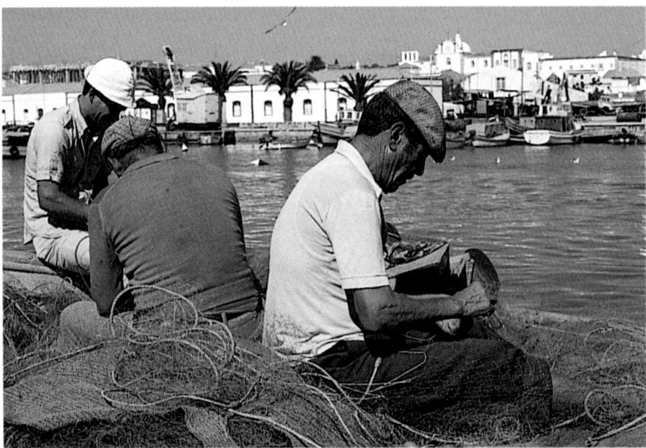

▲ ***Portuguese fishermen*** *mending their nets at Tavira, on the Algarve. They continue to land sardines and other fish, but the town relies on the tourist trade for most of its income.*

DID YOU KNOW?

Gibraltar is still a British colony, but it is only 6 square kilometres in area. Spain still owns two towns in Morocco: ***Ceuta*** and ***Melilla***. Spain wants Gibraltar – and Morocco wants Ceuta and Melilla. The argument has been going on for nearly 300 years....

THE ALHAMBRA PALACE

This beautiful palace in Granada, Spain, was built by the Moors (Arabs from North Africa). The Moors ruled southern Spain for hundreds of years, until 1492. The Arabs brought new ideas and new crops to Europe, such as oranges, rice and sugar-cane, which are still grown in Spain today.

The photo (left) of the Court of Lions shows the stone lions carved 600 years ago by Arab craftsmen.

▲ ***Village in southern Spain.*** *The old houses crowd closely together, and roads are very narrow: wide enough for a donkey, but not for lorries. People whitewash their houses to reflect the rays of the hot sun. Some of the roofs are used as balconies.*

SPAIN AND PORTUGAL

People visit **Spain** for holidays: the Costa Brava (Rugged Coast), Costa Blanca (White Coast), Costa del Sol (Coast of the Sun) and the Balearic Islands (Majorca, Minorca and Ibiza).

People also enjoy holidays in the **Canary Islands**. These belong to Spain – find them on page 55. These volcanic islands have fertile soil. Some have lava cones and black sand.

In **Portugal** the Algarve coast is the most popular holiday area. **Madeira** is a Portuguese island far out in the Atlantic Ocean (see page 55). It is another holiday area that is also famous for its wine.

SWITZERLAND AND ITALY

SWITZERLAND

AREA 41,284 sq km
POPULATION 8,454,000
MONEY Swiss franc

▲ ***The Matterhorn*** *in the Swiss Alps is 4478 metres high. Glaciers helped carve its shape. Zermatt is the ski resort which gives good views of the peak.*

ITALY is shaped like a boot: its toe seems to be kicking Sicily! The shape is caused by the long range of fold mountains called the Apennines. The great Roman Empire was centred on Italy, and there are many Roman ruins. Yet Italy was only united as a country less than 150 years ago. Italy has lots of big factories. The Fiat car plant in Turin is one of the largest in the world.

The south of Italy and the islands of Sicily and Sardinia have hot, dry summers. These areas are much less rich than the north. Many people have moved to the industrial cities in the north of the country to find work. But government projects are bringing factories and better roads.

In **Switzerland**, most people live in cities north of the Alps. Switzerland is one of the world's richest countries, with modern banks, offices and factories. Rivers, dams and waterfalls in the Alps are used for making hydro-electric power: trains, factories and homes in Switzerland all run on cheap electricity. Cable-cars powered by electricity take skiers and tourists high into the beautiful mountains. Switzerland holds some amazing world records (see below).

▲ ***Venice,*** *in north-east Italy, is a city built in the sea. Everywhere in the old town has to be reached by boat, or on foot, because the 'roads' are canals.*

ITALIAN FOOD

Large plum tomatoes are tinned (above). Many kinds of fruit are dried and used in cakes (right).

Pasta (above) is made from Italian wheat. Spaghetti, macaroni and ravioli are pastas.

WORLD RECORDS IN SWITZERLAND

- The longest and deepest rail tunnel in the world runs through the Alps: the Gotthard Base Tunnel opened in 2016 and is 57 kilometres long.
- The longest stairway is beside the Niesenbahn mountain railway, near Spiez. It has 11,674 steps!
- The steepest railway goes up Mount Pilatus. It has a gradient of 48%.
- Switzerland has been at peace with everyone since 1815. That's quite a record!

▲ ***Vinci, Tuscany,*** *is a small town west of Florence. It was once the home of the famous artist Leonardo. The roofs are covered with pantiles. Lots of olive trees are growing in the fields below the town.*

ITALY

AREA 301,318 sq km
POPULATION 62,390,000
MONEY Euro

OTHER COUNTRIES ON THIS MAP:

Vatican City in Rome;
San Marino within Italy;
Malta, an island country south of Italy.

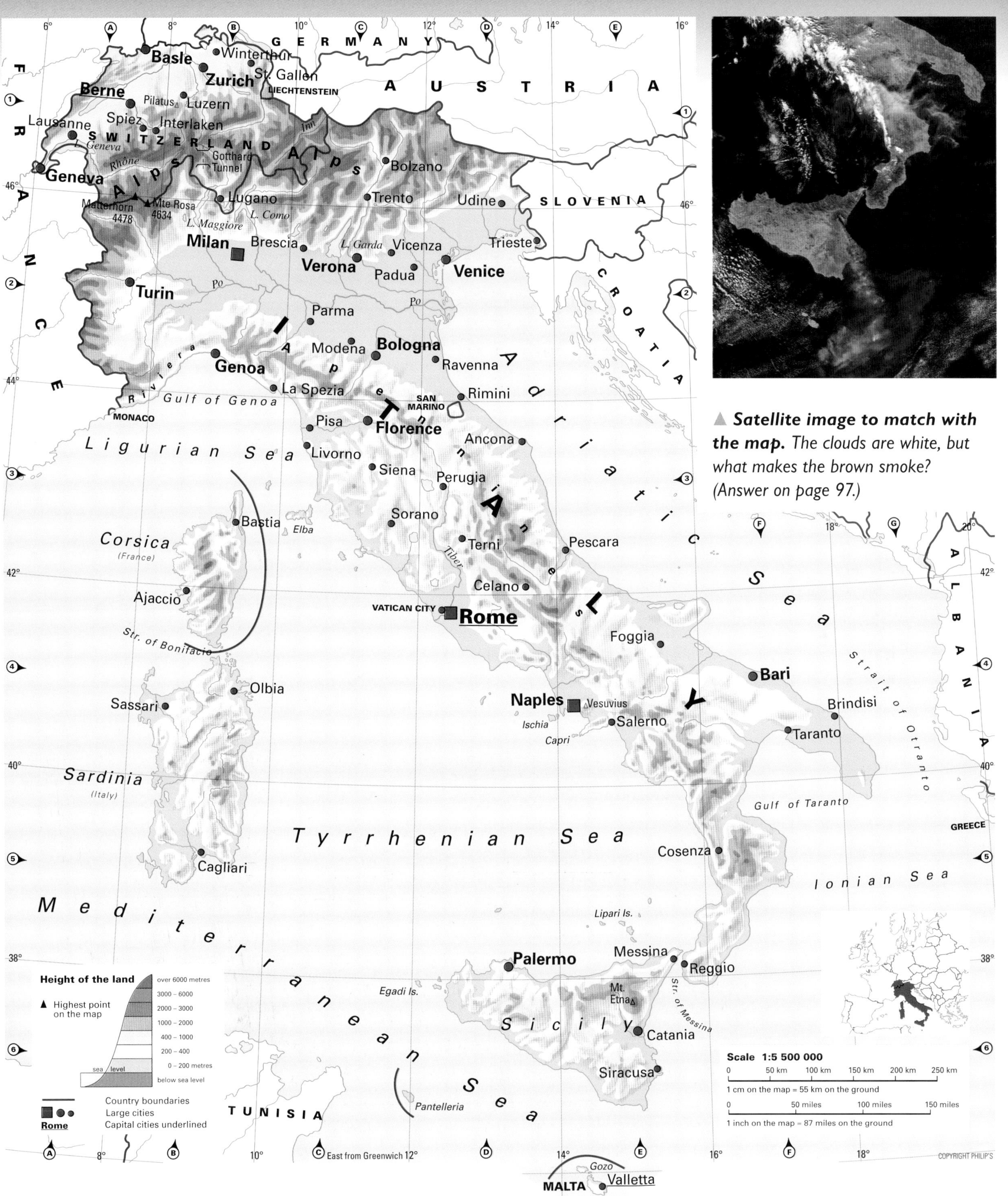

▲ ***Satellite image to match with the map.*** *The clouds are white, but what makes the brown smoke? (Answer on page 97.)*

SOUTH-EAST EUROPE

GREECE

AREA 131,957 sq km
POPULATION 10,570,000
MONEY Euro

BULGARIA

AREA 110,912 sq km
POPULATION 6,919,000
MONEY Lev

ALBANIA

AREA 28,748 sq km
POPULATION 3,088,000
MONEY Lek

MOST of south-east Europe is very mountainous, except near the River Danube. Farmers keep sheep and goats in the mountains and grow grain, vines and sunflowers on the lower land.

The coastlines are popular with tourists. There are many holiday resorts beside the Adriatic Sea (**Croatia**), the Aegean Sea (**Greece** and **Turkey**), and the Black Sea (**Romania** and **Bulgaria**). The Romanians are building new ski villages in their mountains. All these countries are trying to develop new industries, but this is still one of the poorest parts of Europe.

Albania is one of the least-known countries in Europe, although it is now slowly opening up to visits from tourists.

Yugoslavia no longer exists. It was 1 country with 2 alphabets (Latin and Cyrillic), 3 religious groups (Roman Catholic, Orthodox and Muslim), and 4 languages. Now there are 7 countries: **Slovenia**, **Croatia**, **Serbia**, **Montenegro**, **Kosovo**, **Bosnia-Herzegovina** and **North Macedonia**.

▲ ***The town of Korcula, in Croatia,*** *is built on an island – also called Korcula – in the Adriatic Sea, north-west of Dubrovnik. In the distance are the limestone mountains of the mainland. Until 1991, Croatia was part of Yugoslavia, but after some fighting it became independent.*

▲ ***Transylvania, in central Romania,*** *is a scenic area surrounded by high mountains: find the Carpathians on the map. This tractor is preparing the rich soil in the valley for crops.*

THE DANUBE

This stamp shows a boat at the gorge on the River Danube called the Iron Gates, on the southern border of Romania. The Danube flows from Germany to a marshy delta beside the Black Sea.

THE CORINTH CANAL

A cruise ship being towed through the Corinth Canal in southern Greece. The canal was cut in 1893 and is 6.4 kilometres long. It links the Gulf of Corinth with the Aegean Sea.

Α	Β	Γ	Δ	Ε	Ζ	Η	Θ	Ι	Κ	Λ	Μ	Ν	Ξ	Ο	Π	Ρ	Σ	Τ	Υ	Φ	Χ	Ψ	Ω
A	V/B	G	D	E	Z	E	TH	I	K	L	M	N	X	O	P	R	S	T	Y	F	CH	PS	O

▲ ***The Greek alphabet:*** *the Greeks developed their alphabet before the Romans, and they still use it. Some letters are the same as ours (A, B ...), and some look the same but have a different sound (P, H ...). The other letters are completely different. Some Greek letters appear in the Cyrillic alphabet, which is used in Bulgaria, the former Yugoslavia, and Russia (see page 41). The word 'alphabet' is formed from the first two Greek letters: alpha and beta. The Greek letter for D is called 'delta': also the name for some river mouths that have a similar shape (page 96).*

▲ ***The Acropolis of Athens, Greece.*** *The monuments on this hill above the capital city are the ruins of temples built about 2400 years ago. Ruins of ancient Greek cities can be found in many of the countries shown on the map.*

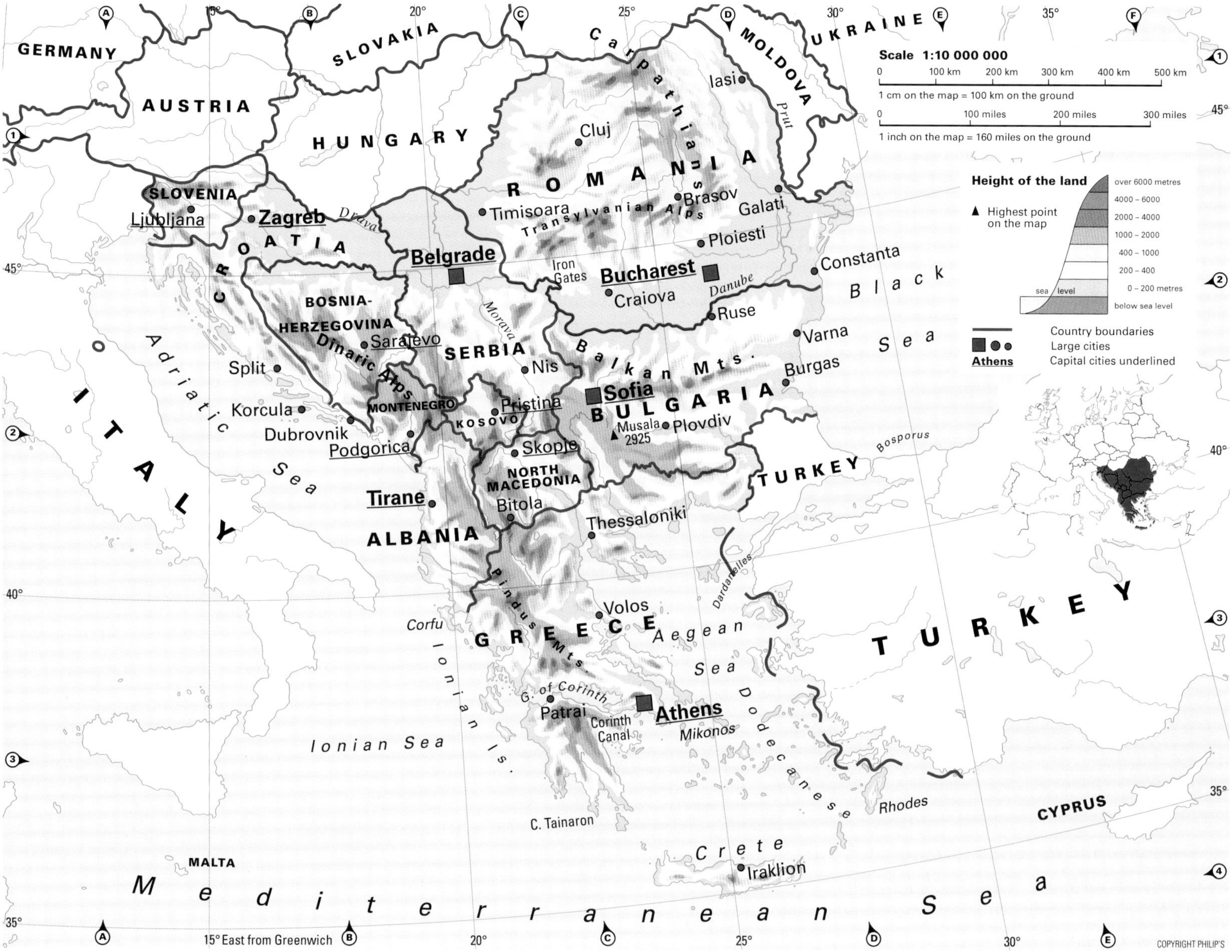

Scale 1:10 000 000

0 100 km 200 km 300 km 400 km 500 km

1 cm on the map = 100 km on the ground

0 100 miles 200 miles 300 miles

1 inch on the map = 160 miles on the ground

Height of the land

▲ Highest point on the map

over 6000 metres; 4000 – 6000; 2000 – 4000; 1000 – 2000; 400 – 1000; 200 – 400; 0 – 200 metres; sea level; below sea level

Country boundaries

Large cities

Athens Capital cities underlined

15° East from Greenwich

COPYRIGHT PHILIP'S

EASTERN EUROPE

POLAND

AREA 323,250 sq km
POPULATION 38,186,000
MONEY Zloty

HUNGARY

AREA 93,032 sq km
POPULATION 9,728,000
MONEY Forint

UKRAINE

AREA 603,700 sq km
POPULATION 43,746,000
MONEY Hryvnia

SEVEN countries from Eastern Europe joined the European Union in 2004: Estonia, Latvia, Lithuania, Poland, Czechia, Slovakia and Hungary.

Poland has a coastline on the Baltic Sea. There are huge shipbuilding factories at Gdansk. Towns in the south have big factories, too, where there is plenty of coal. Most of Poland is flat farmland. The magnificent mountains in the far south are being 'rediscovered' by tourists.

Czechoslovakia split into two countries in 1993. **Czechia** is west of **Slovakia**. Both countries have beautiful hills and mountains, with fine pine trees. Skoda cars come from Czechia. Further south is **Hungary**, a small country with SEVEN neighbours – can you name them? Most of Hungary is good farmland on plains and hills.

Polish, Czech and Slovak are all Slavic languages. Hungarian is totally different: it came from central Asia. Some Hungarian speakers also live in Slovakia and Romania.

Six countries on this map were part of the USSR (Soviet Union) until 1991.

▲ ***Budapest, on the River Danube.*** *Buda and Pest were twin cities on either side of the River Danube. Now they have become Budapest, capital of Hungary. The river Danube is an important international waterway that flows through 9 countries.*

▲ ***Town square in Telc, Czechia.*** *These houses date from the 1500s, when the town was rebuilt after a great fire. This is a popular place for tourists to visit. The historic centres of many towns in Eastern Europe are carefully preserved. Some have been totally rebuilt in the old style after wartime bombing.*

BELARUS

AREA 207,600 sq km
POPULATION 9,442,000
MONEY Belarusian ruble

CZECHIA

AREA 78,866 sq km
POPULATION 10,703,000
MONEY Czech koruna

SLOVAKIA

AREA 49,012 sq km
POPULATION 5,436,000
MONEY Euro

▲ ***Church in Ukraine,*** *where many people are Orthodox Christians. The Ukraine is Europe's biggest country, apart from Russia. The population is nearly as big as the UK or France.*

CAN YOU FIND THESE ON THE MAP?

- 4 seas (1 in the north; 3 in the south).
- A lake shared by 2 countries.
- A river with 4 lakes (these lakes have been made by dams).
- A river with a 3-letter name.
- A city with a 14-letter name.
- 2 capital cities very near the sea.
- A mountain over 2500 metres high (the highest part of the mountain ridge in the picture, right).
- A peninsula that is joined to the rest of Ukraine by a very narrow piece of land.

Estonia, **Latvia** and **Lithuania** are called 'the Baltic republics' because they lie alongside the coast of the Baltic Sea. **Belarus** ('White Russia') and little **Moldova** are landlocked countries, like several others on this map.

Ukraine is the largest country completely in Europe, but it is also one of the poorest. It has large areas of fertile farmland. Europe's largest coalfield is in the east, and there is iron ore for its steelworks. Crimea is now under the control of Russia.

▲ ***The border of Poland (right) and Slovakia (left)*** *runs along a high ridge of the Tatra Mountains. Can you find this border on the map below?*

Scale 1:10 000 000

0 100 km 200 km 300 km 400 km 500 km

1 cm on the map = 100 km on the ground

0 100 miles 200 miles 300 miles

1 inch on the map = 160 miles on the ground

Height of the land: over 6000 metres; 4000 – 6000; 2000 – 4000; 1000 – 2000; 400 – 1000; 200 – 400; 0 – 200 metres; sea level; below sea level

▲ Highest point on the map

Country boundaries

Large cities

Warsaw — Capital cities underlined

NORWAY, SWEDEN, DENMARK, GERMANY, RUSSIA, (RUSSIA), ESTONIA, LATVIA, LITHUANIA, BELARUS, POLAND, CZECHIA, SLOVAKIA, AUSTRIA, HUNGARY, UKRAINE, MOLDOVA, ROMANIA, ITALY, SLOVENIA, CROATIA, BOSNIA-HERZEGOVINA, SERBIA

Baltic Sea, Saaremaa, L. Chudskoye, Adriatic Sea, Sea of Azov, Black Sea, Crimea (under Russian control)

Oder, Vistula, Pripet, Dnepr, Dnestr, Bug, Prut, Danube, Carpathians, Tatra Mts., 2655

Tallinn, Tartu, Riga, Daugavpils, Kaunas, Vilnius, Vitsyebsk, Minsk, Homyel, Brest, Gdansk, Szczecin, Bialystok, Poznan, Warsaw, Lodz, Wroclaw, Lublin, Krakow, Prague, Ostrava, Brno, Bratislava, Budapest, Szeged, Lviv, Chernobyl, Kiev, Zhytomyr, Kharkiv, Lugansk, Dnipro, Donetsk, Mariupol, Chisinau, Odesa, Sevastopol

10° 15° 20° 25° 30° 35° 40° 45° 50° 55° East from Greenwich

COPYRIGHT PHILIP'S

ASIA

THE world's largest continent is Asia, which stretches from the cold Arctic Ocean in the north to the warm Indian Ocean in the south.

Mainland Asia nearly reaches the Equator in Malaysia. Several Asian islands are on the Equator: Sumatra, Borneo and Sulawesi. In the west, Asia reaches Europe and the Mediterranean, and in the east Asia reaches the Pacific Ocean. In the centre are the high, empty plateaus of Tibet and Mongolia, where winters are bitterly cold.

Two countries cover over half of Asia: Russia and China. India looks quite small – yet it is over ten times as big as Italy or the UK! But some of Asia's important countries are very small indeed, such as Lebanon and Israel in south-west Asia (Middle East); Singapore and Brunei in south-east Asia (Far East).

Over half the world's population lives in Asia. Seven of the world's 'top ten' most populated countries are here (see page 9). The coastal areas of south and east Asia are the most crowded parts. But people in these areas are in danger from typhoons or cyclones (also called hurricanes) and tsunamis (huge waves caused by earthquakes under the sea).

▲ ***This Buddhist shrine*** *is like many found in Nepal. It has been decorated with prayer flags and painted eyes.*

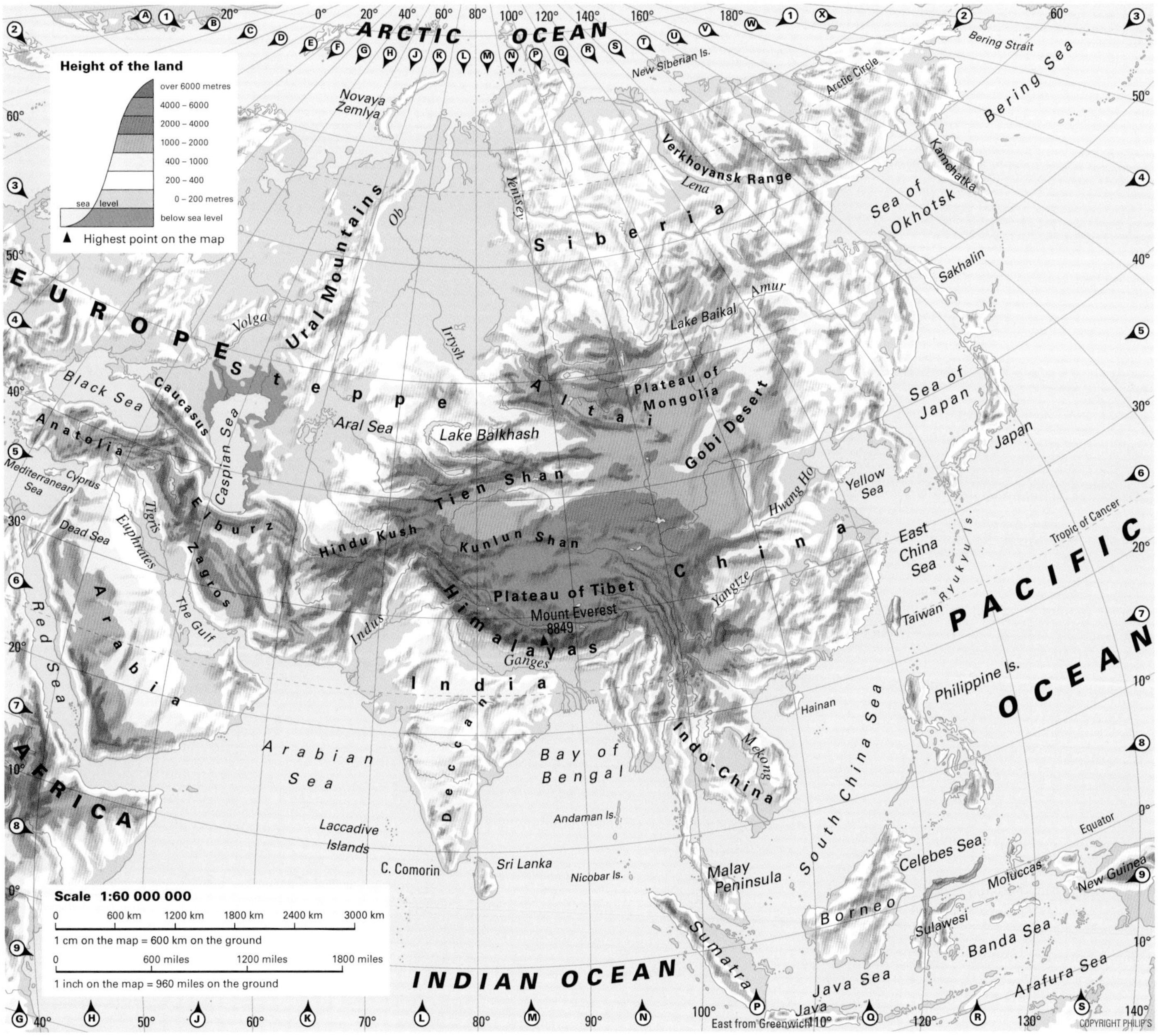

Height of the land

- over 6000 metres
- 4000 – 6000
- 2000 – 4000
- 1000 – 2000
- 400 – 1000
- 200 – 400
- 0 – 200 metres
- below sea level
- sea level
- ▲ Highest point on the map

Scale 1:60 000 000

0 – 600 km – 1200 km – 1800 km – 2400 km – 3000 km

1 cm on the map = 600 km on the ground

0 – 600 miles – 1200 miles – 1800 miles

1 inch on the map = 960 miles on the ground

澳 1

埃 2

香 3

美 4

台 5

Turn to page which countrie script here.

ASIA FACTS

AREA 44,387,000 sq km (including Asiatic Russia)
HIGHEST POINT Mount Everest (Nepal/China), 8849 metres (A world record as well as an Asian record.)
LOWEST POINT Shores of Dead Sea (Israel/Jordan), 400 metres below sea level (A world record as well as an Asian record.)
LONGEST RIVERS Yangtze (China), 6380 km; Yenisey (Russia), 5540 km
BIGGEST COUNTRY Russia, 17,075,400 sq km (A world record as well as an Asian record.)
SMALLEST COUNTRY The Maldives, 298 sq km
LARGEST LAKE Caspian Sea, 371,000 sq km (A world record as well as an Asian record.) The Caspian Sea is shared by five countries – which are they? (*Answers on page 97.*)

▲ ***Himalayan Mountains, Nepal.*** *The photograph shows Annapurna I. Annapurna I is 8078 metres high and was first climbed in 1950. There are four other peaks in the group that are over 7500 metres high. The Himalayas are the world's highest mountain range, containing all the world's 'top ten' highest peaks, including Mount Everest.*

洲及港國灣

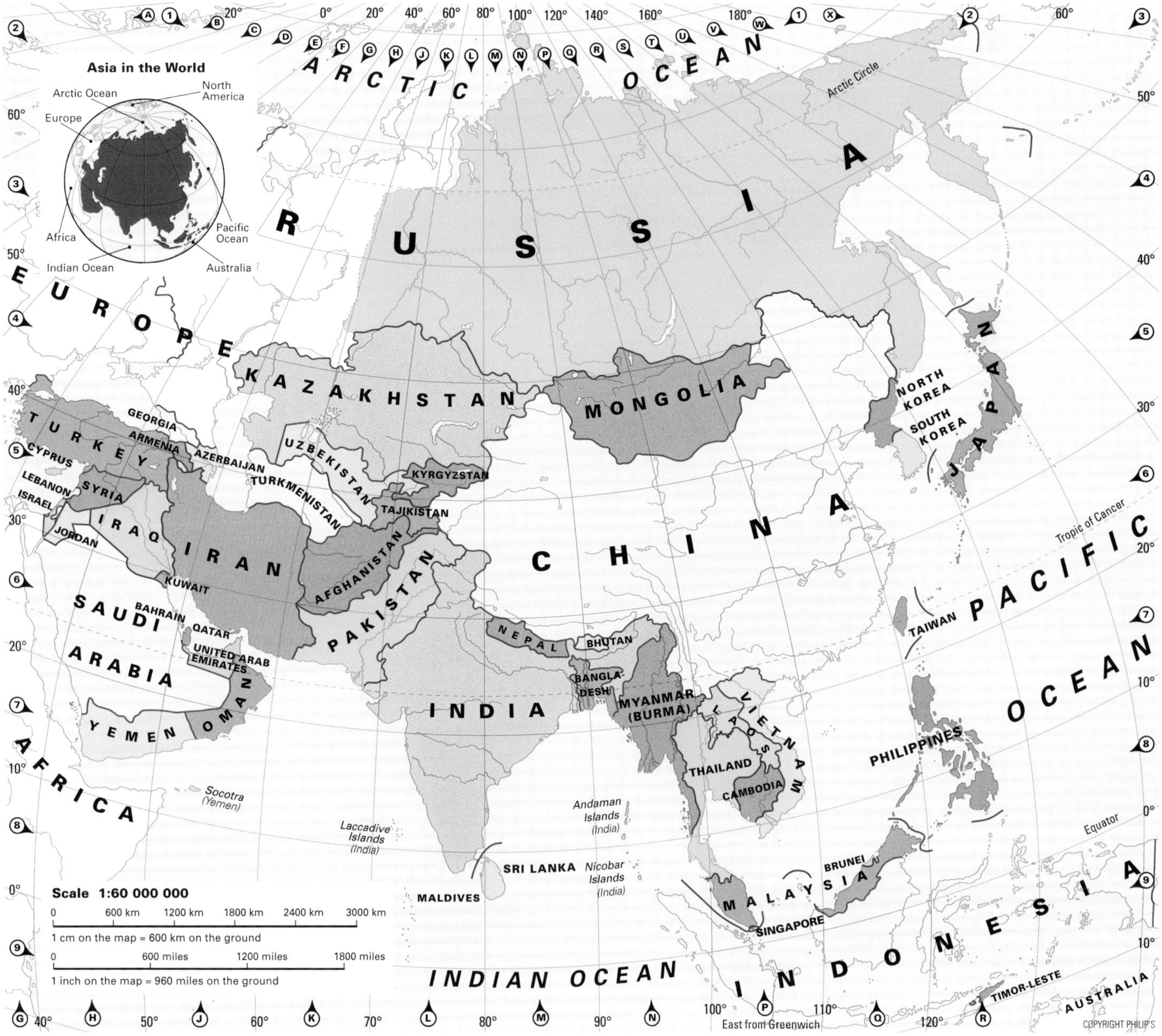

7 to find out
re in Chinese

Asia in the World
Arctic Ocean
North America
Europe
Africa
Pacific Ocean
Indian Ocean
Australia

ARCTIC OCEAN
RUSSIA
EUROPE
KAZAKHSTAN
MONGOLIA
NORTH KOREA
SOUTH KOREA
JAPAN
GEORGIA
ARMENIA
AZERBAIJAN
TURKEY
CYPRUS
LEBANON
ISRAEL
SYRIA
UZBEKISTAN
TURKMENISTAN
KYRGYZSTAN
TAJIKISTAN
IRAQ
JORDAN
IRAN
AFGHANISTAN
PAKISTAN
CHINA
KUWAIT
BAHRAIN
QATAR
SAUDI ARABIA
UNITED ARAB EMIRATES
OMAN
YEMEN
NEPAL
BHUTAN
BANGLADESH
INDIA
MYANMAR (BURMA)
LAOS
VIETNAM
THAILAND
CAMBODIA
TAIWAN
PHILIPPINES
PACIFIC OCEAN
AFRICA
Socotra (Yemen)
Laccadive Islands (India)
Andaman Islands (India)
Nicobar Islands (India)
SRI LANKA
MALDIVES
MALAYSIA
BRUNEI
SINGAPORE
INDONESIA
TIMOR-LESTE
AUSTRALIA
INDIAN OCEAN
Arctic Circle
Tropic of Cancer
Equator
East from Greenwich

Scale 1:60 000 000
0 600 km 1200 km 1800 km 2400 km 3000 km
1 cm on the map = 600 km on the ground
0 600 miles 1200 miles 1800 miles
1 inch on the map = 960 miles on the ground

RUSSIA AND NEIGHBOURS

RUSSIA

AREA 17,075,400 sq km
POPULATION 142,321,000
MONEY Russian ruble

KAZAKHSTAN

AREA 2,724,900 sq km
POPULATION 19,246,000
MONEY Tenge

TURKMENISTAN

AREA 488,100 sq km
POPULATION 5,580,000
MONEY Manat

RUSSIA stretches across two continents, Europe and Asia. Most of the people live in the European part, west of the Ural Mountains. Some people have moved east to new towns in Siberia.

Because Russia is so huge, there are many different climates and almost all crops can be grown. The far north is snow-covered for most of the year (see page 88). Further south is the largest forest in the world – a vast area of coniferous trees stretching from the Baltic Sea to the Sea of Okhotsk in the far east. Grassy plains, called the steppes, are found south of the forest. In some parts, grain is grown on huge farms. Russia also has large deposits of many different minerals and can supply most of the needs of its many factories.

The republics of central Asia are mostly in a desert area – hot in summer but bitterly cold in winter. With irrigation, crops such as sugar-cane and cotton grow well. Space rockets are launched from the 'Cosmodrome' in the desert of Kazakhstan.

▲ ***St Basil's cathedral, Moscow,*** *is at one end of Red Square. It is famous for its brightly coloured domes: each one is different. In the background are the domes and towers of buildings inside the Kremlin walls. 'Kremlin' means 'fortress'. The Moscow Kremlin has a cathedral and offices of the government of Russia.*

▲ ***In Uzbekistan,*** *people still use traditional looms like this one, for weaving silk, cotton and wool – but there is modern industry as well. Uzbekistan is one of the 15 countries created when the USSR broke up in 1991. Can you name them? (Page 37 will help; answers on page 97.)*

THE ARAL SEA ...

... is getting smaller. This ship was once in the Aral Sea, but is now on dry land. This salty lake is drying up because rivers do not refill it with enough water. The water is used to irrigate fields instead.

▲ ***Siberia*** *has the world's largest forest. It stretches from the Ural Mountains to the far east of Russia. Most of the trees are conifers. They can survive the Siberian winters, which are long and extremely cold.*

А	Б	В	Г	Д	Е	Ё	Ж	З	И	Й	К	Л	М	Н	О	П	Р	С	Т	У	Ф	Х	Ц	Ч	Ш	Щ	Ю	Я
A	B	V	G	D	E	YO	ZH	Z	I	Y	K	L	M	N	O	P	R	S	T	U	F	KH	TS	CH	SH	SHCH	YU	YA

▲ ***Russian is written in the Cyrillic alphabet.*** *This is partly based on Latin letters (the same as English letters) and partly on Greek letters (see page 35).*

The alphabet was invented centuries ago by St Cyril, so that the Russian church could show it was separate from both the Roman and the Greek churches. In Cyrillic, R is written P, and S is written C. So the Metro is written METPO.

CAN YOU UNDERSTAND THIS MESSAGE?

Use the key above: Х А Б А Р О В С К (square S4) is on the River А М У Р (see square S3 on the map). Now work out what the sign on the railway carriage (right) says. It is not as hard as it looks! Uzbekistan and some other republics of Central Asia are keeping the same language but changing their alphabet from Cyrillic to 'Latin' (as used in English and many other languages).

TRANS-SIBERIAN RAILWAY

It takes a week to cross Russia by train, and you must change your watch seven times. Here is the distance chart and timetable (only the main stops are shown).

МОСКВА-ВЛАДИВОСТОК

This is the plate on the side of the train. The translation is on page 97. This is one of the world's most exciting train journeys.

DISTANCE (IN KM)	TOWN	TIME (IN MOSCOW)	DAY
0	Moscow	15:05	1
957	Kirov	04:00	2
1818	Yekaterinburg	16:25	2
2716	Omsk	03:13	3
3343	Novosibirsk	10:44	3
4104	Krasnoyarsk	22:31	3
5184	Irkutsk	16:23	4
5647	Ulan Ude	00:02	5
6204	Chita	09:23	5
7313	Skovorodino	05:20	6
8531	Khabarovsk	01:10	7
9297	Vladivostok	13:30*	7

* This is 20:30 local time in Vladivostok.

At these stations, there is time for a quick walk – and some bartering. But don't forget to allow another week to come back!

Scale 1:45 000 000
0 450 km 900 km 1350 km 1800 km
1 cm on the map = 450 km on the ground
0 450 miles 900 miles
1 inch on the map = 720 miles on the ground

Height of the land
over 6000 metres
4000 – 6000
2000 – 4000
1000 – 2000
400 – 1000
200 – 400
0 – 200 metres
below sea level
▲ Highest point on the map
Country boundaries
Large cities
Capital cities underlined

80° East from Greenwich 90°

MIDDLE EAST

SAUDI ARABIA

AREA 2,149,690 sq km
POPULATION 34,784,000
MONEY Saudi riyal

JORDAN

AREA 89,342 sq km
POPULATION 10,910,000
MONEY Jordan dinar

IRAN

AREA 1,648,195 sq km
POPULATION 85,889,000
MONEY Iranian rial

THE 'Middle East' is another name for 'south-west Asia'. It is the part of Asia which is closest to Europe and Africa. In fact, it is the only place where three continents meet. Turkey is partly in Europe and mostly in Asia. Of all the countries on this map, Turkey and Iran have the most people.

Most of the Middle East is semi-desert or desert. Yet many great civilizations have existed here, such as the Assyrian, the Babylonian and the Persian. Their monuments are found in the fertile valleys of the largest rivers, the Tigris and the Euphrates. During the fighting in Iraq, some historic buildings were destroyed and many people were killed.

Scarce water is used to irrigate crops in some places. In others, herds of sheep and goats are kept. Only camels can be kept in the driest desert areas. Dates from **Iraq** come from desert oases; oranges come from irrigated land in **Israel**. So much water is being taken from the River Jordan that the Dead Sea is getting smaller. Some countries make fresh water from salt water, but it is expensive.

▲ ***Craft stall in San'a, Yemen.*** *These men are making decorative daggers which are worn by men and older boys in Yemen. This small workshop opens directly off one of the narrow streets in the old part of San'a, the capital of Yemen. Craft industries still thrive in towns and villages all over the Middle East.*

IRAQ

AREA 438,317 sq km
POPULATION 39,650,000
MONEY Iraqi dinar

CONSTRUCTION

▲ ***Progress in Qatar:*** *is shown by the highways and high-rise office blocks being built with money from oil.*

▲ ***Yemen:*** *this is an ancient multi-storey building made of mud bricks and built on top of a cliff.*

HOLY CITIES OF THE MIDDLE EAST

Jerusalem: a Jewish boy's Bar Mitzvah ceremony at the West Wall ('Wailing Wall'). The huge stones (in the background, on the right) are all that remains of the Jewish temple. Jerusalem is a holy city for Jews, Christians and Muslims. People of all three religions live here and many pilgrims and tourists visit the city.

Mecca: crowds of pilgrims surround the Kaaba (the huge black stone, centre) inside the Great Mosque. Mecca is the holiest city of Islam as it is where the prophet Mohammed was born. Muslims try to come to worship here at least once in their lifetime. But wherever they are, they face towards Mecca when they pray.

The Middle East has changed dramatically in the last 60 years. Oil was found beneath the Arabian desert and around the Persian Gulf. It is pumped out from below the desert and mountains and even from under the sea. The demand for oil has grown in Europe and all over the world. The sale of oil has made some countries very rich, especially **Saudi Arabia**, **Kuwait** and **Qatar**. Often the rulers have benefited most, but they have also used the money to build schools, hospitals, roads and office blocks. The 'oil boom' has meant that many foreign workers have come to these countries to construct modern buildings like the ones in the photo of Dubai.

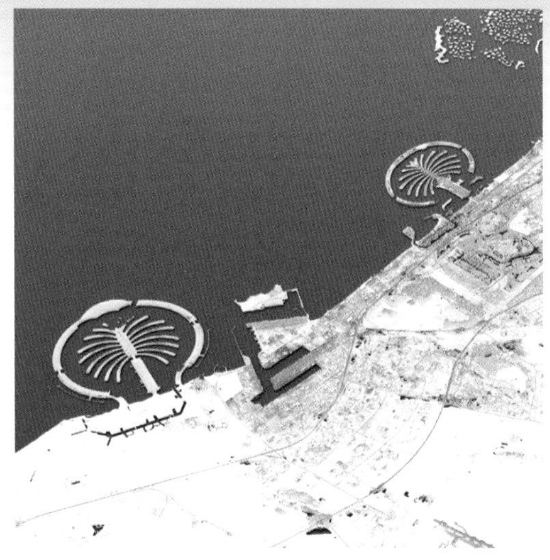

▲ ***Dubai in the United Arab Emirates*** *is a modern city in the desert by the Persian Gulf. Man-made islands are being built in the shape of palm trees.*

▲ ***A camel in the desert of Jordan.*** *This boy is hoping tourists might want a ride in Wadi Rum, a dry valley in southern Jordan.*

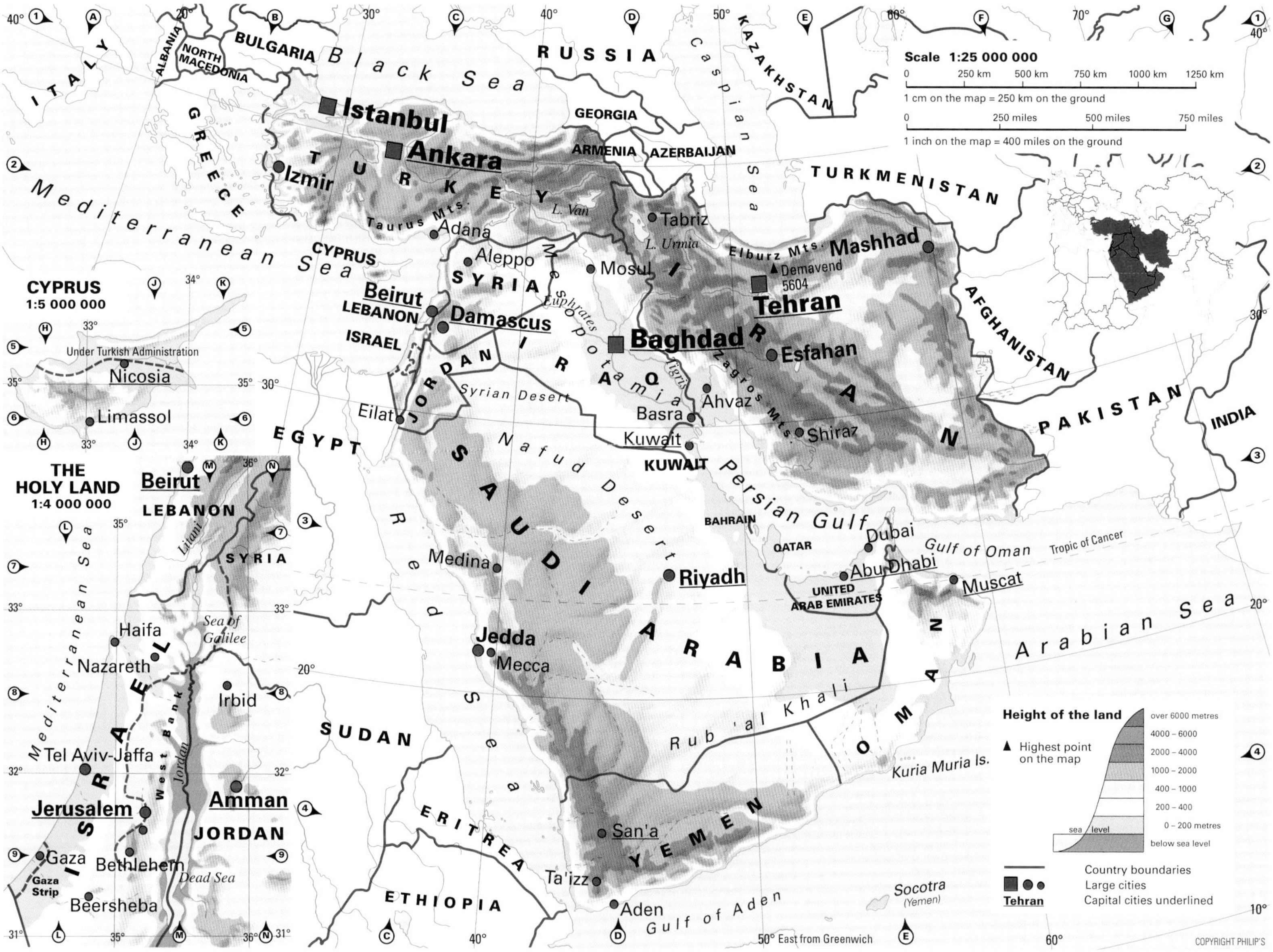

Scale 1:25 000 000

0 250 km 500 km 750 km 1000 km 1250 km

1 cm on the map = 250 km on the ground

0 250 miles 500 miles 750 miles

1 inch on the map = 400 miles on the ground

RUSSIA, KAZAKHSTAN, TURKMENISTAN, AFGHANISTAN, PAKISTAN, INDIA, ITALY, ALBANIA, NORTH MACEDONIA, BULGARIA, GREECE, TURKEY, GEORGIA, ARMENIA, AZERBAIJAN, CYPRUS, SYRIA, LEBANON, ISRAEL, JORDAN, IRAQ, IRAN, EGYPT, KUWAIT, BAHRAIN, QATAR, UNITED ARAB EMIRATES, SAUDI ARABIA, OMAN, YEMEN, SUDAN, ERITREA, ETHIOPIA

Black Sea, Caspian Sea, Mediterranean Sea, Red Sea, Persian Gulf, Gulf of Oman, Arabian Sea, Gulf of Aden, Tropic of Cancer

Istanbul, Ankara, Izmir, Adana, Aleppo, Beirut, Damascus, Mosul, Tabriz, Tehran, Mashhad, Baghdad, Esfahan, Ahvaz, Basra, Shiraz, Kuwait, Eilat, Medina, Riyadh, Dubai, Abu Dhabi, Muscat, Jedda, Mecca, San'a, Ta'izz, Aden

Taurus Mts., L. Van, L. Urmia, Elburz Mts., Demavend 5604, Zagros Mts., Mesopotamia, Euphrates, Tigris, Syrian Desert, Nafud Desert, Rub 'al Khali, Kuria Muria Is., Socotra (Yemen)

CYPRUS 1:5 000 000

Under Turkish Administration, Nicosia, Limassol

THE HOLY LAND 1:4 000 000

Beirut, LEBANON, Litani, SYRIA, Mediterranean Sea, Haifa, Sea of Galilee, Nazareth, Irbid, ISRAEL, West Bank, Jordan, Tel Aviv-Jaffa, Amman, Jerusalem, JORDAN, Gaza, Gaza Strip, Bethlehem, Dead Sea, Beersheba

Height of the land: over 6000 metres; 4000 – 6000; 2000 – 4000; 1000 – 2000; 400 – 1000; 200 – 400; 0 – 200 metres; sea level; below sea level

▲ Highest point on the map

Country boundaries

Large cities

Capital cities underlined (Tehran)

50° East from Greenwich

SOUTH ASIA

INDIA

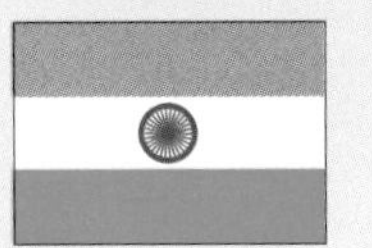

AREA 3,287,263 sq km
POPULATION 1,339,331,000
MONEY Indian rupee
CAPITAL New Delhi

PAKISTAN

AREA 796,095 sq km
POPULATION 238,181,000
MONEY Pakistani rupee
CAPITAL Islamabad

SRI LANKA

AREA 65,610 sq km
POPULATION 23,044,000
MONEY Sri Lankan rupee

THE world's highest mountains appear on this map, including Mount Everest. The Himalayas form a great mountain chain which joins on to other high mountain areas, such as the Hindu Kush.

More than 1400 million people live in south Asia. The deserts and mountains do not have many people, but the river valleys, plains and plateaus are crowded.

Afghanistan, **Bhutan** and **Nepal** are rugged, mountainous countries.

Bangladesh is very different: it is mostly flat, low-lying land where the great rivers Ganges and Brahmaputra reach the sea.

Pakistan has very little rain, but the River Indus is used to irrigate crops.

India is the largest country. It stretches 3300 kilometres from the Himalayas to Cape Comorin. Most people live in the villages, but towns and cities are growing fast and are overcrowded. There are many modern factories, and India makes more films than any other country.

Sri Lanka (once called Ceylon) is a mountainous island off the coast of India.

The Maldives are a chain of low, flat, coral islands in the Indian Ocean.

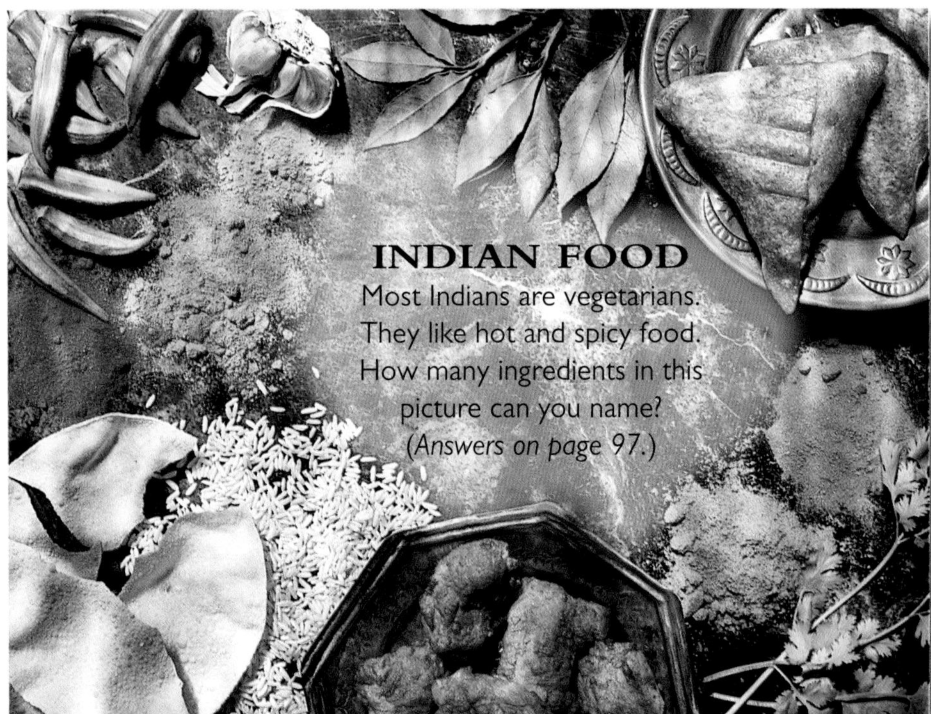

INDIAN FOOD

Most Indians are vegetarians. They like hot and spicy food. How many ingredients in this picture can you name? (*Answers on page 97.*)

▲ ***Wool for carpets.*** *This lady in northern India is winding wool which will be used to make carpets. She sits in the courtyard of her house, where the ploughs and pots and pans are also kept.*

TEA PLANTATIONS

Tea is an important crop in the hills of Sri Lanka where nights are cool, and there is plenty of rain. Women pick the new young leaves from the bushes (as shown on the stamp). The leaves are then dried and crushed, and packed into large tea chests for storage. 'Ceylon Tea' is one of Sri Lanka's most important exports. Where does the tea you drink come from?

AFGHANISTAN

AREA 652,090 sq km
POPULATION 37,466,000
MONEY Afghani

NEPAL

AREA 147,181 sq km
POPULATION 30,425,000
MONEY Nepalese rupee

Religion is very important in the lives of people in south Asia.

Hinduism is the oldest religion, and most people in India and Nepal are Hindus.

Buddhism began in India, but only Sri Lanka and Bhutan are mainly Buddhist today.

Islam is the religion of most people in Afghanistan, Pakistan and Bangladesh. There are many Muslims in India, too

Many **Sikhs** live in northern India; there are also **Christian** groups in all these countries.

Rice is an important food crop in south Asia. It grows best where the land is flat, and where the weather is hot and wet. In a good year, rice grows in the wet fields and is ready for harvesting after four or five months. If the monsoon fails and there is a drought, the seedlings will shrivel up; too much rain and the seedlings will drown. If the rice crop fails, many people go hungry. Where irrigation is available, the farmer can control the water supply and may be able to grow two rice crops a year.

► ***The Markhor** is a rare goat with curled horns that lives in the mountains of Pakistan and Afghanistan.*

▲ ***Planting rice, Kashmir, India.** These men are planting out rice seedlings in the wet soil.*

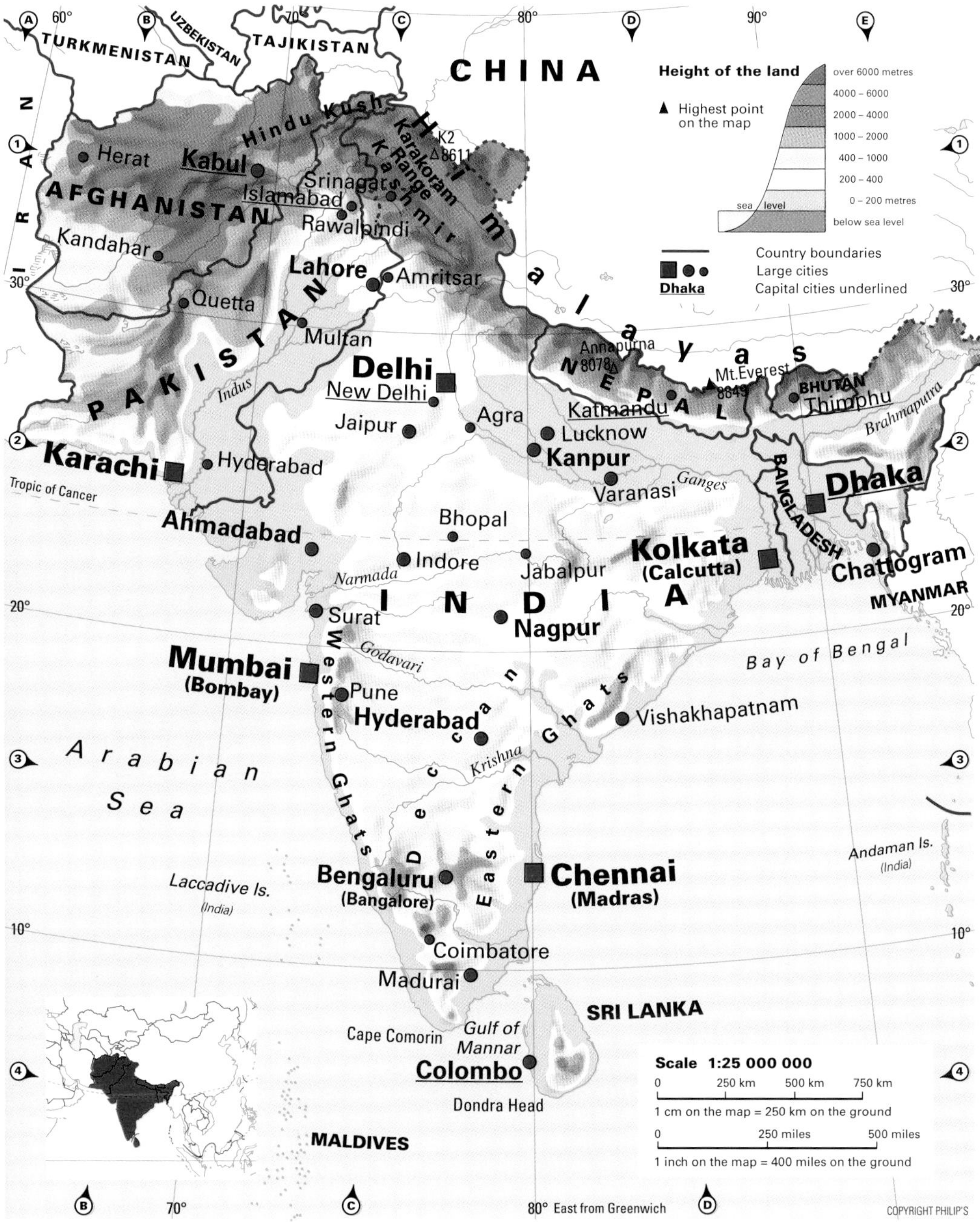

MOUNT EVEREST

Mount Everest is the world's highest mountain – 8849 metres above sea level. It was not climbed until 1953.

Everest is on the border of Nepal and Tibet (now part of China) – find it on the map in square D2. It is called 'Sagarmatha' in Nepalese, and in Chinese it is known as 'Qomolangma' (Queen of Mountains).

The photograph shows a glacier below the icy summit, and the bare rock that climbers have to cross. At this height, the air is very thin, so climbing is very hard and most climbers carry oxygen with them.

SOUTH-EAST ASIA

PHILIPPINES

AREA 300,000 sq km
POPULATION 110,818,000
MONEY Philippine peso

THAILAND

AREA 513,115 sq km
POPULATION 69,481,000
MONEY Baht

SINGAPORE

AREA 683 sq km
POPULATION 5,866,000
MONEY Singapore dollar

▲ ***Singapore** is the world's most crowded country. Most smaller old shops and houses have been replaced by new skyscrapers.*

THE Equator crosses South-east Asia, so it is always hot. Heavy tropical rainstorms are common. The mainland and most of the islands are very mountainous.

Indonesia is the biggest country, by both area and population. It used to be called the Dutch East Indies.

The Philippines is another large group of islands, south of China. They were Spanish until 1898.

Malaysia includes part of the mainland and most of northern Borneo.

Brunei is a very small but a very rich country on the island of Borneo.

Myanmar (Burma) was counted as part of British India. It became independent in 1948.

Vietnam, **Laos** and **Cambodia** were once called French Indo-China.

Thailand has always been independent, and has a king.

▲ ***Rice terraces, Bali.** Rice grows on terraces cut into the mountainside in Bali. Each terrace is sown and harvested by hand. Bali is a small island east of Java. Some people claim that it is the most beautiful island of Indonesia, and in all the world!*

GROWING RICE

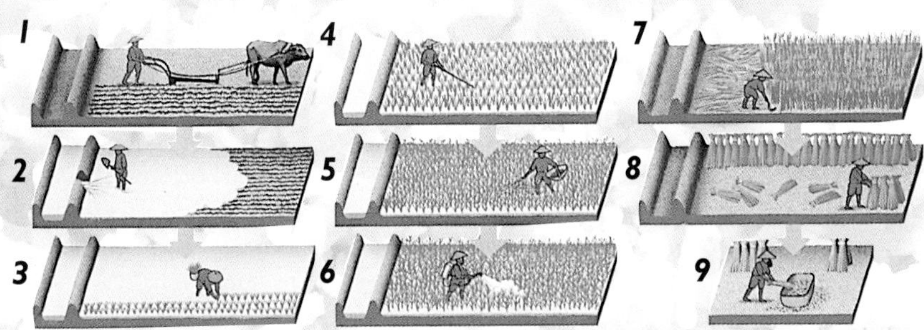

1 Ploughing
2 Irrigation
3 Transplanting
4 Weeding
5 Fertilizing
6 Spraying
7 Harvesting
8 Drying
9 Threshing

Rice is the world's most important crop. The nine stages in growing rice are shown above. It is hot, hard work. Rice needs plenty of water as well as hot sunshine. New varieties of plants yield more rice, but they also need more fertilizer, more water and more care.

▲ ***Floating market in Thailand.** Farmers bring their fruit and vegetables by boat to a market at Damnoen Saduak, to the west of Bangkok. Fish are cooked on some of the boats and sold for lunch.*

The mountains of South-east Asia are covered with thick tropical forest (look at the stamp of Laos). Rare animals and plants live here, but they will not survive if the forest is cut down These areas are very difficult to reach and have few people. The large rivers are important routes inland. Their valleys and deltas are very crowded indeed.

Java, Bali and Singapore are among the most crowded islands in the world – yet several bigger islands, such as Sulawesi and Borneo, have very small populations.

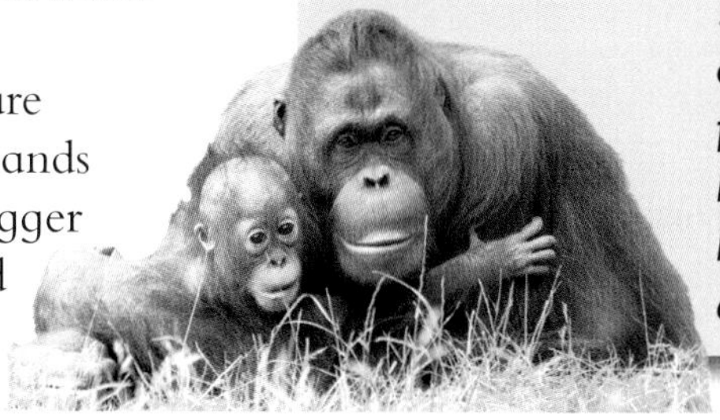

▼ ***Borneo** is a large island shared by 3 countries. Its forests are home to the rare Orang-utan.*

République Démocratique Populaire Lao
Postes 1982
2K

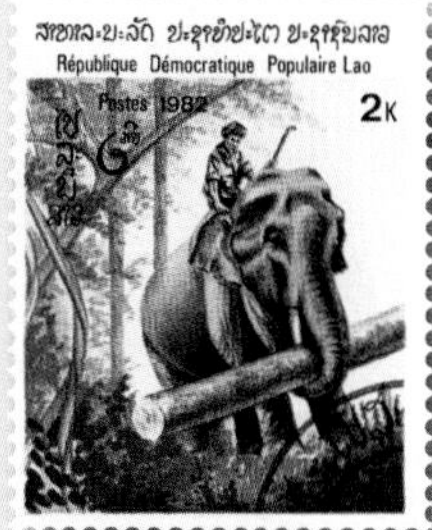

▲ ***Laos.** Elephants carry huge logs from the jungle. Laos was called Lanxang – 'land of a million elephants'.*

5
Thống nhất
BƯU CHÍNH
VIỆT NAM

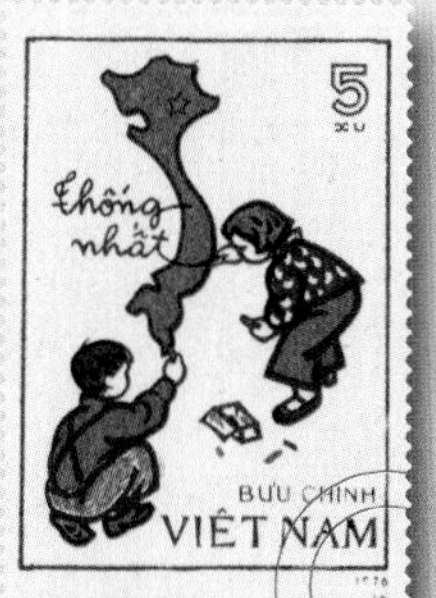

▲ ***Vietnam.** These young children are learning to draw a map of their country.*

PELITA REPUBLIK INDONESIA

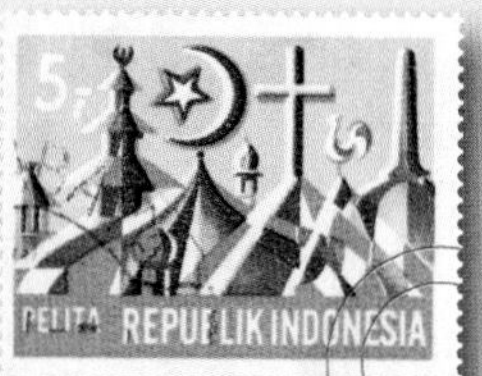

▲ ***Indonesia** is mainly an Islamic country. The moon and star (seen here above a mosque) are traditional symbols of Islam.*

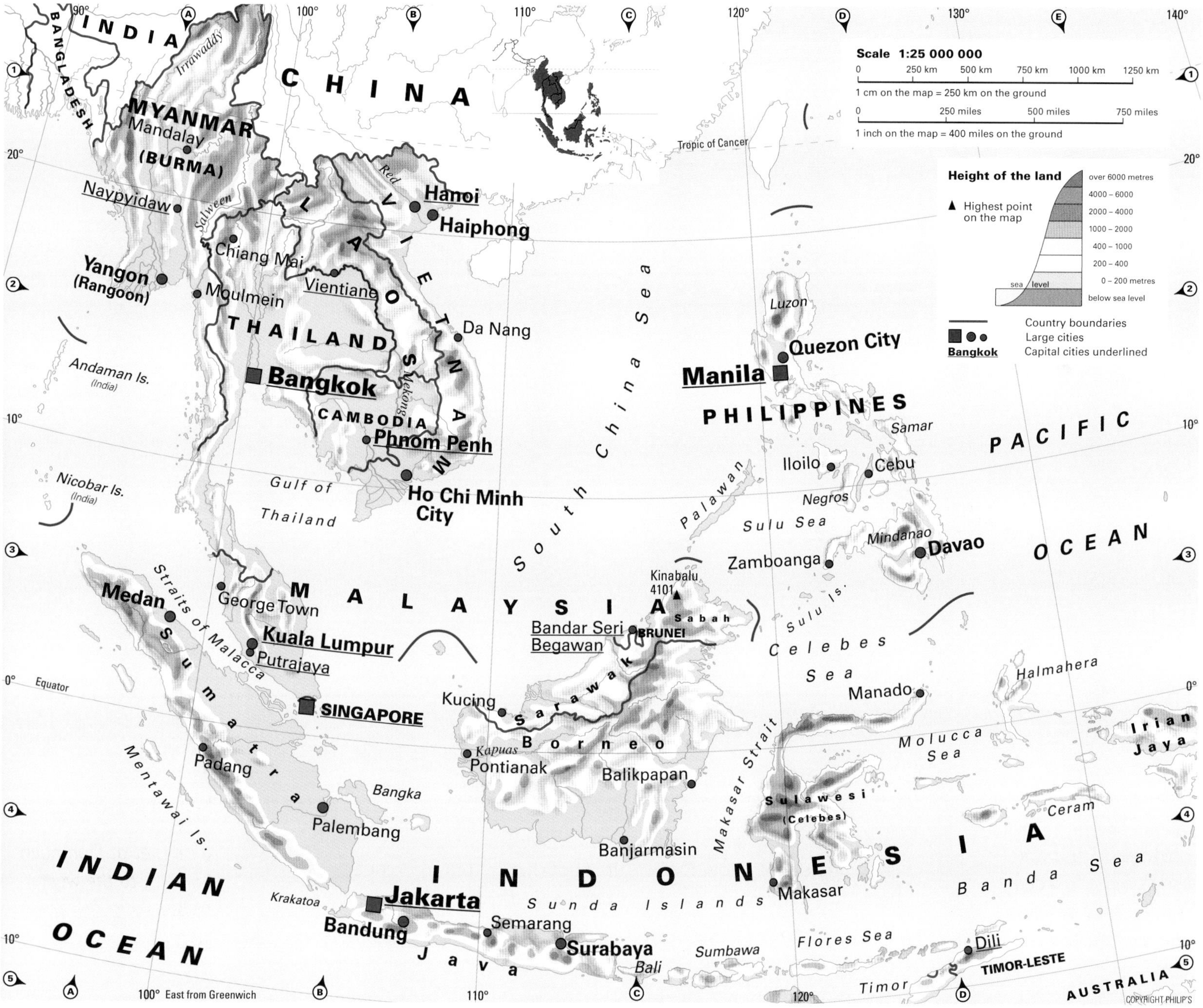

Scale 1:25 000 000
0 250 km 500 km 750 km 1000 km 1250 km
1 cm on the map = 250 km on the ground
0 250 miles 500 miles 750 miles
1 inch on the map = 400 miles on the ground
Height of the land
over 6000 metres
4000 – 6000
2000 – 4000
1000 – 2000
400 – 1000
200 – 400
0 – 200 metres
sea level
below sea level
▲ Highest point on the map
Country boundaries
Large cities
Bangkok
Capital cities underlined
INDIA
BANGLADESH
CHINA
MYANMAR (BURMA)
Mandalay
Naypyidaw
Yangon (Rangoon)
Moulmein
Irrawaddy
Salween
Red
Hanoi
Haiphong
LAOS
Vientiane
VIETNAM
Da Nang
Chiang Mai
THAILAND
Bangkok
Mekong
CAMBODIA
Phnom Penh
Ho Chi Minh City
Gulf of Thailand
Andaman Is. (India)
Nicobar Is. (India)
Tropic of Cancer
South China Sea
Luzon
Quezon City
Manila
PHILIPPINES
Samar
Iloilo
Cebu
Negros
Palawan
Sulu Sea
Mindanao
Davao
Zamboanga
PACIFIC OCEAN
Kinabalu 4101
Sabah
BRUNEI
Bandar Seri Begawan
MALAYSIA
George Town
Medan
Kuala Lumpur
Putrajaya
Straits of Malacca
SINGAPORE
Sumatra
Sulu Is.
Celebes Sea
Manado
Halmahera
Irian Jaya
Kuching
Sarawak
Borneo
Kapuas
Pontianak
Balikpapan
Makasar Strait
Molucca Sea
Sulawesi (Celebes)
Ceram
Mentawai Is.
Padang
Bangka
Palembang
Banjarmasin
INDONESIA
INDIAN OCEAN
Krakatoa
Jakarta
Bandung
Semarang
Sunda Islands
Makasar
Banda Sea
Java
Surabaya
Bali
Sumbawa
Flores Sea
Dili
TIMOR-LESTE
Timor
AUSTRALIA
Equator
100° East from Greenwich
90° 100° 110° 120° 130° 140°
20° 10° 0°
A B C D E
1 2 3 4 5
COPYRIGHT PHILIP'S

CHINA AND MONGOLIA

CHINA

AREA 9,596,961 sq km
POPULATION 1,397,898,000
MONEY Yuan

MONGOLIA

AREA 1,566,500 sq km
POPULATION 3,199,000
MONEY Tugrik

CHINA has over a billion people – more than any other country in the world. The map shows that there are many high mountains in China, such as the huge plateau of Tibet and the rugged mountains of the south-west where the Giant Pandas live. Not many people live in these mountains, nor in the deserts of the north, near Mongolia.

So the lower land of eastern China is very crowded indeed. Rice grows well south of the River Yangtze. North of the Yangtze, where the winters are colder, wheat and maize are important food crops, but it is hard to grow enough.

Taiwan is an island country which used to be called Formosa, or nationalist China. It is not communist and is not part of China.

Mongolia is a large desert country between Russia and China. Everywhere is more than 1000 metres above sea level. It is the emptiest country in the world, with an average of only 2 people for every square kilometre.

▲ ***The Forbidden City*** *in Beijing was once the home of the emperors of China. Over 15 million people now visit it every year. Can you see the modern city in the distance?*

▲ ***Mongolia:*** *the Mongols were famous for their skill with bows and arrows. Today, archery is one of the main sports, along with horse-racing and wrestling.*

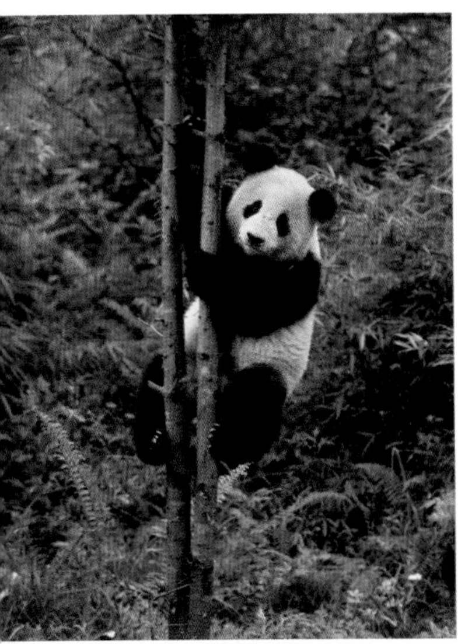

▲ ***Giant Pandas*** *live in the remote mountains in south-west China. Their main food is bamboo. This panda lives in a special reserve because a lot of the bamboo forests have been cut down to make more farmland.*

▲ ***The Great Wall of China*** *was over 5000 kilometres long (see map) – by far the longest man-made structure in the world. Building started 2000 years ago to keep China's enemies out. Notice the fortified towers.*

This Chinese painting shows the amazing mountains of southern China. They are made of limestone and their strange shapes are real!

CHINESE NEW YEAR

This giant dragon is being carried in the New Year procession in Hong Kong. Chinese people all over the world celebrate New Year (or Spring Festival) in February.

▲ ***Shanghai** is a large city and important port of China. The skyscrapers are in the new Pudong area on the east bank of the Huangpu river. In the centre is the Oriental Pearl Tower.*

FACT BOX

- One out of every five people in the world is Chinese.
- The world's highest railway goes to Lhasa in Tibet, which is 3500 metres above sea level.
- The Chinese invented the compass, paper and printing.
- The Three Gorges Dam on the River Yangtze is the world's largest hydro-electric scheme.
- China is one of the world's biggest exporters of goods. What can you find that is 'Made in China'?

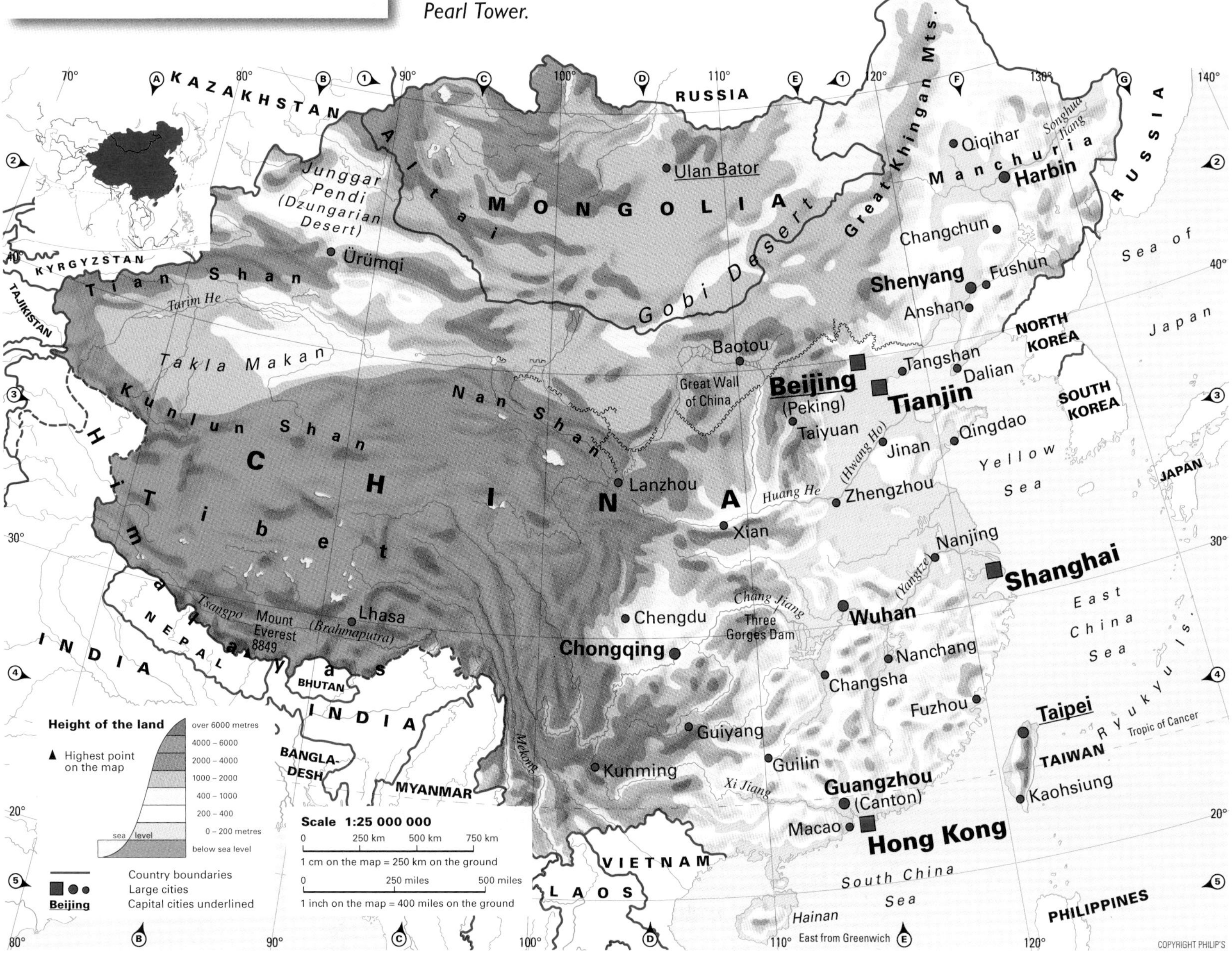

KAZAKHSTAN
RUSSIA
MONGOLIA
Ulan Bator
Junggar Pendi (Dzungarian Desert)
Altai
Gobi Desert
Great Khingan Mts.
Manchuria
Qiqihar
Harbin
Songhua Jiang
Changchun
Shenyang
Fushun
Anshan
KYRGYZSTAN
TAJIKISTAN
Tian Shan
Ürümqi
Tarim He
Takla Makan
Kunlun Shan
Nan Shan
Baotou
Great Wall of China
Beijing (Peking)
Tianjin
Tangshan
Dalian
Taiyuan
Jinan
Qingdao
Huang He (Hwang Ho)
Zhengzhou
Lanzhou
Xian
CHINA
Tibet
Himalayas
Lhasa
Tsangpo (Brahmaputra)
Mount Everest 8849
NEPAL
INDIA
BHUTAN
BANGLADESH
MYANMAR
Mekong
Chengdu
Chongqing
Chang Jiang (Yangtze)
Three Gorges Dam
Wuhan
Nanjing
Shanghai
Nanchang
Changsha
Fuzhou
Guiyang
Kunming
Guilin
Xi Jiang
Guangzhou (Canton)
Macao
Hong Kong
Taipei
TAIWAN
Kaohsiung
Ryukyu Is.
Tropic of Cancer
NORTH KOREA
SOUTH KOREA
JAPAN
Sea of Japan
Yellow Sea
East China Sea
South China Sea
Hainan
VIETNAM
LAOS
PHILIPPINES

Height of the land
over 6000 metres
4000 – 6000
2000 – 4000
1000 – 2000
400 – 1000
200 – 400
0 – 200 metres
below sea level
sea level
▲ Highest point on the map
Country boundaries
Large cities
Beijing — Capital cities underlined

Scale 1:25 000 000
0 250 km 500 km 750 km
1 cm on the map = 250 km on the ground
0 250 miles 500 miles
1 inch on the map = 400 miles on the ground

East from Greenwich

JAPAN AND KOREA

JAPAN

AREA 377,829 sq km
POPULATION 124,687,000
MONEY Yen
CAPITAL Tokyo
MAIN ISLAND Honshu

NORTH KOREA

AREA 120,538 sq km
POPULATION 25,831,000
MONEY North Korean won
CAPITAL Pyongyang

SOUTH KOREA

AREA 99,268 sq km
POPULATION 51,715,000
MONEY South Korean won
CAPITAL Seoul

JAPAN is quite a small country: it is smaller than France or Spain. But Japan has a big population – over twice as many people as France or Spain. Outside the big cities, most of Japan is still beautiful countryside.

This small country is mostly mountainous and many of the mountains are volcanoes. At school, children practise what to do when there is an earthquake, tsunami (a huge wave) or a volcanic eruption.

Japan has very few mines and hardly any oil, yet it has become well known for making electrical goods, cars and many other 'hi-tech' items that are sold all over the world.

▲ ***Mount Fuji, beyond fields of tea.*** *Mount Fuji (Fuji-san) is Japan's most famous mountain. It is an old volcano, 3776 metres high. Tea is important in Japan. It is usually drunk as 'green tea' and often with great ceremony.*

▲ ***A busy street in Kyoto.*** *This city was the capital of Japan for over 1000 years – until 1868. It is famous for its cooking, its gardens and shrines. High mountains surround the city on three sides.*

▲ ***Bullet train, or Shinkansen.*** *Japan's 'bullet trains' go like a bullet from a gun! The trains run on new tracks with no sharp curves to slow them down. They provide a superb service except when there is an earthquake warning.*

TEMPLES

▲ **Horyu Temple, at Nara, Japan.** The beautiful temple on the right is called a pagoda. Japanese pagodas are carefully preserved. Their unusual shape originally came partly from Indian temples and also partly from Chinese temples.

PUZZLE

▼ **Decorations for a Buddhist festival in South Korea.**

- What are they?
- What are they made of?

(Answers on page 97.)

JAPAN AND KOREA

▲ ***South Korea.*** *Seoul has been the capital of Korea since 1392 – but is now only the capital of South Korea. These children are playing on one of the many hills in the city.*

There are booming cities in the south of Japan, with highly skilled, hard-working people. Many of them live in the city suburbs and travel to work in overcrowded trains. Most Japanese families have small, space-saving homes. The main room is usually a living room by day, then the beds are unrolled for the night.

In southern Japan, rice is the main food crop. Some of the hillsides look like giant steps because they are terraced to make flat fields. But northern Japan has very cold winters.

Korea is sandwiched between China and Japan, and has often been ruled by one or other country. Since the end of the Korean War in 1953, it has been divided into two countries by a high fence that is well guarded. Find the border on the map.

North Korea is a communist country. It has lots of valuable minerals, but the people are poor.

South Korea is smaller but it has a lot more people. It has become rich and exports items such as ships, electronic goods, trainers and jeans.

RUSSIA
CHINA
NORTH KOREA
SOUTH KOREA
JAPAN
HOKKAIDO
HONSHU
SHIKOKU
KYUSHU
Sea of Japan (East Sea)
Sea of Okhotsk
Yellow Sea
PACIFIC OCEAN
La Perouse Strait
Nemuro Str.
Tsugaru Strait
Korea Strait
Inland Sea
Kunashir
Wakkanai
Asahigawa
Otaru
Sapporo
Kushiro
Hakodate
Aomori
Hachinohe
Akita
Kitakami
Sendai
Sado
Niigata
Fukushima
Hitachi
Utsunomiya
Tone
Toyama
Nagano
Kanazawa
Tokyo
Kawasaki
Yokohama
Mt. Fuji 3776
Gifu
Kiso
Nagoya
Hamamatsu
Kyoto
Nara
Osaka
Sakai
Kobe
Okayama
Hiroshima
Matsuyama
Kitakyushu
Fukuoka
Nagasaki
Kumamoto
Kagoshima
Tanega I.
Izu Islands
Oki Islands
Tsushima
Jeju-do
Chongjin
Hyesan
Kanggye
Kimchaek
Sinuiju
Hamhung
Wonsan
Nampo
Pyongyang
Kaesong
Incheon
Seoul
Gangneung
Daejeon
Gunsan
Pohang
Daegu
Ulsan
Gwangju
Busan

Height of the land
over 6000 metres
4000 – 6000
2000 – 4000
1000 – 2000
400 – 1000
200 – 400
0 – 200 metres
below sea level
sea level
▲ Highest point on the map
Country boundaries
Large cities
Capital cities underlined

Scale 1:10 000 000
0 100 km 200 km 300 km 400 km 500 km
1 cm on the map = 100 km on the ground
0 100 miles 200 miles 300 miles
1 inch on the map = 160 miles on the ground

East from Greenwich

AFRICA

MOST of the countries of Africa have quite small populations – except for Nigeria and Egypt. But everywhere the population is growing fast. It is difficult to provide enough schools and clinics for all the children and there are not enough good jobs.

Imagine travelling southwards across Africa, along the 20°E line of longitude. You start in **Libya**. Your first 1000 kilometres will be across the great Sahara Desert (where you must travel in winter) – sand, rock and the high rugged Tibesti Mountains. Then you reach thorn bushes, in the semi-desert Sahel area of **Chad**.

By 15°N you are into savanna – very long grass and scattered trees. You cross the country known as **CAR** for short. The land becomes greener and at about 5°N you reach the equatorial rainforest . . . a real jungle! You are now in **Congo**.

Then the same story happens in reverse – savanna in **Angola**; then semi-desert (the Kalahari and the Karoo). Now you come down to green fields, fruit trees and vines that are grown in the far south. Finally, you reach the coast at the Cape of Good Hope – a journey of nearly 8000 kilometres.

▲ ***The grasslands of the Savanna*** *provide grazing for large animals.*

▲ ***Children in Ghana.*** *Everywhere in Africa, there are lots of children. The fathers of these children are fishermen: in the background you can see nets drying and big dug-out canoes. The canoes are made from the huge trees of the rainforest, and can cope with big waves in the Gulf of Guinea.*

Height of the land

▲ Highest point on the map

over 6000 metres
4000 – 6000
2000 – 4000
1000 – 2000
400 – 1000
200 – 400
0 – 200 metres
sea level
below sea level

Scale 1:55 000 000

0 500 km 1000 km 1500 km 2000 km 2500 km

1 cm on the map = 550 km on the ground

0 500 miles 1000 miles 1500 miles

1 inch on the map = 870 miles on the ground

WHERE DO NAMES COME FROM

CHAD Named from Lake Chad
GAMBIA, NIGER, NIGERIA From big rivers
GHANA, BENIN, MALI Names of great empires in West Africa a long time ago
NAMIBIA From the Namib Desert
SIERRA LEONE 'Lion Mountain' (Portuguese)
SUDAN Named after the region south of the Sahara
TANZANIA From Tanganyika (the mainland) and the island of Zanzibar

▲ ***The pyramids of Egypt** are tombs built by slaves over 4500 years ago. The picture shows the largest, which are at Giza, near Cairo. They are still the largest buildings in the whole of Africa. They are near the River Nile, in the Sahara Desert.*

EUROPE
Mediterranean Sea
ASIA
Madeira (Portugal)
MOROCCO
Canary Islands (Spain)
WESTERN SAHARA
TUNISIA
ALGERIA
LIBYA
EGYPT
Suez Canal
Red Sea
Tropic of Cancer
MAURITANIA
MALI
NIGER
CHAD
SUDAN
ERITREA
SENEGAL
GUINEA-BISSAU
GUINEA
BURKINA FASO
BENIN
DJIBOUTI
SIERRA LEONE
COTE D'IVOIRE
GHANA
TOGO
NIGERIA
SOUTH SUDAN
ETHIOPIA
LIBERIA
CAMEROON
CENTRAL AFRICAN REPUBLIC
SOMALI REPUBLIC
EQUATORIAL GUINEA
DEMOCRATIC REPUBLIC of the CONGO
UGANDA
KENYA
Equator
SÃO TOMÉ & PRÍNCIPE
GABON
CONGO
RWANDA
BURUNDI
SEYCHELLES →
ATLANTIC OCEAN
CABINDA (Angola)
TANZANIA
Ascension Island (U.K.)
ANGOLA
ZAMBIA
MALAWI
COMOROS
Mayotte (France)
MOZAMBIQUE
MADAGASCAR
ZIMBABWE
MAURITIUS
Réunion (France)
NAMIBIA
BOTSWANA
Tropic of Capricorn
ESWATINI
LESOTHO
SOUTH AFRICA
INDIAN OCEAN

Africa in the World
Mediterranean Sea
Europe
Asia
South America
Atlantic Ocean
Indian Ocean

Scale 1:55 000 000
0 500 km 1000 km 1500 km 2000 km 2500 km
1 cm on the map = 550 km on the ground
0 500 miles 1000 miles 1500 miles
1 inch on the map = 870 miles on the ground

West from Greenwich | East from Greenwich

COINS OF AFRICA

All the 56 countries of Africa have their own banknotes and stamps. Most countries have coins as well. Pictures on the coins usually show something about the country. The 5 Bututs coin from the Gambia (above) shows a fine sailing ship. There is Arabic writing because many people are Muslims. The 10 Kobo coin from Nigeria (right) shows palm trees.

AFRICAN FACTS

AREA 30,319,000 sq km
HIGHEST POINT Mount Kilimanjaro (Tanzania), 5895 metres
LOWEST POINT Shores of Lake Assal (Djibouti), 155 metres below sea level
LONGEST RIVER Nile, 6695 km (also a world record)
LARGEST LAKE Lake Victoria (East Africa), 69,484 sq km
BIGGEST COUNTRY Algeria, 2,381,741 sq km
SMALLEST COUNTRIES
Mainland: Gambia, 11,295 sq km;
Islands: Seychelles, 455 sq km (see page 9)

NORTH AFRICA

TUNISIA

AREA 163,610 sq km
POPULATION 11,811,000
MONEY Tunisian dinar

MOROCCO

AREA 446,550 sq km
POPULATION 36,562,000
MONEY Moroccan dirham

MALI

AREA 1,240,192 sq km
POPULATION 20,138,000
MONEY CFA franc

MOST of North Africa is desert – but not all. The coastlines and mountains of north-west Africa get winter rain: good crops are grown and the coasts of Tunisia and Morocco are popular with tourists.

Most of these countries are Islamic. **Morocco** has the oldest university in the world: the Islamic University in Fez. **South Sudan** is the only country that is mainly Christian. It was part of **Sudan**, but became an independent country in 2011 after a long civil war.

People can live in the desert if there is water. Some modern settlements have been built deep in the desert where there are valuable minerals, and water is pumped from underground. These minerals are the main reason why some countries are richer than others. **Algeria** and **Libya** have plenty of oil beneath the desert.

South of the Sahara is the 'Sahel' – a large semi-desert area. Some years have good rains; some years very little rain. **Mali**, **Niger**, **Chad** and **South Sudan** are among the poorest nations in the world.

▲ ***A market near Timbuktu, in Mali,*** *is a place to meet as well as to trade. People bring the goods they hope to sell in locally made baskets or in re-used cartons which they balance on their heads.*

EGYPT

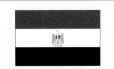

AREA 1,001,449 sq km
POPULATION 106,437,000
MONEY Egyptian pound

SUEZ CANAL

This old print shows the procession of ships through the Suez Canal at its opening in December 1869. The canal links the Mediterranean with the Red Sea (see map: G1). It was dug in 1859–69 by Arabs, organized by a Frenchman, Ferdinand de Lesseps. Before the canal opened, the route by sea from Europe to India and the Far East was around the whole of Africa.

▲ ***Oasis near Lake Djerid, Tunisia.*** *Water is just below the ground, so date palms can grow well. But in the background, great sand dunes loom on the skyline. If they advance, they may cover the oasis and kill the crops.*

▲ ***Mosque in Morocco.*** *This tower is a minaret: part of an Islamic mosque. It is used to announce the times of prayer to all the village. The village is in the Ziz River valley, south of the Atlas Mountains of Morocco. Notice the flat roofs of the houses and the date palms.*

Egypt is a desert country; its fertile land is 'the gift of the River Nile'. It has the biggest population of any North African country. Its capital, Cairo, is one of the biggest cities in the world. The River Nile brings water to the valley and delta. The land on either side of the Nile is carefully farmed using irrigation and is crowded with people. The rest of Egypt is almost empty. Find Cairo and the River Nile on the world population map on page 11 which shows the crowded and empty areas very clearly. The lack of rain has helped to preserve many of the monuments, palaces and tombs built by the ancient Egyptians. The pyramids at Giza, near Cairo, are about 4500 years old (page 53). They are the only one of the Seven Wonders of the ancient world still surviving.

THE SAHARA DESERT

The Sahara is the biggest desert in the world. It is over 9 million sq km in size. From west to east it is over 5000 km; from north to south it extends about 2000 km and it is still growing.

The hottest shade temperture recorded in Africa, 55°C, was in Kebili, Tunisia, in 1931.

The sunniest place in the world, over 4300 hours of sunshine per year, is in the eastern Sahara.

The highest sand dunes in the world, 430 metres high, are in central Algeria.

The longest river in the world is the River Nile, 6695 km long.

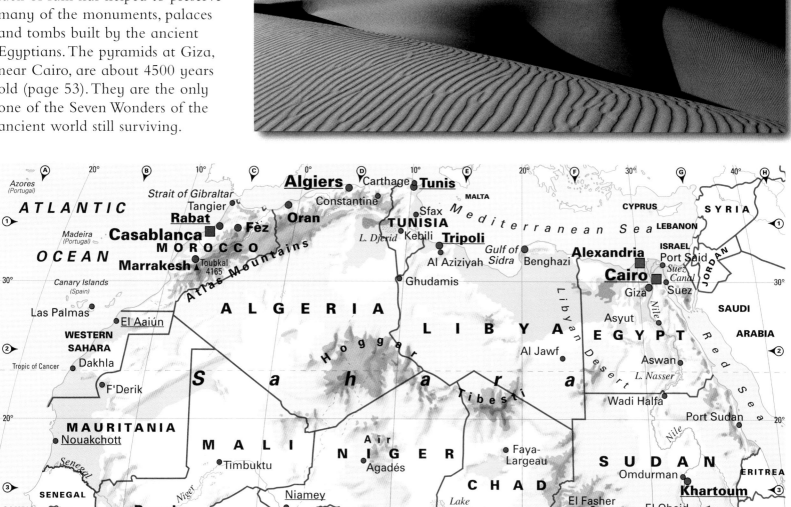

Height of the land
▲ Highest point on the map

over 6000 metres
4000 – 6000
2000 – 4000
1000 – 2000
400 – 1000
200 – 400
0 – 200 metres
below sea level

Country boundaries
Large cities
Capital cities underlined

Scale 1:30 000 000
0 300 km 600 km 900 km 1200 km
1 cm on the map = 300 km on the ground
0 300 miles 600 miles
1 inch on the map = 480 miles on the ground

West from Greenwich 0° East from Greenwich

COPYRIGHT PHILIP'S

WEST AFRICA

NIGERIA

AREA 923,768 sq km
POPULATION 219,464,000
MONEY Naira

THE GAMBIA

AREA 11,295 sq km
POPULATION 2,221,000
MONEY Dalasi

COTE D'IVOIRE

AREA 322,463 sq km
POPULATION 28,088,000
MONEY CFA franc

THERE are lots of countries in West Africa. In the last 300 years, European countries grabbed parts of the coastline and later they took over the inland areas as well. Now, all the countries are independent, but still use the language of those who once ruled them. English, French, Spanish or Portuguese is spoken. Many Africans speak a European language as well as one or more African languages.

Nigeria is the largest and most important country in West Africa. It has over 180 million people – more than any other African country. About half the people are Muslims, the other half are mainly Christians. Although English is the official language, there are about 240 other languages in Nigeria!

In many parts of West Africa, there is rapid progress. Most children now go to primary school, and the main cities have television and airports. But many people are still very poor. Civil war has made poverty much worse in some countries – for example, in **Sierra Leone** and **Liberia**.

▲ ***Village in Cameroon:*** *building houses with mud for the walls and tall grass for thatch. These materials are free and the homes are less hot than those with corrugated iron roofs.*

LIBERIA

AREA 111,369 sq km
POPULATION 5,214,000
MONEY Liberian dollar

▲ ***Women pounding yams, Benin.*** *They use a large wooden bowl and long pestles (pounding sticks) to break up and mash the yams. These root crops are eaten at most meals. It is very hard work: much easier if it is shared! They are probably singing to help keep a rhythm for using the pestles. The baby will love this!*

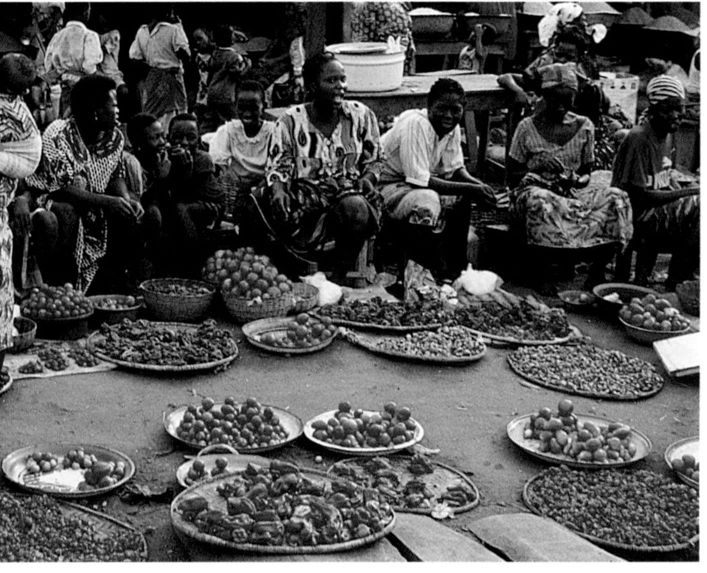

▲ ***Market day, Nigeria.*** *Red peppers for sale in Benin City, in southern Nigeria. Red peppers are very popular in West Africa – they give a strong flavour in cooking. Markets are important in both towns and villages throughout Africa.*

OIL IN NIGERIA

Nigeria pumps up lots of oil from under the delta of the River Niger. Oil has brought money for some people but pollution for others. The oil is used for fuel and chemicals. Nigeria also GROWS oil that is used in food, soaps and cosmetics. It is made from fruit that grows on palm trees - see the harvest picture on the next page.

The southern part of West Africa, near the Equator, is forested. The tall trees are being felled for their hardwood. Many crops are grown in the forest area and sold overseas: cocoa (for chocolate-making); coffee, pineapples and bananas; rubber (for car and lorry tyres). The main food crops are root crops, such as cassava and yams.

Further north, the trees thin out and there is savanna. The tall grass with some trees is suitable for cattle farming. There are big herds of cattle, and beautiful leather goods are on sale in the markets. Cotton and groundnuts (peanuts) are grown in the savanna lands. The main food crops are grass-like: rice, maize and millet. In the far north of West Africa there is semi-desert called the Sahel. The Sahara is advancing southwards and Lake Chad has shrunk in size.

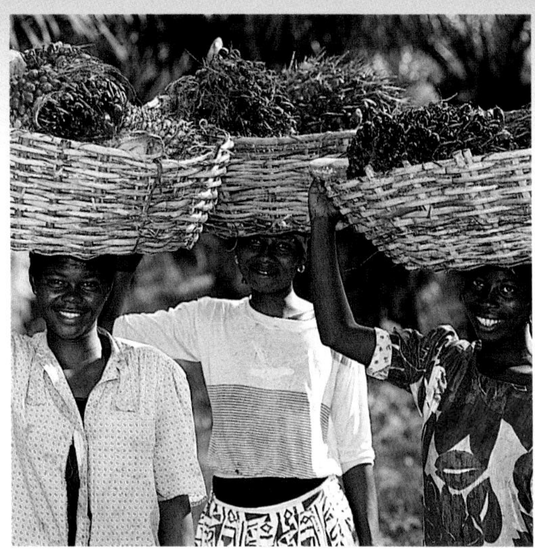

▲ ***Palm-oil harvest, Ghana.*** *These people are carrying heavy baskets full of oil-palm fruit. The oil palm grows in the hot, wet climate of the tropical forest. The fruits grow in bunches, with as many as 3000 bright-red palm fruits in a bunch. The fruit and the kernels are crushed in a factory to obtain oils. These oils are very useful for cooking and in making soap.*

▲ ***Yeji ferry, Ghana.*** *This big ferry carries lorries, cars, people and their heavy loads across Lake Volta. This man-made lake flooded Ghana's main road to the north. As the water rose in the new lake, the trees and much of the wildlife died. A fifteenth of all Ghana's land was 'lost' under the lake, and new villages had to be built.*

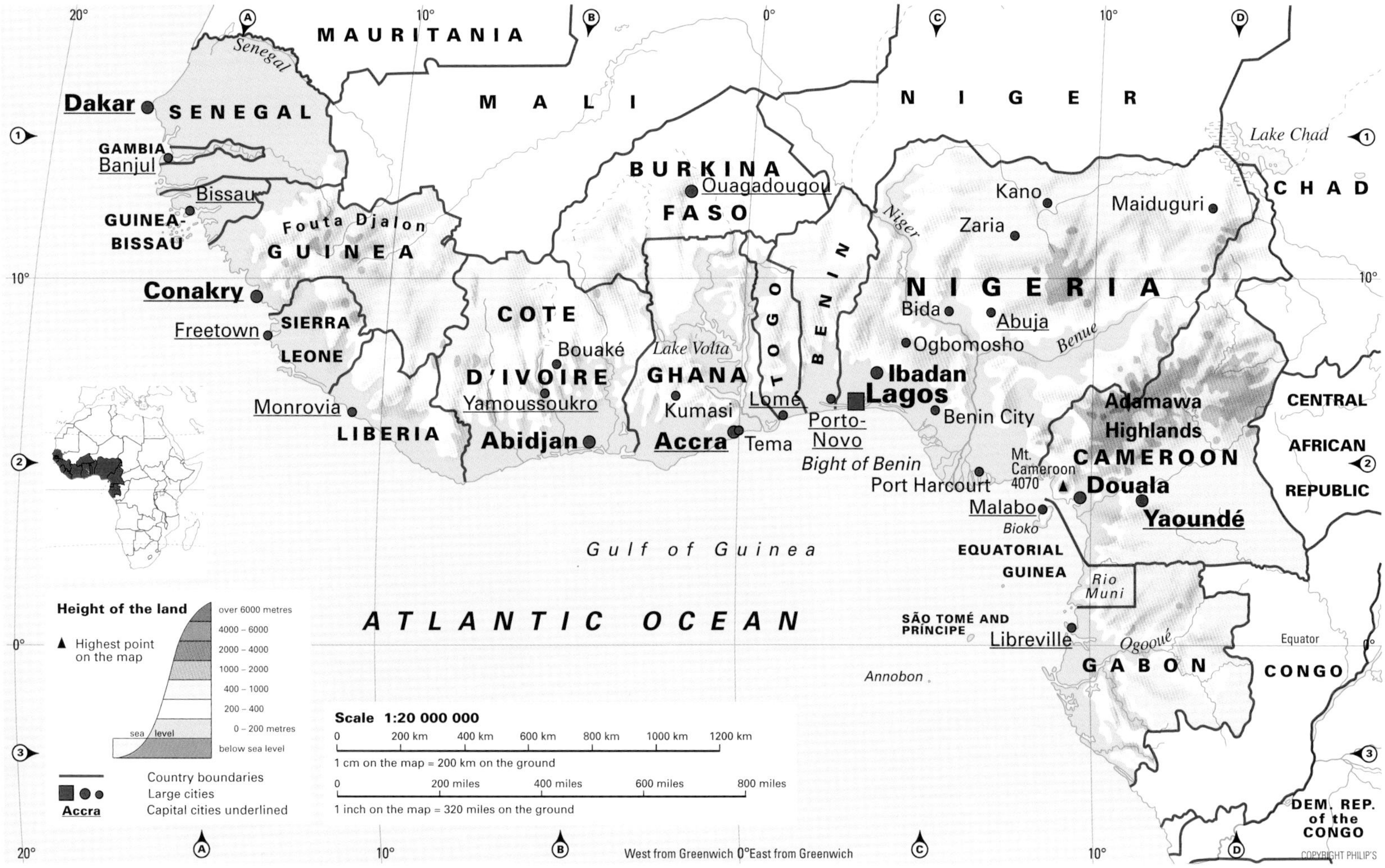

MAURITANIA
MALI
NIGER
SENEGAL
Dakar
GAMBIA
Banjul
Bissau
GUINEA-BISSAU
Fouta Djalon
GUINEA
Conakry
SIERRA LEONE
Freetown
Monrovia
LIBERIA
COTE D'IVOIRE
Bouaké
Yamoussoukro
Abidjan
BURKINA FASO
Ouagadougou
Lake Volta
GHANA
Kumasi
Accra
Tema
TOGO
Lomé
BENIN
Porto-Novo
Bight of Benin
NIGERIA
Kano
Zaria
Maiduguri
Bida
Abuja
Ogbomosho
Ibadan
Lagos
Benin City
Port Harcourt
Niger
Benue
Lake Chad
CHAD
Adamawa Highlands
Mt. Cameroon 4070
CAMEROON
Douala
Yaoundé
Malabo
Bioko
EQUATORIAL GUINEA
Rio Muni
CENTRAL AFRICAN REPUBLIC
Gulf of Guinea
ATLANTIC OCEAN
SÃO TOMÉ AND PRÍNCIPE
Annobon
Libreville
Ogooué
GABON
CONGO
Equator
DEM. REP. of the CONGO

Height of the land
▲ Highest point on the map
over 6000 metres
4000 – 6000
2000 – 4000
1000 – 2000
400 – 1000
200 – 400
0 – 200 metres
sea level
below sea level

Country boundaries
Large cities
Capital cities underlined
Accra

Scale 1:20 000 000
0 200 km 400 km 600 km 800 km 1000 km 1200 km
1 cm on the map = 200 km on the ground
0 200 miles 400 miles 600 miles 800 miles
1 inch on the map = 320 miles on the ground

West from Greenwich 0° East from Greenwich

CENTRAL AND EAST AFRICA

KENYA

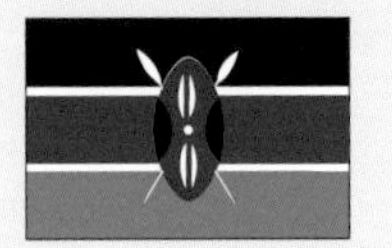

AREA 580,367 sq km
POPULATION 54,685,000
MONEY Kenyan shilling

ETHIOPIA

AREA 1,104,300 sq km
POPULATION 110,871,000
MONEY Birr

CONGO (DEM. REP.)

AREA 2,344,858 sq km
POPULATION 105,045,000
MONEY Congolese franc

CENTRAL Africa is mostly lowland, with magnificent trees in the equatorial rainforest near the River Congo. Some timber is used for buildings and canoes (see photograph right); some is exported. The cleared land can grow many tropical crops.

East Africa is mostly high savanna land with long grass, and scattered trees. Some parts are reserved for wild animals; in other parts, there are large farms for export crops such as coffee and tea. But in most of East Africa, the people keep cattle and grow crops for their own needs.

The **Somali Republic**, **Djibouti** and **Eritrea** are desert areas, but the mountain areas of **Ethiopia** get plenty of rain. If the rains fail, the crops fail and people go hungry. This part is sometimes called 'the Horn of Africa' because of its shape. Wars here have made the famines even worse.

In 1994 and 1995, a civil war in **Rwanda** led to a million deaths and more than a million refugees travelling to **Congo** and **Tanzania**. Wars like this damage people, the animals and the environment.

▲ ***In a game reserve in Kenya,*** *a group of zebra graze the savanna grassland. In the dry season, the grass is brown, but in the rainy season it is tall and green. The game reserves are carefully managed and people come from all over the world to see the wildlife.*

▲ ***Gorillas in Rwanda.*** *These gorillas live high up in the forested mountains. They are at risk as the trees are being cut down.*

▲ ***The River Congo at Mbandaka.*** *Children who live near the river learn to paddle a dug-out canoe from an early age. The boats are hollowed out of a single tree with an axe. The River Congo is an important transport route. Mbandaka is a river port about four days by steamer from Kinshasa.*

FARMING IN EAST AFRICA

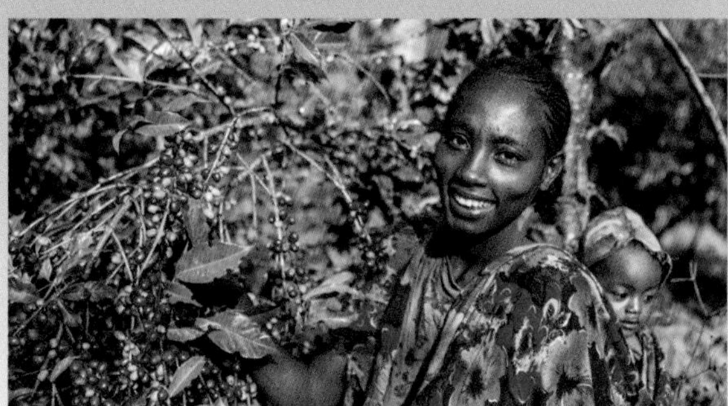

Picking coffee: Inside the cherry-like fruits are the beans that are dried, roasted and ground up to make coffee. This is an important 'cash crop' which farmers can sell. Other 'cash crops' are sisal (for making rope and sacks), cotton, tobacco and tea.

▲ ***Nairobi in Kenya*** *started to be built in the 1890s as a railway depot and became the capital in 1901 – yet 120 years ago there was no town here.*

In all these countries, there are many signs of development: new farm projects, new ports and roads, new clinics and schools. But there is much poverty, too, and people are moving to the cities and towns in the hope of finding work.

The population of this area is growing fast. It has doubled in less than 25 years. Some of these countries have the world's highest population growth rates, and more than half the population is young.

▲ ***Mount Kilimanjaro, Tanzania.*** *Africa's highest mountain is the beautiful cone of an old volcano. It is near the Equator, but high enough to have snow all year.*

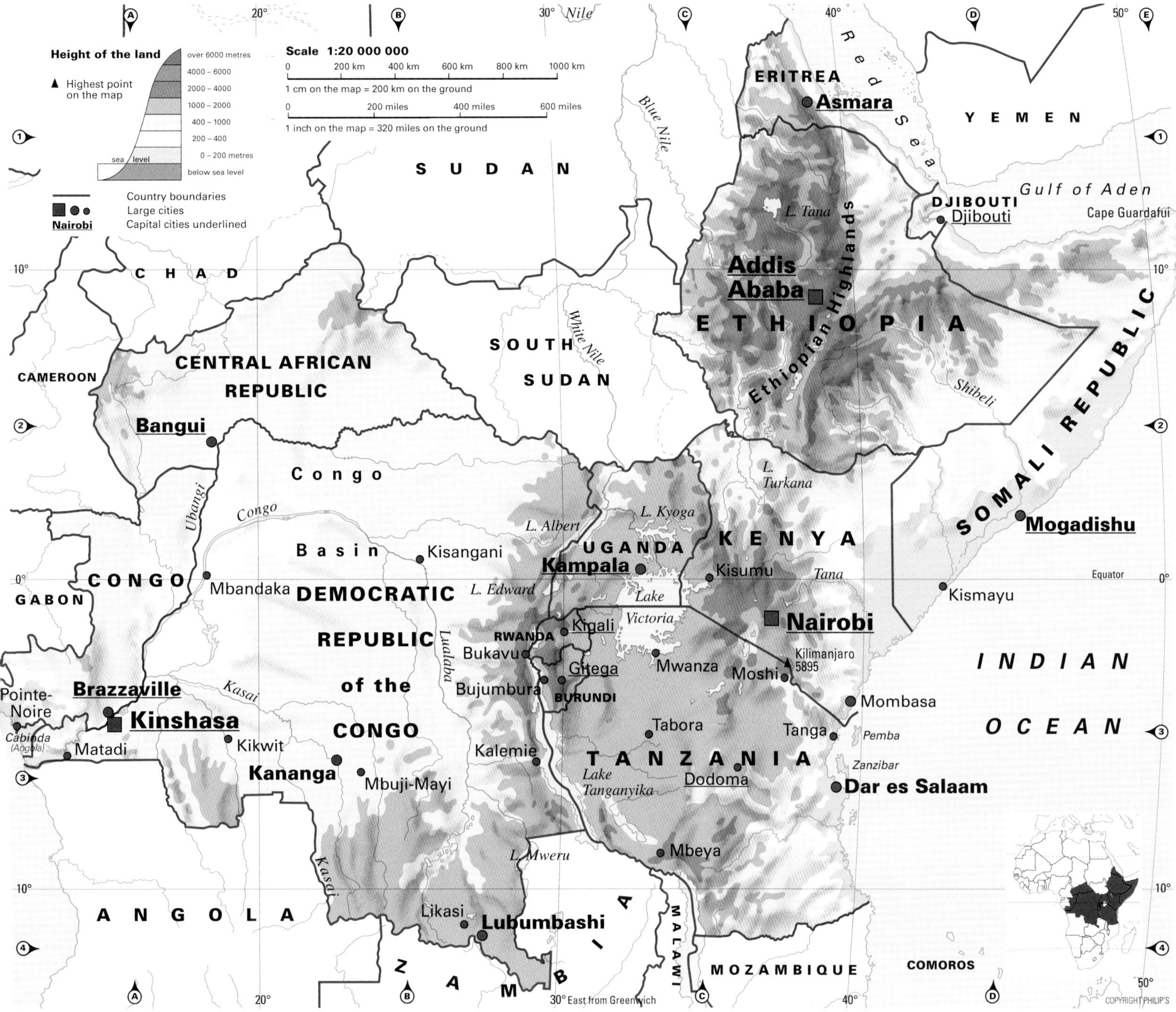

Height of the land
over 6000 metres
4000 – 6000
2000 – 4000
1000 – 2000
400 – 1000
200 – 400
0 – 200 metres
sea level
below sea level
▲ Highest point on the map

Country boundaries
Large cities
Capital cities underlined
Nairobi

Scale 1:20 000 000
0 200 km 400 km 600 km 800 km 1000 km
1 cm on the map = 200 km on the ground
0 200 miles 400 miles 600 miles
1 inch on the map = 320 miles on the ground

SUDAN
SOUTH SUDAN
CHAD
CENTRAL AFRICAN REPUBLIC
CAMEROON
Bangui
ERITREA
Asmara
YEMEN
DJIBOUTI
Djibouti
Gulf of Aden
Cape Guardafui
Red Sea
Blue Nile
White Nile
L. Tana
Addis Ababa
ETHIOPIA
Ethiopian Highlands
Shibeli
SOMALI REPUBLIC
Mogadishu
Kismayu
L. Turkana
KENYA
Tana
Kisumu
Nairobi
Kilimanjaro 5895
Moshi
Mombasa
UGANDA
Kampala
L. Kyoga
L. Albert
L. Edward
Lake Victoria
RWANDA
Kigali
BURUNDI
Gitega
Bujumbura
Bukavu
Mwanza
Congo Basin
Congo
Ubangi
Kisangani
Mbandaka
CONGO
GABON
DEMOCRATIC REPUBLIC of the CONGO
Lualaba
Kasai
Brazzaville
Kinshasa
Pointe-Noire
Cabinda (Angola)
Matadi
Kikwit
Kananga
Mbuji-Mayi
Kalemie
Lake Tanganyika
TANZANIA
Tabora
Dodoma
Tanga
Pemba
Zanzibar
Dar es Salaam
Mbeya
L. Mweru
Likasi
Lubumbashi
ANGOLA
ZAMBIA
MALAWI
MOZAMBIQUE
COMOROS
INDIAN OCEAN
Equator
30° East from Greenwich
COPYRIGHT PHILIP'S

SOUTHERN AFRICA

ANGOLA

AREA 1,246,700 sq km
POPULATION 33,643,000
MONEY Kwanza

ZAMBIA

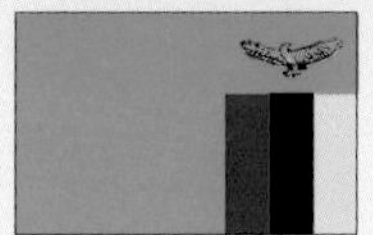

AREA 752,618 sq km
POPULATION 19,078,000
MONEY Zambian kwacha

SOUTH AFRICA

AREA 1,221,037 sq km
POPULATION 56,979,000
MONEY Rand

MOST of southern Africa is a high, flat plateau. The rivers cannot be used by ships because of big waterfalls like the Victoria Falls (see photograph right). But the rivers can be useful. Two huge dams have been built on the River Zambezi – at Kariba (in Zambia) and at Cahora Bassa (in Mozambique). The map shows the lakes behind each dam. The power of the falling water is used to make electricity.

Angola and **Mozambique** used to be Portuguese colonies, and Portuguese is still their official language – though many different African languages are spoken, too. Most of the other countries shown on the map have English as their official language.

Look at the map to find six countries of Southern Africa that have no coastline. It is more difficult and expensive for them to bring goods in and export their products. Railways and roads leading to ports in neighbouring countries are very important. **Zambia** has large copper mines and **Botswana** has the world's richest diamond mine.

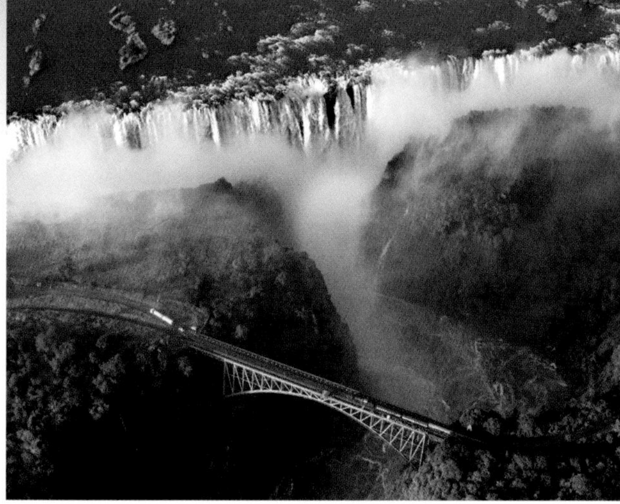

▲ ***The Victoria Falls from the air.*** *The River Zambezi plunges over the falls into a narrow gorge. Africans call the falls Mosi-oa-tunya – 'the smoke that thunders'. They were named after the English Queen Victoria by the explorer David Livingstone. The falls are more than a kilometre wide and over 100 metres high. This is the border of Zimbabwe and Zambia, which are linked by the bridge at the bottom of the image.*

MOZAMBIQUE

AREA 801,590 sq km
POPULATION 30,888,000
MONEY Metical

▲ ***Cape Town, South Africa.*** *There are tall buildings in the city centre. The flat-topped mountain in the distance is 'Table Mountain'. It looks as flat as a table. When cloud covers it, it is called 'the tablecloth'. Cape Town is near the Cape of Good Hope, in the far south of Africa.*

A VILLAGE IN ZAMBIA

A Zambian girl drew this picture of her village during a lesson at her school. Her village is close to the River Zambezi in the west of Zambia. Look for a well, a man hoeing, a fisherman and a man looking after cattle. On the road there is a bus, a car and a van.

▲ ***Ring-tailed Lemur, Madagascar.*** *The island of Madagascar has wonderful forests and some of its wildlife is unique. But several species are under threat of extinction.*

The **Republic of South Africa** is the wealthiest country in Africa. The world's largest diamond was found here. It has the world's richest gold mine and the world's deepest mine. People rushed to the area around Johannesburg when gold was found in the 1880s. Now it is South Africa's largest city.

Most of the people are still very poor. For many years, black people were kept apart from the rich white people who used to rule the country. In 1994 they gained the vote and now they govern the country.

Namibia and **Botswana** are dry areas, with small numbers of people. Some of the rivers in this area never reach the sea. The map on this page shows big swamps and 'salt pans': these are the places where the river water evaporates.

Lesotho is a small mountainous country, completely surrounded by the Republic of South Africa.

Madagascar is the fourth largest island in the world. It is a long way from the rest of Africa. Most of its animals and plants are found nowhere else on Earth.

▲ ***Children in Mozambique*** *hope for a better future. Their country is one of the poorest in Africa, and has also suffered from disastrous floods and drought.*

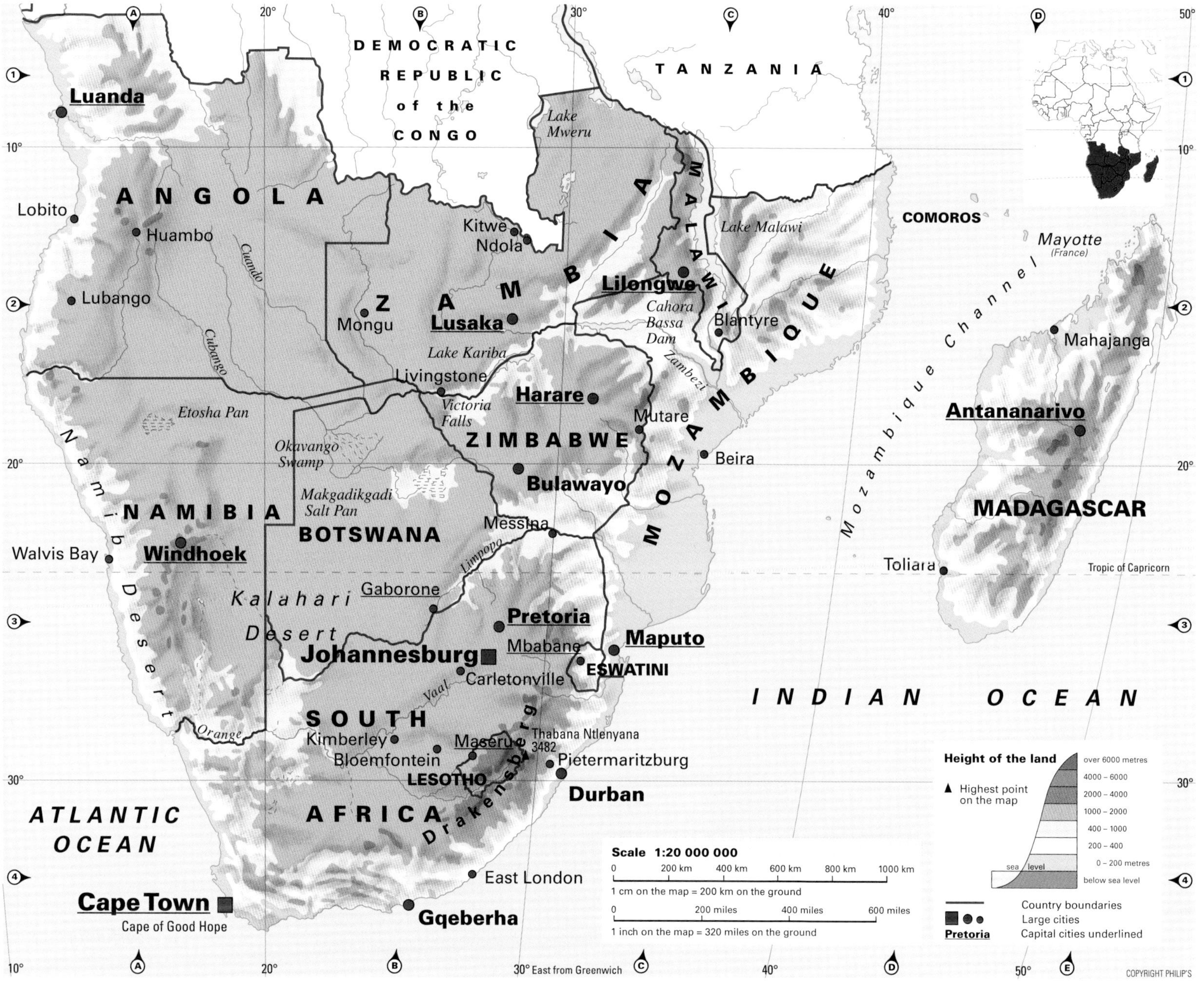

DEMOCRATIC REPUBLIC of the CONGO
TANZANIA
Luanda
Lobito
Huambo
Lubango
ANGOLA
Cuando
Cubango
Lake Mweru
Kitwe
Ndola
ZAMBIA
Mongu
Lusaka
Lake Kariba
Livingstone
Victoria Falls
MALAWI
Lake Malawi
Lilongwe
Cahora Bassa Dam
Blantyre
Zambezi
COMOROS
Mayotte (France)
Mozambique Channel
Mahajanga
Antananarivo
MADAGASCAR
Toliara
Tropic of Capricorn
Harare
ZIMBABWE
Mutare
Beira
Bulawayo
MOZAMBIQUE
Etosha Pan
Okavango Swamp
Makgadikgadi Salt Pan
BOTSWANA
Messina
Limpopo
Namib Desert
NAMIBIA
Walvis Bay
Windhoek
Kalahari Desert
Gaborone
Pretoria
Maputo
Mbabane
ESWATINI
Johannesburg
Carletonville
Vaal
Orange
SOUTH AFRICA
Kimberley
Bloemfontein
Maseru
LESOTHO
Thabana Ntlenyana 3482
Pietermaritzburg
Durban
Drakensberg
East London
Gqeberha
Cape Town
Cape of Good Hope
ATLANTIC OCEAN
INDIAN OCEAN
10° 20° 30° East from Greenwich 40° 50°

Scale 1:20 000 000
0 200 km 400 km 600 km 800 km 1000 km
1 cm on the map = 200 km on the ground
0 200 miles 400 miles 600 miles
1 inch on the map = 320 miles on the ground

Height of the land: over 6000 metres; 4000 – 6000; 2000 – 4000; 1000 – 2000; 400 – 1000; 200 – 400; 0 – 200 metres; sea level; below sea level

▲ Highest point on the map

Country boundaries
Large cities
Capital cities underlined (Pretoria)

South Africa has two joint capital cities: most of the government offices are in Pretoria, but the parliament meets in Cape Town. So both cities are underlined.

THE PACIFIC

THIS map shows half the world. Guess which place is furthest from a continent: it is to be found somewhere in the south Pacific. The Pacific Ocean also includes the deepest place in the world: the Mariana Trench (11,022 metres deep).

There are thousands of islands in the Pacific. Some are volcanic mountains, while many others are low, flat coral islands. Coral also grows around the volcanoes.

A few islands have valuable minerals – for example Bougainville (copper) and Nauru (phosphates). But some islands will disappear if the sea level rises.

Castaway Island is one of the 300 islands that are part of Fiji. This island with white sand beaches and coconut palms is surrounded by coral reefs.

INTERNATIONAL DATE LINE

Find this imaginary line on the map. When it is Sunday midday in London it is already Sunday evening in Australia and nearly *Monday* in New Zealand. But travel west and it is Sunday morning in the USA and *Sunday* is beginning in the Cook Islands. The date changes at the Date Line. Use a globe to help you understand why this is.

▲ ***Coral reef in French Polynesia,*** *from the air. Coral BELOW sea level is ALIVE! A reef is built up from the shells of dead coral. Gradually plants colonize parts of the reef.*

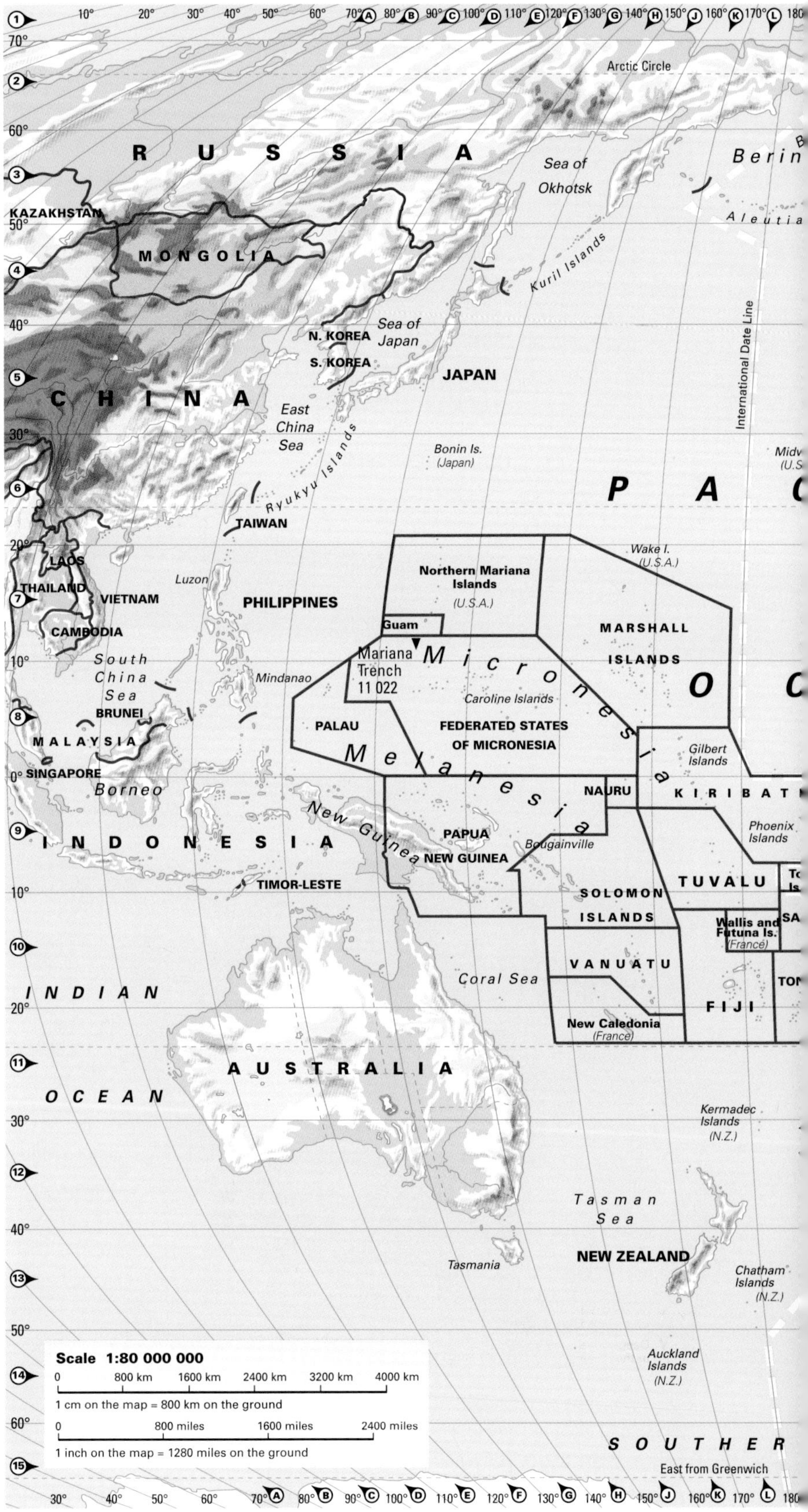

Most islanders are farmers. Many tropical food crops such as sweet potatoes, cassava and coconuts grow well; sugar-cane, bananas and pineapples are important exports. And, with so much sea, fishing is also important. Islands big enough for a full-sized airport, such as Fiji, the Samoan islands, Tahiti, and Hawaii (see page 72), now have tourists coming to enjoy the beautiful beaches.

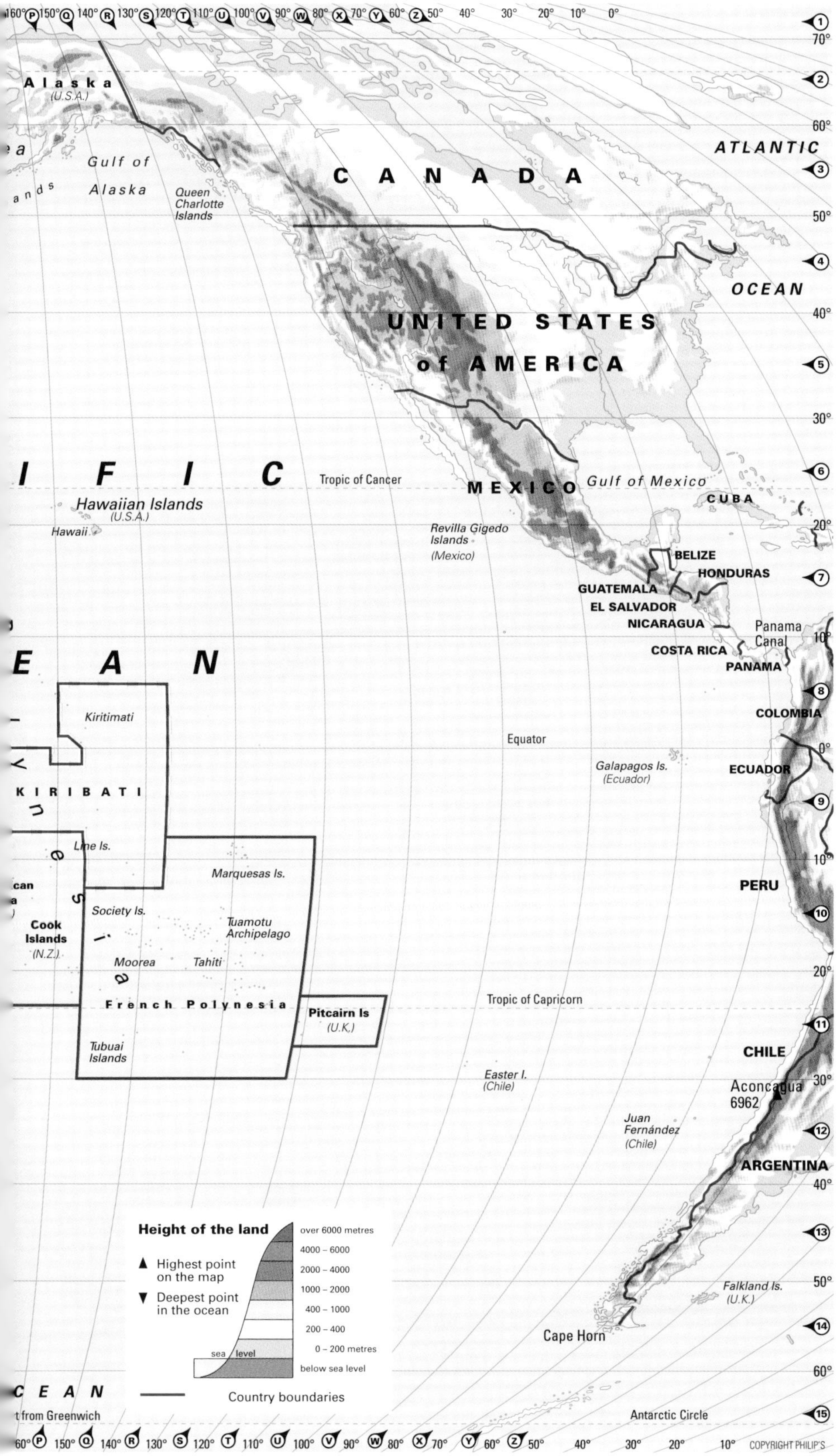

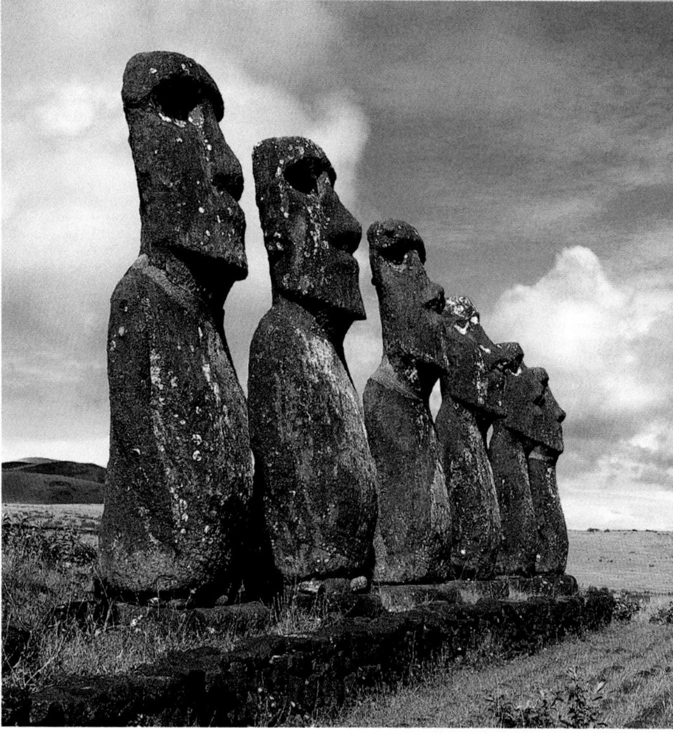

▲ ***Easter Island, South Pacific.*** *These huge stone sculptures each weigh about 50 tonnes! They were cut long ago with simple stone axes, and lifted with ropes and ramps – an amazing achievement for people who had no metal, no wheels and no machines. Look for Easter Island on the map (in square U11): it is one of the most remote places in the world. It is now owned by Chile, 3860 kilometres away in South America.*

Alaska (U.S.A.)
Gulf of Alaska
Queen Charlotte Islands
CANADA
ATLANTIC OCEAN
UNITED STATES of AMERICA
Tropic of Cancer
MEXICO
Gulf of Mexico
CUBA
Hawaiian Islands (U.S.A.)
Hawaii
Revilla Gigedo Islands (Mexico)
BELIZE
HONDURAS
GUATEMALA
EL SALVADOR
NICARAGUA
COSTA RICA
PANAMA
Panama Canal
COLOMBIA
Equator
Galapagos Is. (Ecuador)
ECUADOR
Kiritimati
KIRIBATI
Line Is.
Marquesas Is.
Society Is.
Tuamotu Archipelago
Cook Islands (N.Z.)
Moorea
Tahiti
French Polynesia
Pitcairn Is (U.K.)
Tubuai Islands
PERU
Tropic of Capricorn
Easter I. (Chile)
CHILE
Aconcagua 6962
Juan Fernández (Chile)
ARGENTINA
Falkland Is. (U.K.)
Cape Horn
Antarctic Circle
Height of the land
▲ Highest point on the map
▼ Deepest point in the ocean
over 6000 metres
4000 – 6000
2000 – 4000
1000 – 2000
400 – 1000
200 – 400
0 – 200 metres
sea level
below sea level
Country boundaries
COPYRIGHT PHILIP'S

PACIFIC FACTS

OCEAN AREA 155,557,000 sq km – the world's biggest ocean

HIGHEST POINT Mount Wilhelm (Papua New Guinea), 4508 metres

LOWEST POINT ON LAND Lake Eyre (Australia), 16 metres below sea level

DEEPEST PART OF OCEAN Mariana Trench, 11,022 metres below surface. This is the deepest place on Earth.

LONGEST RIVER Murray–Darling (Australia), 3750 km

LARGEST LAKE Lake Eyre (Australia), 8900 sq km

BIGGEST COUNTRY Australia, 7,741,220 sq km

SMALLEST COUNTRY Nauru, 21 sq km

Most Pacific countries are large groups of small islands. Their boundaries are out at sea – just lines on a map. For example, Kiribati is 33 small coral atolls spread over 5,000,000 square kilometres of ocean.

AUSTRALIA

AUSTRALIA

AREA 7,741,220 sq km
POPULATION 25,810,000
MONEY Australian dollar

AUSTRALIA is the world's largest island, but the world's smallest continent. It is the sixth-largest country in the world, smaller than the USA or Canada, but more than twice the size of India. Yet Australia's total population is small for such a large country. Most Australians are descended from people who came from Europe in the past 150 years.

Only a few people live in the mountains or in the outback – the enormous area of semi-desert and desert that makes up most of the country. The few outback people live on huge sheep and cattle farms, in mining towns, or on special reserves for the original Australians – the Aborigines. The north of Australia is tropical – and very hot.

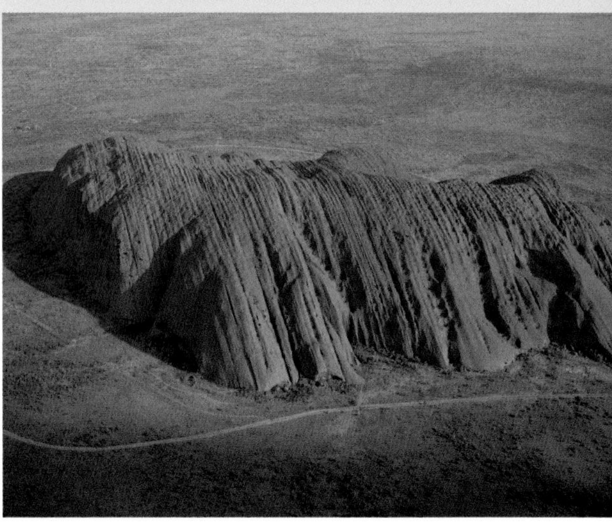

▲ ***Ayers Rock*** *rises steeply out of the dry plains in central Australia. It is 348 metres high. The sides have deep gullies and strange caves. For the Aborigines, it is a holy place called Uluru. Many tourists come for the hard climb or to watch the rock glow deep red at sunset.*

▲ ***The Flying Doctor Service*** *aeroplane is used to take people from remote areas to hospital, or to fly doctors to remote farms. People in the outback use 2-way radios to get medical advice and to keep in touch with one another.*

▲ ***Sydney Opera House*** *cost millions of dollars to build and has become the new symbol of Sydney. It is by the harbour, below the famous harbour bridge (in the background) which was built in Newcastle, UK!*

THE GREAT BARRIER REEF

The Great Barrier Reef is the world's largest living thing! It is an area of coral over 2000 kilometres long, which grows in the warm sea near the coast of Queensland. The reef is also home to colourful fish that swim among the coral. They can be seen from glass-bottomed boats.

AUSTRALIAN ANIMALS

Australia is not joined to any other continent. It has been a separate island for millions of years, and has developed its own unique wildlife. Most of the world's marsupials live in Australia.

The map shows that all the state capitals are on the coast. Canberra is a planned city built inland which became the national capital in 1927. Most Australians live near the coast and most live in towns. Sydney is by far the largest city. Yet much of the coast is almost uninhabited. The Great Divide separates the green coastal lowlands from the dry interior. The Nullarbor ('no tree') Plain is a desert by the sea.

TRICK QUESTION

Which was the biggest island in the world, before Australia was discovered? Think very carefully – then turn to page 97.

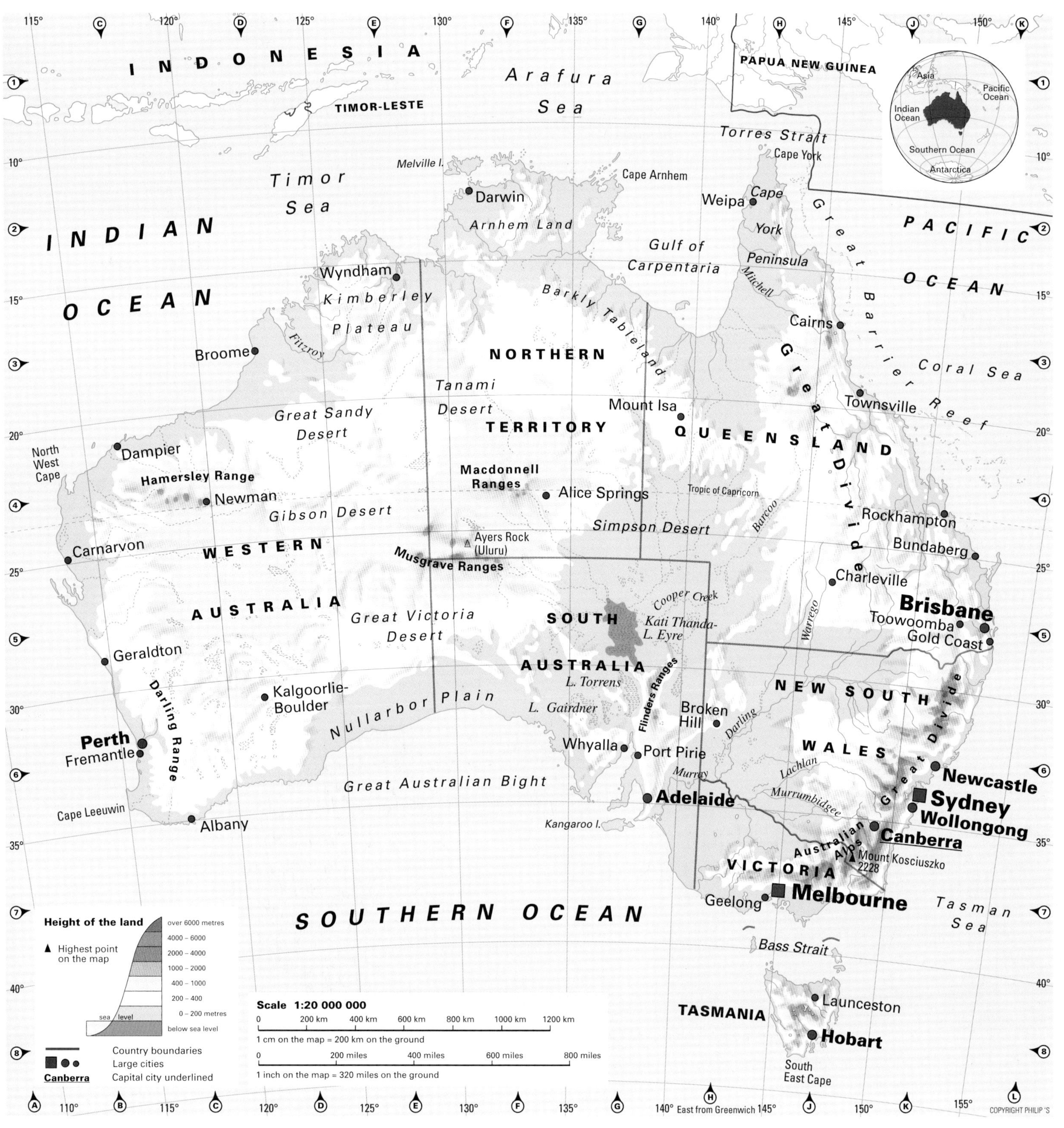

NEW ZEALAND

THE ANTIPODES

New Zealand is on the opposite side of the Earth from Europe. This 'double map' is printed as if you were looking right through a transparent globe. It shows that the far north of New Zealand is at the same latitude as North Africa, and that the far south of New Zealand is at the same latitude as the centre of France. Now turn the map upside down!

THE two main islands that make up New Zealand are 2000 km east of Australia. Only 4 and a half million people live in the whole country. The capital is Wellington, near the centre of New Zealand, but the largest city is Auckland in the north.

The original inhabitants were the Maoris, but now they are only about 15 per cent of the population. Some place-names are Maori words, such as Rotorua, Whangarei and Wanganui.

South Island is the largest island, but has fewer people than North Island. There are more sheep than people! The Canterbury Plains are a very important farming area. Aoraki Mount Cook, the highest point in New Zealand, is in the spectacular Southern Alps. Tourists visit the far south to see the glaciers and fjords. The fast-flowing rivers are used for hydro-electricity.

▲ ***Auckland** is sometimes called 'the city of sails' because so many people own or sail a yacht here. The city centre looks out over two huge natural harbours that are ideal for sailing. To the north is Waitemara Harbour and to the south is the shallow Manukau Harbour. Auckland is New Zealand's biggest city, and also an important port for huge container ships.*

NEW ZEALAND

AREA 270,534 sq km
POPULATION 4,991,000
CURRENCY NZ dollar

▲ ***The Southern Alps** stretch the length of South Island. The fine scenery attracts tourists, and the grassland is used for sheep-grazing.*

KIWI FRUIT . . .

. . . were known as 'Chinese Gooseberries' until New Zealanders (nicknamed 'Kiwis') improved them, renamed them, and promoted them. Now they are a successful export crop for farmers, and many other countries also grow them – it is interesting to find out where YOUR kiwi fruit comes from.

▲ ***This Maori boy** wears traditional war paint and beads. The Maoris lived in New Zealand before the Europeans came. Today, most live in North Island and many of their traditions have become part of New Zealand life.*

North Island has a warmer climate than South Island. In some places you can see hot springs and boiling mud pools and there are also volcanoes. Fine trees and giant ferns grow in the forests, but much of the forest has been cleared for farming. Cattle are kept on the rich grasslands for meat and milk. Many different kinds of fruit grow well, including apples, kiwi fruit and pears, which are exported.

On the map below you can find: a sea and a bay named after the Dutch explorer Abel Tasman; a strait (sea channel) and a mountain named after the British explorer James Cook.

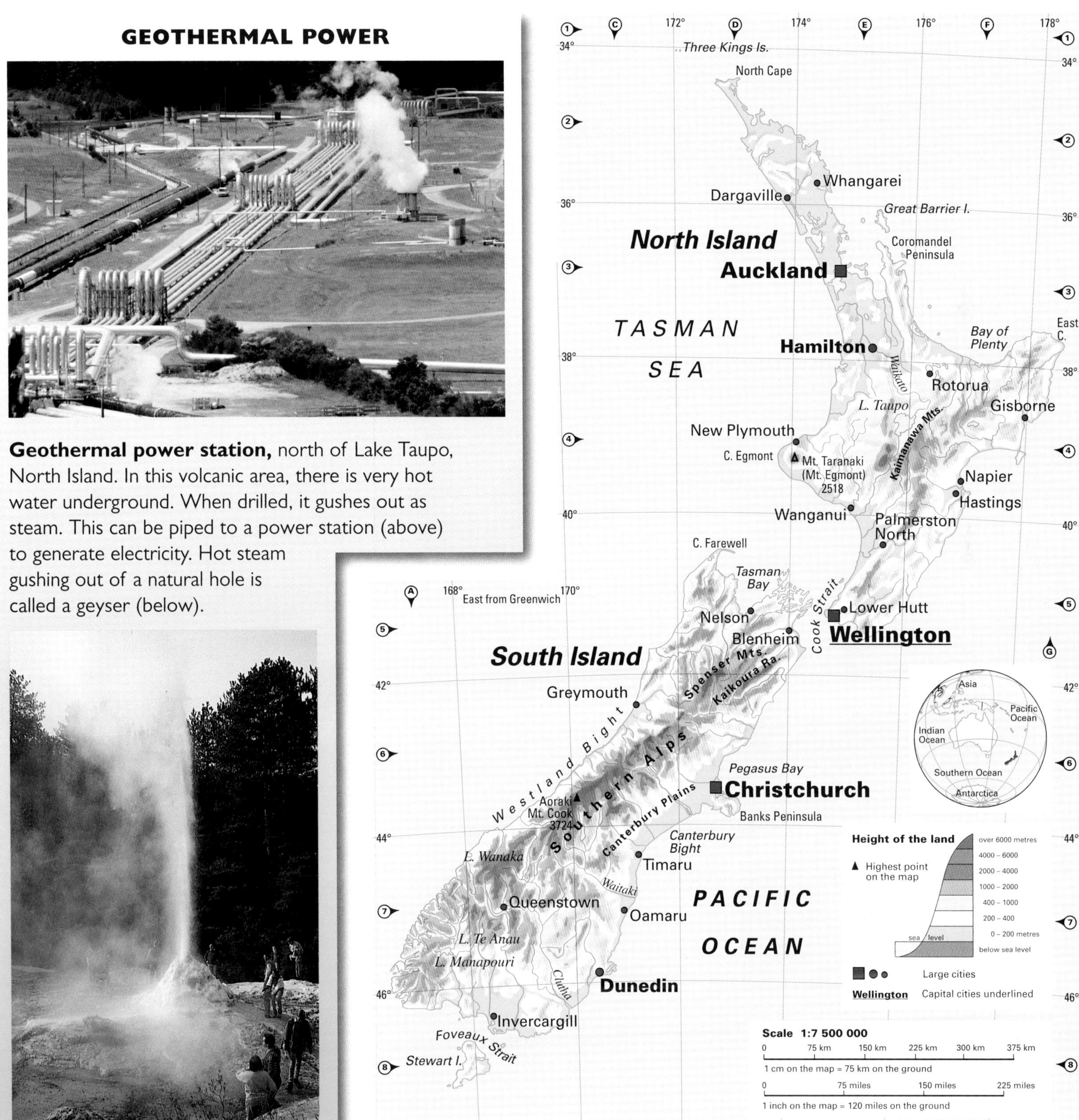

GEOTHERMAL POWER

Geothermal power station, north of Lake Taupo, North Island. In this volcanic area, there is very hot water underground. When drilled, it gushes out as steam. This can be piped to a power station (above) to generate electricity. Hot steam gushing out of a natural hole is called a geyser (below).

NORTH AMERICA

NORTH America includes many Arctic islands, a huge mainland area (quite narrow in Central America) and the islands in the Caribbean Sea. The map shows the great mountain ranges, including the Rockies, which are the most impressive feature of this continent.

Almost all of the west is high and mountainous, yet Death Valley is *below* sea level. The rocks have been folded into mountain ranges, but the highest peaks are volcanoes. The Appalachian Mountains in the east are also fold mountains. In between are the Great Plains (known as the Prairies in Canada), which are flat and fertile. The Canadian Shield in the far north is made of very old hard rocks.

▲ ***Flyovers, Los Angeles, USA.*** *There are three levels of road at this road junction in Los Angeles; sometimes there are traffic jams as well! In 1994, a huge earthquake destroyed many road bridges.*

The political map of North America is quite a simple one. The boundary between **Canada** and the **USA** is mostly on exactly latitude 49°N. Look at the Great Lakes on both maps. Four of the five have one shore in Canada and one shore in the USA★.

Canada's two biggest cities, Toronto and Montreal, are south of the 49° line Find them on the map on page 71.

Greenland used to be a colony of Denmark, but now it is self-governing. Most of Greenland is covered by ice all year. See page 88 for more about Greenland and the Arctic Ocean, and page 73 for Alaska (which is part of the USA).

★ *Which lakes? Answer on page 97.*

Mexico and the seven countries of Central America have more complicated boundaries. Six of these countries have two coastlines. The map shows that one country has a coastline only on the Pacific Ocean, and one has a coastline only on the Caribbean Sea★. These countries are Spanish-speaking: in fact there are more Spanish speakers here than in Spain. Some of Mexico and all of Central America are tropical.

The **West Indies** are made up of islands. Some countries have lots of islands; some islands are one or two countries. They are shown in more detail on page 81. **Cuba** is the biggest island country. One island has TWO countries on it★. They are shown in more detail on page 81. This area is often called 'The Caribbean'. Some West Indians have emigrated to the USA, Britain and France.

★ *Which ones? Answer on page 97.*

▲ ***Market in St George's, Grenada.*** *The West Indies have hot sunshine and plenty of rain. This is an ideal climate for growing vegetables and fruit. These stalls are stacked high with local produce. Many islands have volcanic soil which is rich in minerals and very fertile.*

Grenada is an island country which grows and exports bananas and nutmeg. Find it on the map on page 81.

North Pole
ASIA
ARCTIC OCEAN
GREENLAND
ICELAND
Arctic Circle
Alaska (part of U.S.A.)
CANADA
Great Lakes
PACIFIC OCEAN
UNITED STATES OF AMERICA (U.S.A.)
ATLANTIC OCEAN
BERMUDA
Tropic of Cancer
BAHAMAS
Gulf of Mexico
MEXICO
CUBA
HAITI
DOMINICAN REP.
PUERTO RICO
JAMAICA
DOMINICA
ST. LUCIA
ST. VINCENT
BARBADOS
GRENADA
Caribbean Sea
BELIZE
HONDURAS
GUATEMALA
EL SALVADOR
NICARAGUA
Panama Canal
COSTA RICA
PANAMA
SOUTH AMERICA
Equator
100° West from Greenwich

North America in the World
Arctic Ocean
Asia
Europe
Africa
Pacific Ocean
South America
Atlantic Ocean

Scale 1:50 000 000
0 500 km 1000 km 1500 km 2000 km 2500 km
1 cm on the map = 500 km on the ground
0 500 miles 1000 miles 1500 miles
1 inch on the map = 800 miles on the ground

NORTH AMERICA FACTS

AREA 24,249,000 sq km
HIGHEST POINT Denali (Mt. McKinley) (Alaska), 6190 metres
LOWEST POINT Death Valley (California), 86 metres below sea level
LONGEST RIVERS
Red Rock–Missouri–Mississippi, 5970 km
Mackenzie–Peace, 4240 km
LARGEST LAKE Lake Superior*, 82,350 sq km
BIGGEST COUNTRY
Canada, 9,970,610 sq km
SMALLEST COUNTRY Grenada (West Indies), 344 sq km
RICHEST COUNTRY USA
POOREST COUNTRY Haiti
MOST CROWDED COUNTRY Barbados
LEAST CROWDED COUNTRY Canada
* *The world's largest freshwater lake*

CANADA

CANADA

AREA 9,970,610 sq km
POPULATION 37,943,000
MONEY Canadian dollar
CAPITAL Ottawa

ONLY one country in the world is bigger than Canada*, but 37 countries have more people than Canada. Most of Canada is almost empty. Some of the northern islands are uninhabited. Very few people live in the Northwest Territories, or in the western mountains, or near Hudson Bay. The farmland of the prairies (see the top stamp) is uncrowded too. So ... where do Canadians live?

The answer is that more Canadians live in cities than in the countryside. The map shows where the biggest cities are – all of them are in the southern part of Canada, and none are as far north as Norway or Sweden in Europe. Toronto is on the same latitude as Venice and Milan.

These photographs show Canada in summer. In winter, it is very cold indeed in both central and northern Canada. Children go to school even when it is 40° below zero. The mildest winters are in the south-west, around Vancouver.

* *Which country? See page 9.*

▲ **The Niagara Falls** are between Lake Erie and Lake Ontario, on the border of the USA and Canada. One part is called the Horseshoe Falls: can you see why?

▲ **In western Canada,** the Rocky Mountains are home to the large brown bears known as 'grizzlys'. The Rockies stretch for 4800 km through both Canada and the USA. They were a great barrier to the early explorers and to the early settlers, railway engineers and road builders.

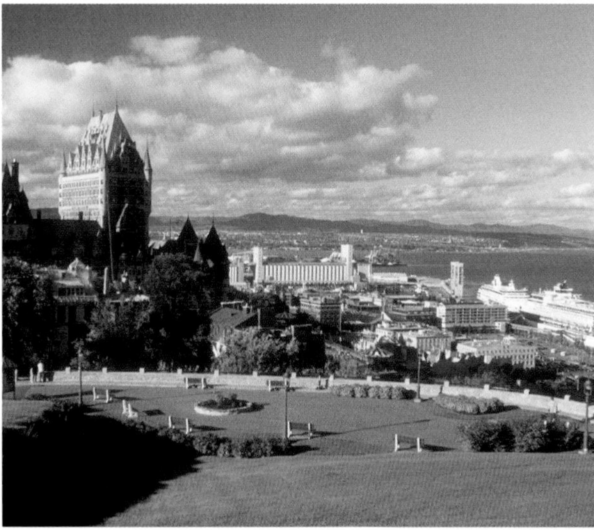

▲ ***Quebec City.*** *The Chateau Frontenac (seen on the left) is built in the style of a French chateau (castle). This part of Canada was once owned by the French, and the people still speak French. On the right is the port beside the River St Lawrence. Large ocean-going ships can dock here.*

▲ ***The Prairies*** *are a vast area of fairly flat and fertile land between the Rocky Mountains and Lake Winnipeg and the Great Lakes. Wheat and other crops are grown for export. You can work out why this area is named 'the bread-basket of Canada'. Many farmers have kept their old red barns for storing machinery. The harvested wheat is taken to large silos beside the railway line.*

▲ ***A long-distance train*** *travels through a pass in the Rocky Mountains. The trans-Canada railway helped to unite Canada as one country.*

LANGUAGES IN CANADA

Canada has two official languages: French and English. So Canadian stamps say 'Postes/Postage', instead of only 'Postage'. Most of the French-speaking Canadians live in the province of Quebec, which once belonged to France. The biggest city in Quebec is Montreal: it is four times as big as Ottawa, the capital of Canada.

▲ ***Vancouver, British Columbia:*** *the biggest city in the west of Canada.*

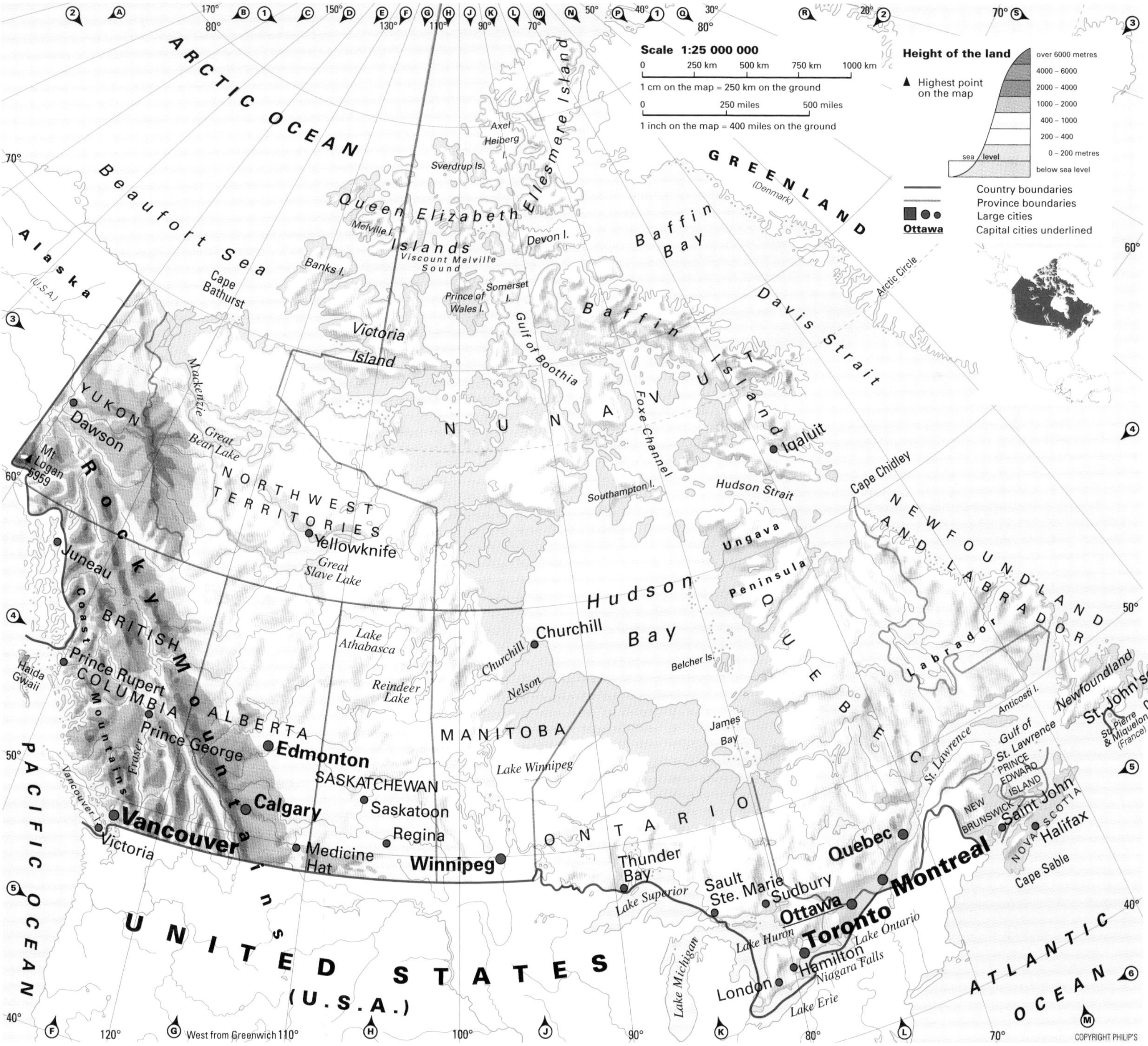

Scale 1:25 000 000

0 – 250 km – 500 km – 750 km – 1000 km

1 cm on the map = 250 km on the ground

0 – 250 miles – 500 miles

1 inch on the map = 400 miles on the ground

Height of the land

▲ Highest point on the map

over 6000 metres
4000 – 6000
2000 – 4000
1000 – 2000
400 – 1000
200 – 400
0 – 200 metres
sea level
below sea level

Country boundaries
Province boundaries
Large cities
Ottawa – Capital cities underlined

USA

WHO are 'the Americans'? Of every 100 people in the USA, over 80 have ancestors from Europe. The first colonists came from Britain, France and Spain, but later on, people came from almost all parts of Europe to the United States.

About 12 people out of every 100 came from West Africa, brought to the USA as slaves to work in the southern states. By 1865, the slaves were free. Many black Americans now live in the north-east. More recently, many Spanish-speaking people have arrived from Mexico and Puerto Rico.

There are now fewer than 1 million American Indians in the USA, some of whom live on special reservations.

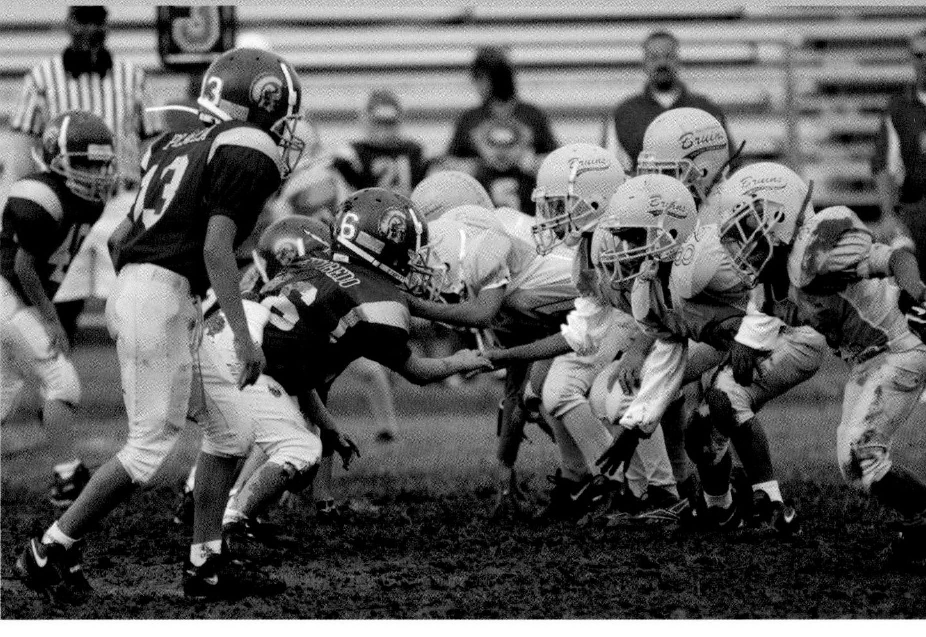

▲ ***American football*** *is a popular sport in the USA. Two teams of 11 people compete for points by trying to get the ball over their opponents' 'end zone'. Teams travel huge distances to compete with each other.*

STARS AND STRIPES

In 1776 there were only 13 states in the USA: so the US flag had 13 stars and 13 stripes. As more and more states joined

the USA, more stars were added to the flag. Now there are 50 states, and 50 stars.

HAWAII

Kauai
Oahu
Honolulu
PACIFIC OCEAN
Hawaiian Islands
Molokai
Maui
Mauna Kea 4205
Mauna Loa 4169
Hawaii
Scale 1:10 000 000
0 100 km 200 km 300 km
1 cm on the map = 100 km on the ground
160° West from Greenwich 158°

Hawaii *is the newest state in the USA: it became a state in 1959. The picture shows Waikiki beach in Honolulu, the biggest city. Honolulu is on Oahu island. These faraway Pacific islands are the tops of volcanoes, over 3000 km from mainland USA (see map page 63). Hawaii island itself has a very active volcano in the south. If the height of Mauna Kea is measured from the seabed, it is 10,023 metres: the world's highest mountain. The islands are the most southerly part of the USA.*

▲ ***The bald eagle*** *(above) is the USA's national bird. This bird of prey is unique to North America and can be found in Canada, Alaska, the USA and northern Mexico.*

USA

AREA 9,629,091 sq km
POPULATION 334,998,000
MONEY US dollar
CAPITAL Washington, DC

The maps show the 50 states of the USA. The first 13 states were on the east coast. They were settled by Europeans who had sailed across the Atlantic Ocean. As the Americans moved westwards, so more states were formed. The western states are bigger than the states in the east. You can see their straight boundaries on the map: those boundaries were drawn *before* the settlers arrived.

DISTANCE CHART

Read the chart just like a tables-chart, or a graph. The distance chart shows how big the USA is. How far is it from Seattle to Miami? Or from New Orleans to Chicago? (*Answers on page 97.*)

Road distances in km

	New York	Miami	Chicago	New Orleans	Seattle
Miami	2138				
Chicago	1346	2198			
New Orleans	2131	1406	1488		
Seattle	4613	5445	3288	4211	
San Francisco	4850	4915	3499	3622	1352

ALASKA

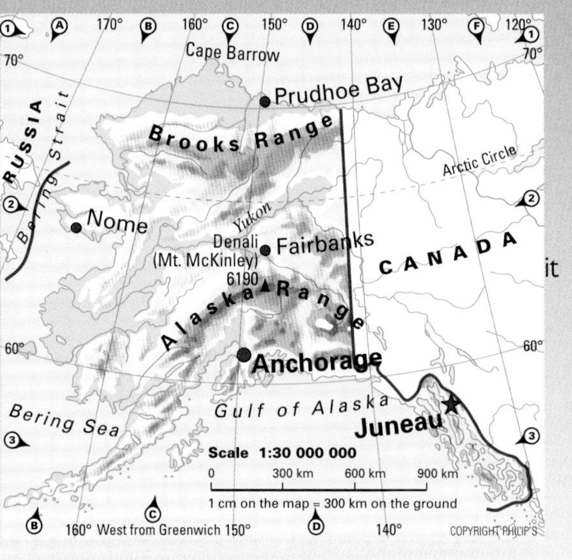

Alaska is the biggest state of the USA – but has the fewest people. It was bought from Russia in 1867 for $7 million: the best bargain ever, particularly as oil was discovered a hundred years later. Oil has helped Alaska to become rich. Timber and fish are the other main products. Much of Alaska is mountainous or covered in forest. In the north, there is darkness all day in December, and months of ice-cold weather. But in the short summer, visitors love the long days and short nights. Farming is not possible in most of Alaska – except in the far south.

DID YOU KNOW? The Bering Strait is the only sea route from the Pacific to the Arctic Ocean, but it is often frozen over.

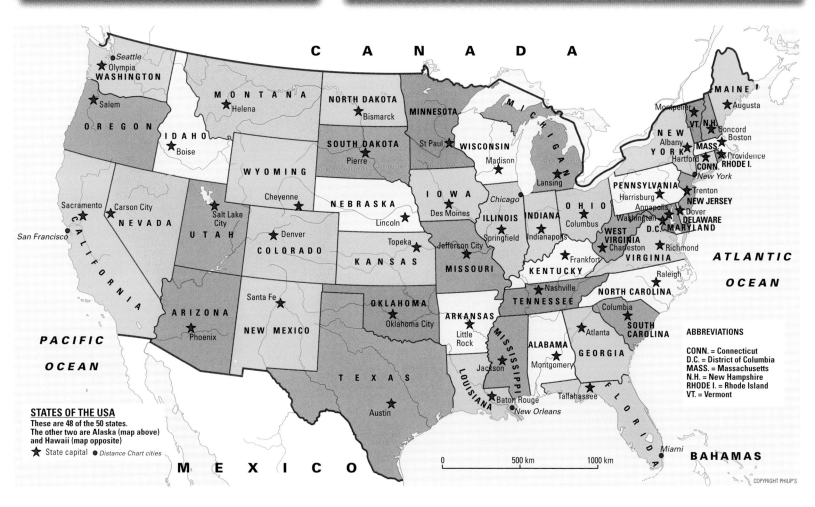

STATES OF THE USA

These are 48 of the 50 states. The other two are Alaska (map above) and Hawaii (map opposite)

★ State capital ● *Distance Chart cities*

0 500 km 1000 km

ABBREVIATIONS

CONN. = Connecticut
D.C. = District of Columbia
MASS. = Massachusetts
N.H. = New Hampshire
RHODE I. = Rhode Island
VT. = Vermont

EASTERN USA

NEW YORK

OHIO

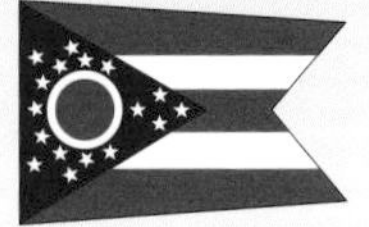

MARYLAND

THE map shows only half the USA, but over three-quarters of the population live in this half of the country.

The great cities of the north-east were the first big industrial areas in America. Pittsburgh's American football team is still called the Pittsburgh Steelers, even though nearly all of the steelworks have closed down.

In recent years, many people have moved from the 'snow-belt' of the north to the 'sun-belt' of the south. New industries are booming in the south, where once there was much poverty. And many older people retire to Florida, where even midwinter feels almost like summer.

In the southern states it is hot enough for cotton, tobacco and peanuts to be successful crops. The palm tree on the flag of South Carolina (below, right) suggests that the climate of this part of America is nearly tropical. Summers are very hot and humid and winters are mostly mild. But hurricanes can cause serious flooding and damage near the coast.

The Appalachian Mountains are beautiful, especially in the autumn (fall), when the leaves turn red. But this area is the poorest part of the USA. Coal mines have closed and farmland is poor. The good farmland is west of the Appalachians, where you can drive for many kilometres past fields of wheat and sweetcorn.

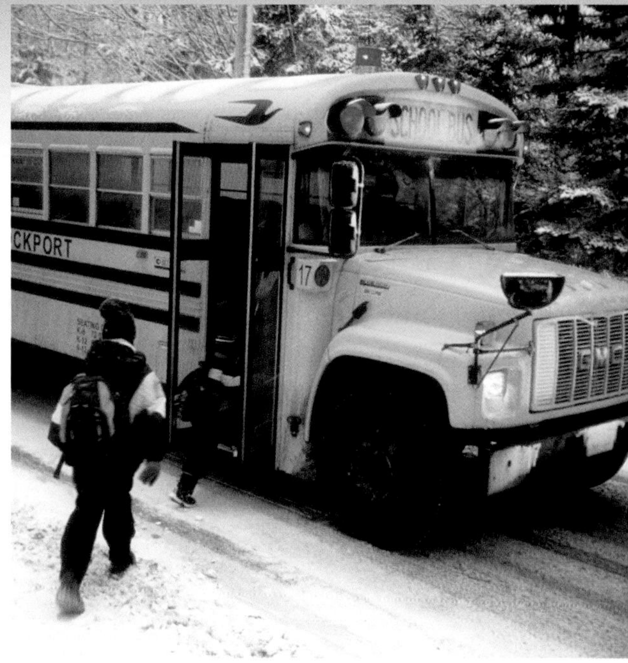

▲ ***The school bus in New Hampshire.*** *The north-east corner of the USA is called New England and was settled by English colonists. The settlers named their towns and villages after places they had known in England. This bus is taking the children to school in the snow!*

WHICH US CITY IS MOST IMPORTANT?

Washington, DC, is the capital city, where the President lives. But New York has far more people and industries than Washington. So both are the most important city – but in different ways.

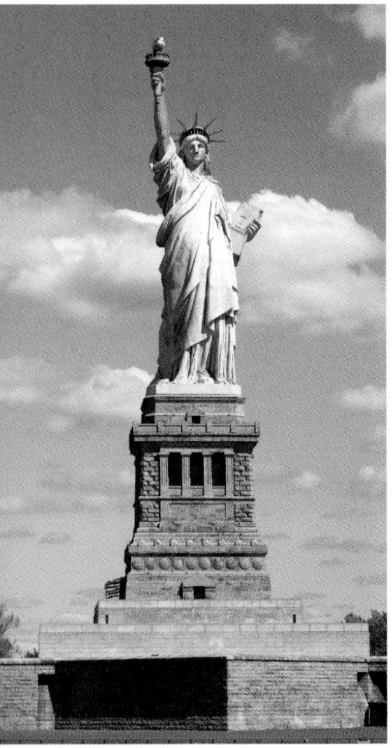

▲ ***The Statue of Liberty*** *stands on an island in New York harbour. When people arrived by ship, the statue was there to greet them! The torch at the top is 93 metres above the ground.*

▲ ***Skyscrapers in Chicago,*** *the biggest inland city in the USA. The world's first skyscraper was built here in 1885. These skyscrapers look out over Lake Michigan. The lake shore can freeze over in winter.*

Every US state has its own flag: six state flags are shown on the page opposite. Several states were named after kings and queens of England – in the days when these states were English colonies. For example, North and South CAROLina use the Latin name for King Charles I; MARYland is named after his wife, Queen Mary, and GEORGia is named after King George II. But LOUISiana is named after King Louis XIV of France because France colonized a vast area along the Mississippi river. The map on page 73 shows the names of all the states.

GREAT LAKES

Try using the first letters of the Great Lakes to make a sentence:

Superior	**S**uper
Michigan	**M**an
Huron	**H**elps
Erie	**E**very
Ontario	**O**ne

If you remember these, you'll never forget the west-to-east order of the five Great Lakes!

THE MISSISSIPPI

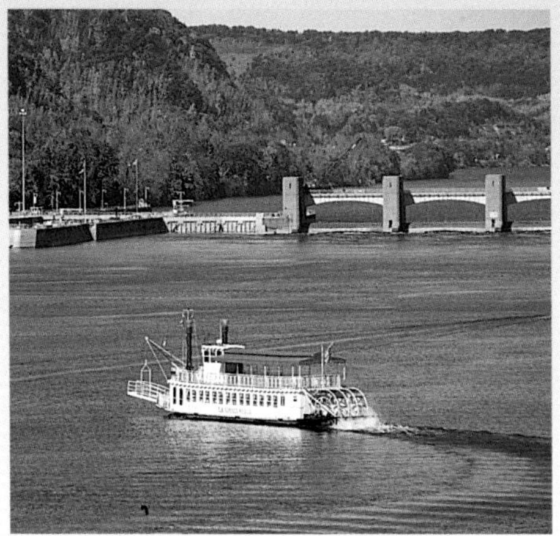

The **Mississippi River** was known as the 'Great River Road' because it was an important route into the heart of the United State of America. 'Stern-wheeler' paddle-steamers travelled the river with cargoes. It is still an important river today. Dams (above) and locks make it easier for big barges to use the river. The dams also help to reduce the risk of floods.

Scale 1:20 000 000
0 200 km 400 km 600 km 800 km
1 cm on the map = 200 km on the ground
0 200 miles 400 miles
1 inch on the map = 320 miles on the ground

Height of the land
▲ Highest point on the map
over 6000 metres
4000 – 6000
2000 – 4000
1000 – 2000
400 – 1000
200 – 400
0 – 200 metres
sea level
below sea level

Country boundaries
Large cities
Washington Capital cities underlined
For the states of the U.S.A. see page 73

CANADA
Great Plains
Appalachian Mts.
Lake Superior
Lake Michigan
Lake Huron
Lake Erie
Lake Ontario
Mississippi
Missouri
Ohio
Tennessee
Arkansas
Red
Hudson
Everglades
Duluth
Fargo
Minneapolis
St. Paul
Sioux Falls
Milwaukee
Detroit
Chicago
Toledo
Omaha
Des Moines
Buffalo
Albany
Boston
C. Cod
Providence
Cleveland
New York
Pittsburgh
Philadelphia
Indianapolis
Columbus
Baltimore
Washington D.C.
Cincinnati
Kansas City
St. Louis
Louisville
Richmond
Norfolk
Wichita
Nashville
Tulsa
Mt Mitchell 2037
Charlotte
Oklahoma City
Memphis
Chattanooga
Atlanta
ATLANTIC OCEAN
Charleston
Fort Worth
Dallas
Montgomery
Austin
Baton Rouge
Jacksonville
New Orleans
Orlando
San Antonio
Houston
Cape Canaveral
Tampa
Palm Beach
Fort Lauderdale
Gulf of Mexico
Miami
BAHAMAS
C. Sable
Key West
West from Greenwich
COPYRIGHT PHILIP'S

▲ ***The everglades of Florida** are an area of tropical wetlands. Lots of birds such as the snowy egret live here (see above). It is also home to more dangerous creatures such as alligators. Can you see the alligator? (Hint: look at the log under the water).*

WESTERN USA

MANY parts of the western USA have hardly any people. The Rocky Mountains are beautiful for holidays, but it is hard to make a living there.

The only big city on the high plateaus west of the Rockies is Salt Lake City, Utah, which was settled by the Mormons. Some former mining towns are now 'ghost towns': when the mines closed, all the people left. The toughest area of all is the desert land of Arizona in the south-west. The mountains and deserts were a great problem to the pioneers, but today the spectacular scenery and wildlife are preserved in large national parks.

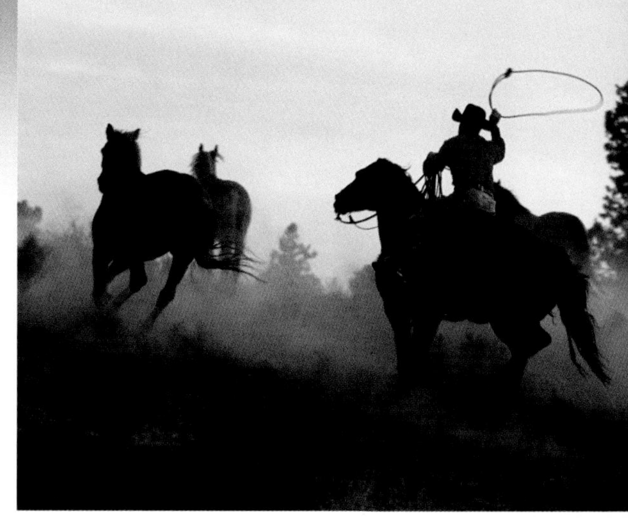

▲ ***The 'Wild West'.*** *Scenes like this one are rare now, except when they are put on for the many tourists who visit the area. But in the days of the 'Wild West', 100 years or more ago, the skills of cowboys were vital for rounding up the cattle that roamed over vast unfenced areas.*

▲ ***Wheat harvest, USA.*** *Huge combine harvesters move across a field of wheat. In the distance is the grain store. Up to 150 years ago, this land was covered in grass and grazed by buffaloes.*

WHAT DO THE NAMES MEAN?

The Spanish were the first settlers in the western USA, and they have left us many Spanish names. Can you match the name and its meaning? (*Answers on page 97.*)

Amarillo (Texas)	The pass
Colorado	Yellow
El Paso (Texas)	The angels
Los Angeles	St Francis
San Jose	Coloured
San Francisco	St Joseph

Energy conservation. A great idea! But Americans use more energy than anyone else in the world.

▲ ***Grand Canyon, Arizona.*** *The Colorado River has cut a huge canyon 1½ kilometres deep and several kilometres wide in this desert area of the USA. The mountains slowly rose, while the river kept carving a deeper valley.*

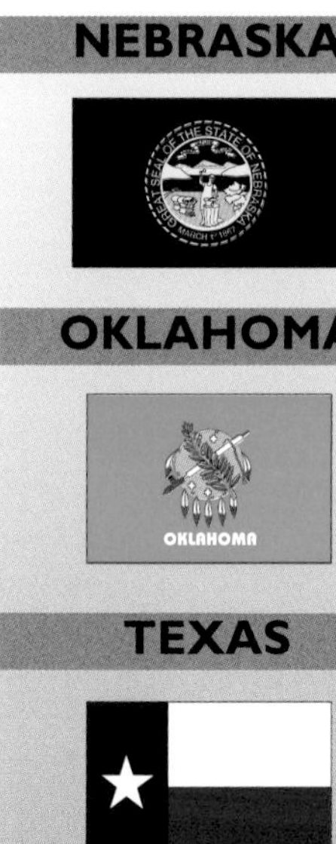

The Great Plains east of the Rocky Mountains are flat but high. Denver is nick-named 'Mile High City'. All of the Great Plains were once grass. Where there is enough rain, they have been ploughed up for crops of wheat and sweetcorn (maize). In drier areas the grassland remains and there are enormous cattle ranches.

The Pacific coastlands of the north-west have plenty of rain and the climate is quite like north-west Europe. The mountains and valleys are thickly forested and timber is an important product. Seattle is on a sheltered inlet of the sea.

CALIFORNIA

California now has more people than any other state, and it is the USA's 'hi-tech' centre. It has many advantages. In the Central Valley, the climate is right for many crops: oranges from California are well known, and grapes grow well and are made into wine. The desert of the south is attractive to retired people – many people migrate here from all over the USA. But there is one big danger: earthquakes! So buildings have to be strengthened.

▲ ***A street-car in San Francisco.*** *Street-cars still climb the steep hills in San Francisco, California. A moving cable runs beneath the street. The car is fixed to the cable and starts with a jerk! In the background you can see an inlet of the Pacific and Alcatraz – once a top-security prison island.*

130° 120° 110° 100° 50° 40° 30°

CANADA

ROCKY MOUNTAINS

GREAT PLAINS

Great Basin

Cascade Range

Sierra Nevada

Coast Range

Wasatch Range

Black Hills

Seattle, Portland, Eugene, Spokane, Boise, Billings, Big Timber, Casper, Reno, Sacramento, San Francisco, San Jose, Fresno, Mt. Whitney 4418, Death Valley, Las Vegas, Salt Lake City, Great Salt Lake, Denver, Pueblo, Grand Canyon, Los Angeles, San Diego, Phoenix, Tucson, Albuquerque, El Paso, Fargo, Duluth, St. Paul, Minneapolis, Sioux Falls, Omaha, Des Moines, Kansas City, Wichita, Tulsa, Oklahoma City, Amarillo, Fort Worth, Dallas, Austin, Houston, San Antonio

Columbia, Snake, Missouri, Yellowstone, Colorado, Arkansas, Red, Rio Grande

PACIFIC OCEAN

MEXICO

Gulf of Mexico

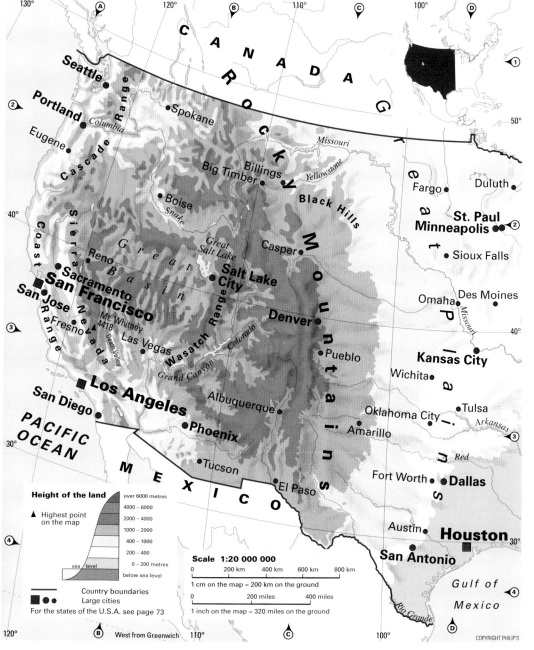

Height of the land

over 6000 metres, 4000 – 6000, 2000 – 4000, 1000 – 2000, 400 – 1000, 200 – 400, 0 – 200 metres, sea level, below sea level

▲ Highest point on the map

Country boundaries

Large cities

For the states of the U.S.A. see page 73

Scale 1:20 000 000

0 200 km 400 km 600 km 800 km

1 cm on the map = 200 km on the ground

0 200 miles 400 miles

1 inch on the map = 320 miles on the ground

West from Greenwich

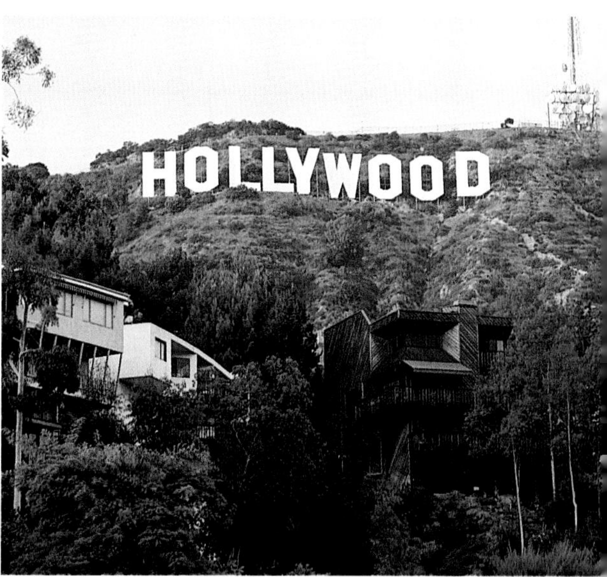

▲ ***Hollywood*** *is a suburb of Los Angeles. Rich film-stars live here in expensive houses. The clear blue skies and lack of rain were helpful to film-makers. But now, Los Angeles has so many cars there is more smog from pollution than clear skies.*

CENTRAL AMERICA

MEXICO

AREA 1,958,201 sq km
POPULATION 130,207,000
MONEY Mexican peso

GUATEMALA

AREA 108,889 sq km
POPULATION 17,423,000
MONEY Quetzal

PANAMA

AREA 75,517 sq km
POPULATION 3,929,000
MONEY Balboa

Mexico is by far the most important country on this map. Over 120 million people live in Mexico – more than in any country in Europe. Mexico City has a population of about 21 million: it is one of the biggest cities in the world. A major earthquake did much damage there in 1985.

Most Mexicans live on the high plateau of central Mexico. Industries are growing fast in Mexico City and near the border with the USA. There are very few people in the northern desert, in Lower California in the north-west, in the southern jungle, or in Yucatan in the east. But tourist resorts thrive on the Yucatan and Pacific coasts.

The other seven countries on this map are quite small. None of them has as many people as Mexico City! These countries were once ruled by Spain, but they have been independent since the 1820s. Civil wars have caused many problems in Central America. But the climate is good for growing many tropical crops, so lots of forest has been cut down for farmland.

▲ ***Ruins at Chichen Itza, Mexico.*** *Great temples were built by the people known as Mayas over a thousand years ago. These amazing ruins are in Yucatan, the most easterly part of Mexico. The tourists look tiny, which shows you how HUGE the pyramid is!*

BELIZE

AREA 22,966 sq km
POPULATION 406,000
MONEY Belize dollar

TORTILLAS – A RECIPE FOR YOU TO COOK

Ingredients: 225 grams of maize flour (sweetcorn flour); salt and water

1. Mix the maize flour, salt and water into a soft dough.
2. Pat into round shapes about ½ centimetre thick, and 12 centimetres across.
3. Melt a little margarine in a frying-pan.
4. Place the tortillas in the hot frying-pan.
5. For best results, turn the tortillas over.
6. Serve at once!

You have now cooked one of the most important meals of Central America. Maize (sweetcorn) was developed as a crop in the Americas, and is now grown in many parts of the world. You eat maize often as Corn Flakes and semolina.

▲ ***The Toucan*** *is sometimes called the 'banana-beak bird', for an obvious reason! It eats fruit and lives in the forest, nesting in a hole in a tree. If the forest is cleared, it will have nowhere to live.*

THE PANAMA CANAL

CARIBBEAN SEA
COLON
Gatun Locks
GATUN
N
W
E
S
GAMBOA
LAKE GATUN
Pedro Miguel Locks
Miraflores Locks
PANAMA
26 metres above sea level
PACIFIC OCEAN

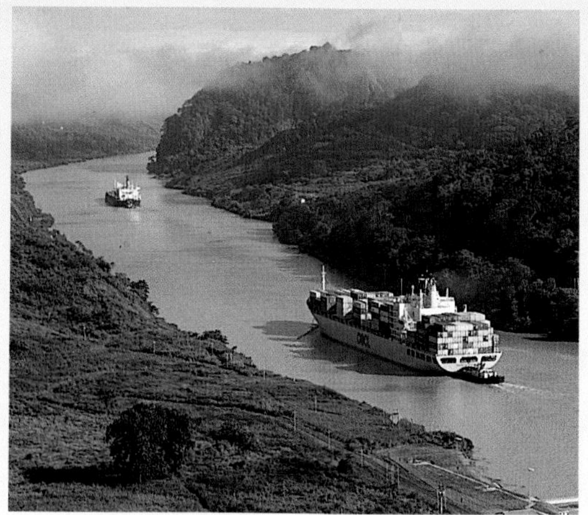

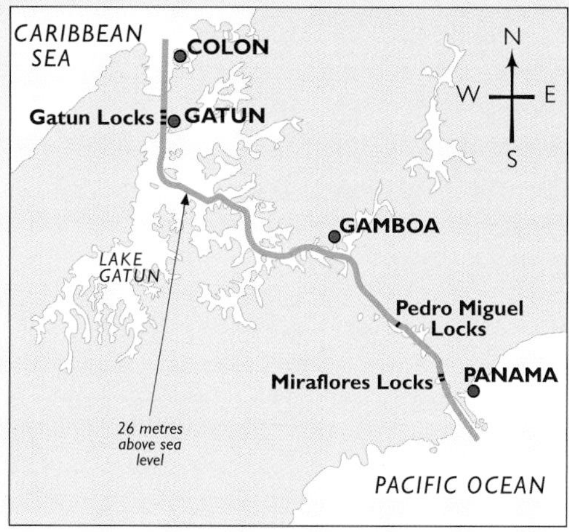

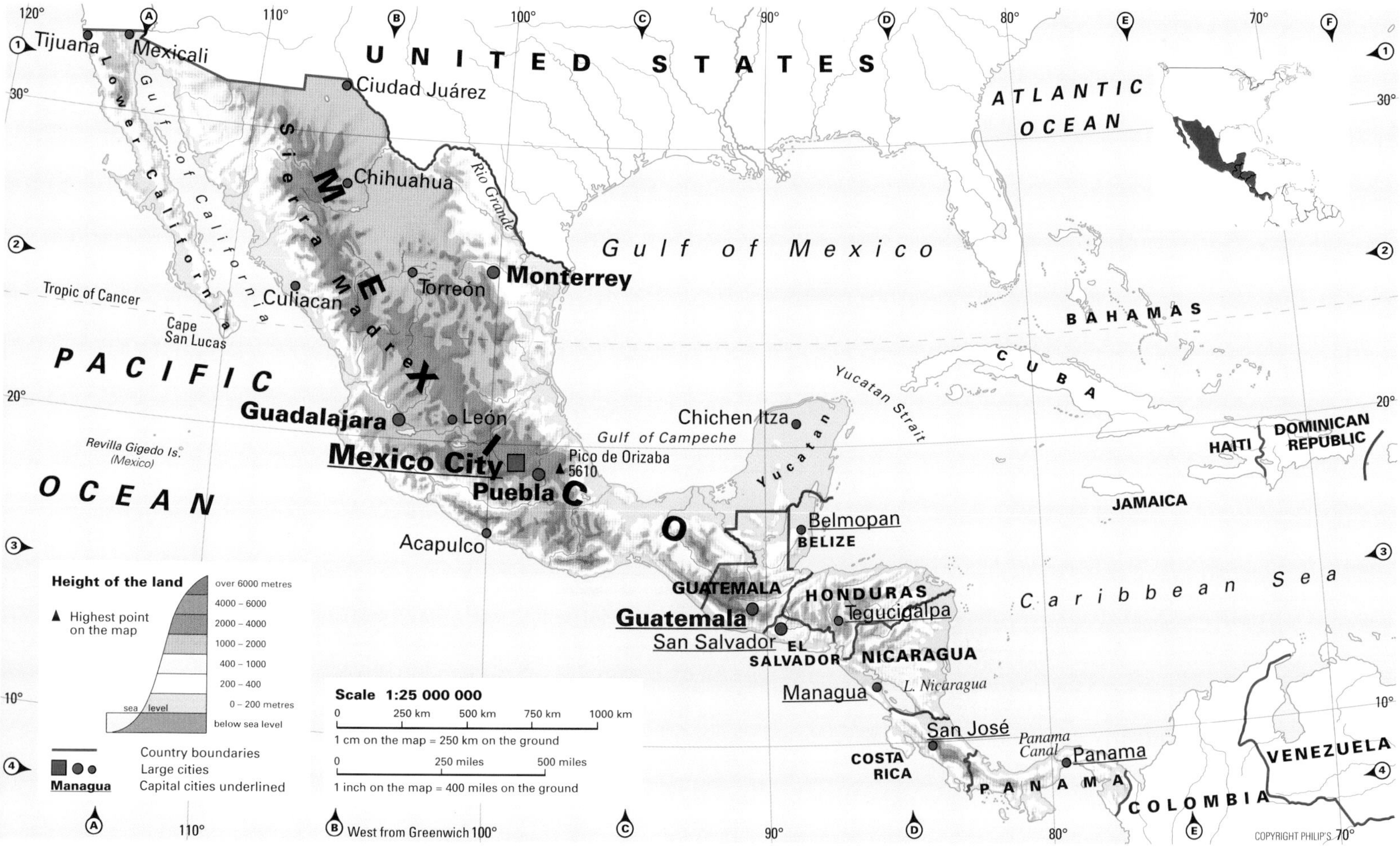

PANAMA CANAL CROSS-SECTION

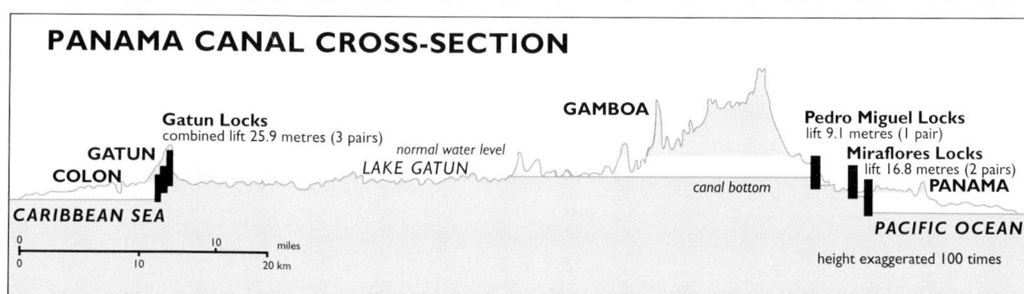

Gatun Locks
combined lift 25.9 metres (3 pairs)
GATUN
COLON
normal water level
LAKE GATUN
GAMBOA
canal bottom
Pedro Miguel Locks
lift 9.1 metres (1 pair)
Miraflores Locks
lift 16.8 metres (2 pairs)
PANAMA
CARIBBEAN SEA
PACIFIC OCEAN
0 10 miles
0 10 20 km
height exaggerated 100 times

The Panama Canal links the Caribbean Sea with the Pacific Ocean. It was opened in 1914. Many workers died of fever while digging the canal through the jungle. It is 82 km long, and the deepest cutting is 82 metres deep – the world's biggest 'ditch'!

There are six locks along the route of the canal. The photograph (left) shows two ships travelling through the canal. The map and diagram show that part of the route is through Lake Gatun, at 26 metres above sea level. So the ships have to pass through three locks at each end.

Over 15,000 ships use the canal each year, and sometimes there are 'traffic jams' at the locks: it is the busiest big-ship canal in the world. Before the Panama Canal was built, the only sea route from the Pacific to the Atlantic was round South America.

In which direction are ships travelling from the Caribbean to the Pacific? Does this surprise you? Look at the map below.

UNITED STATES
MEXICO
Tijuana
Mexicali
Ciudad Juárez
Chihuahua
Rio Grande
Lower California
Gulf of California
Sierra Madre
Monterrey
Torreón
Culiacan
Tropic of Cancer
Cape San Lucas
Gulf of Mexico
ATLANTIC OCEAN
BAHAMAS
CUBA
PACIFIC OCEAN
Guadalajara
León
Revilla Gigedo Is. (Mexico)
Mexico City
Puebla
Pico de Orizaba 5610
Gulf of Campeche
Chichen Itza
Yucatan
Yucatan Strait
Acapulco
Belmopan
BELIZE
HAITI
DOMINICAN REPUBLIC
JAMAICA
Caribbean Sea
GUATEMALA
Guatemala
HONDURAS
Tegucigalpa
San Salvador
EL SALVADOR
NICARAGUA
Managua
L. Nicaragua
San José
COSTA RICA
Panama Canal
Panama
PANAMA
COLOMBIA
VENEZUELA
Height of the land
over 6000 metres
4000 – 6000
2000 – 4000
1000 – 2000
400 – 1000
200 – 400
0 – 200 metres
below sea level
sea level
Highest point on the map
Country boundaries
Large cities
Managua
Capital cities underlined
Scale 1:25 000 000
0 250 km 500 km 750 km 1000 km
1 cm on the map = 250 km on the ground
0 250 miles 500 miles
1 inch on the map = 400 miles on the ground
West from Greenwich
120° 110° 100° 90° 80° 70°
30° 20° 10°
COPYRIGHT PHILIP'S

WEST INDIES

JAMAICA

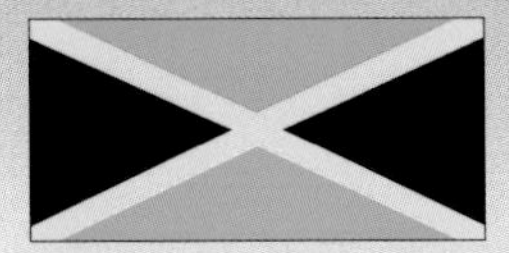

AREA 10,991 sq km
POPULATION 2,817,000
MONEY Jamaican dollar

CUBA

AREA 110,861 sq km
POPULATION 11,032,000
MONEY Cuban peso

HAITI

AREA 27,750 sq km
POPULATION 11,198,000
MONEY Gourde

THE West Indies are a large group of islands in the Caribbean Sea. Some islands are high and volcanic, others are low coral islands – but all of them are beautiful. Most West Indians have African ancestors: they were brought from West Africa as slaves, to work in the sugar and tobacco fields. And in Trinidad, workers came from India as well.

Most of the islands are now independent countries – and tourism is more important than farming in many places. Cruises around the islands are popular. Winter is the best time to visit; summer is very hot and humid, with the risk of hurricanes.

In recent years, many West Indians have emigrated to the UK from Commonwealth islands, to France from Guadeloupe and Martinique, and to the USA from Puerto Rico. The most important crops for export are tobacco, sugar, bananas and special fruit such as nutmegs from Grenada. A few islands have developed their minerals, for example bauxite in Jamaica and oil in Trinidad.

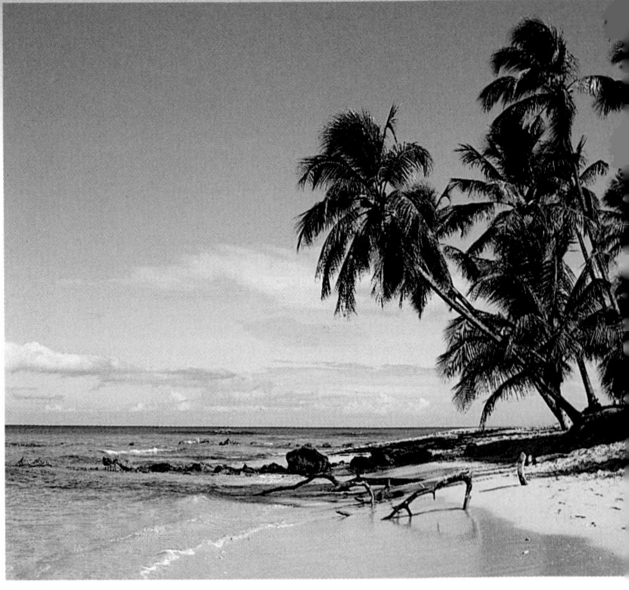

▲ ***Coconut palms and beach, Barbados.*** *It is beautiful – but beware! The tropical sun can quickly burn your skin. And if you seek shade under the coconut palms, you might get hit by a big coconut! Even so, the West Indies are very popular with tourists – especially Americans escaping from cold winters.*

▲ ***Dutch colonial houses, Curaçao.*** *The island of Curaçao has been Dutch for many years. The colonists came from the Netherlands, and tried to build houses just like the ones at home. Several other small West Indian islands still have European connections.*

TOURISM – GOOD & BAD NEWS

Tourism is GOOD news because it brings money and jobs to many West Indian islands. The sunny weather means tourists come all year. There is work in the hotels and restaurants. Farmers can sell more vegetables and a great variety of delicious fruit (left). Beautiful scenery is looked after so that tourists will come and visit – hot springs, waterfalls, old forts and churches as well as coral reefs and lovely beaches. But tourism can also be BAD news … pollution; noise; waste of water; and many local people do not want to be photographed by rich tourists who may not treat them as equals.

The flag of Jamaica (far left) has a meaning: GOLD stands for sunshine and natural resources; GREEN for farming and future hope; BLACK for hardships, past and present.

The West Indies used to be colonies of European countries. Today, most of the islands are independent, but still have close links with Europe.

Look at the map; can you spot★:

- An island that is part of the Netherlands?
- An island owned by the UK?
- An island that is part of France?
- A group of islands – half are owned by the UK; half by the USA?
- An island with two countries?
- The country with the most islands?

(★ *Answers on page 97.*)

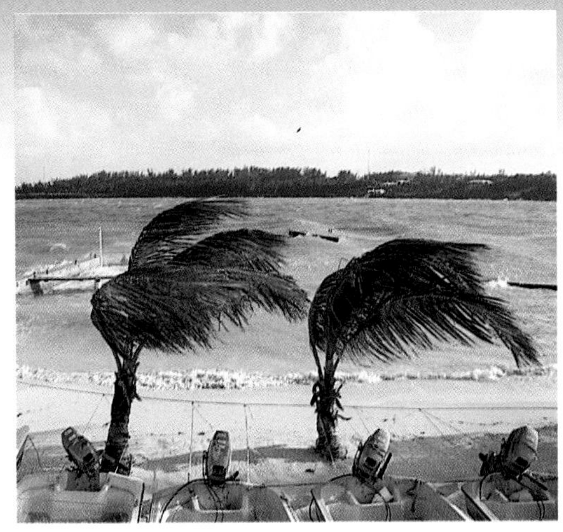

▲ ***Beware of the hurricane season!*** *What a contrast to the peaceful beach (see picture, left)! Violent tropical storms are a danger every summer. Strong winds can reach over 300 kilometres per hour, with torrential rain. They uproot trees and wreck boats and buildings; floods damage crops, roads and bridges.*

▲ ***Cleaning harvested bananas.*** *These bananas have been grown in Guadeloupe. They have to be cleaned before they can be sold. Many people here depend on banana farming to make a living. The bananas travel to other countries in large refrigerated ships.*

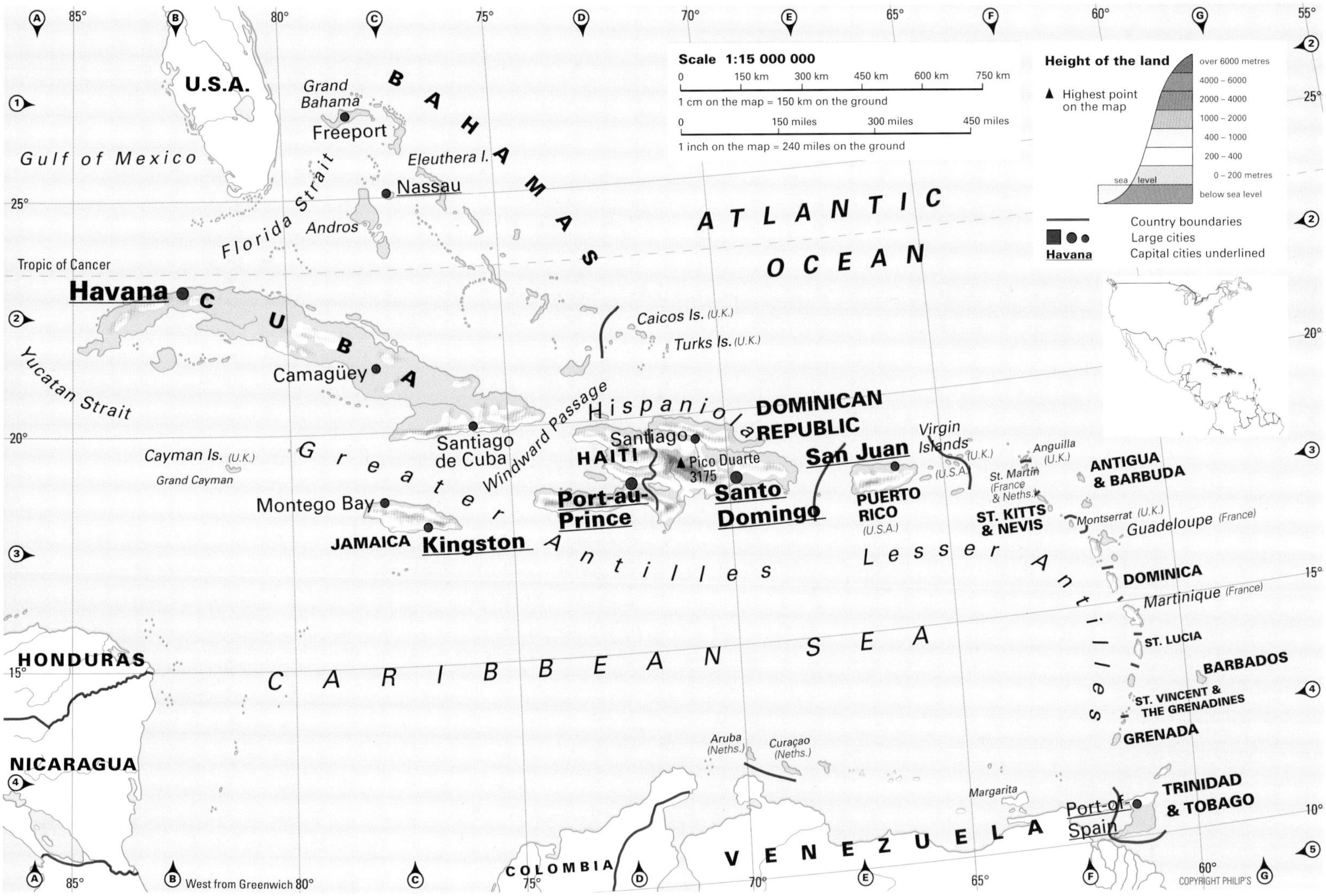

Scale 1:15 000 000
0 150 km 300 km 450 km 600 km 750 km
1 cm on the map = 150 km on the ground
0 150 miles 300 miles 450 miles
1 inch on the map = 240 miles on the ground

Height of the land
▲ Highest point on the map
over 6000 metres
4000 – 6000
2000 – 4000
1000 – 2000
400 – 1000
200 – 400
0 – 200 metres
sea level
below sea level

Country boundaries
Large cities
Capital cities underlined
Havana

U.S.A.
Gulf of Mexico
Grand Bahama
Freeport
BAHAMAS
Eleuthera I.
Nassau
Andros
Florida Strait
Tropic of Cancer
ATLANTIC OCEAN
Havana
CUBA
Camagüey
Yucatan Strait
Caicos Is. (U.K.)
Turks Is. (U.K.)
Windward Passage
Hispaniola
DOMINICAN REPUBLIC
Santiago
▲Pico Duarte 3175
Santo Domingo
HAITI
Port-au-Prince
Santiago de Cuba
Cayman Is. (U.K.)
Grand Cayman
Greater Antilles
Montego Bay
JAMAICA
Kingston
San Juan
PUERTO RICO (U.S.A.)
Virgin Islands (U.K.) (U.S.A.)
Anguilla (U.K.)
St. Martin (France & Neths.)
ANTIGUA & BARBUDA
ST. KITTS & NEVIS
Montserrat (U.K.)
Guadeloupe (France)
Lesser Antilles
DOMINICA
Martinique (France)
ST. LUCIA
BARBADOS
ST. VINCENT & THE GRENADINES
GRENADA
TRINIDAD & TOBAGO
Port-of-Spain
HONDURAS
NICARAGUA
CARIBBEAN SEA
Aruba (Neths.)
Curaçao (Neths.)
Margarita
COLOMBIA
VENEZUELA
West from Greenwich 80°
85° 80° 75° 70° 65° 60° 55°
25° 20° 15° 10°

SOUTH AMERICA

A TOUR of South America would be very exciting. At the Equator are the hot steamy jungles of the Amazon lowlands. To the west comes the great climb up to the Andes Mountains – the world's longest mountain chain. The peaks are so high that even the volcanoes are snow-capped all year. Travellers on buses and trains are offered extra oxygen to breathe, because the air is so thin.

Squeezed between the Andes and the Pacific Ocean in Peru and northern Chile is the world's driest desert – the Atacama Desert, which stretches southwards from the border with Peru for nearly 1600 kilometres. Very few people live here.

Further south in Chile are more wet forests – but these forests are cool. The monkey-puzzle tree originates here. But eastwards, in Argentina, there is less rain and more grass. Cattle on the Pampas are rounded up by cowboys, and crops such as corn (maize) grow well. Further south is the very cold and dry area called Patagonia, where sheep farming is important.

▲ ***Reed boats on Lake Titicaca,*** *the highest navigable lake in the world. It is high in the Andes, at 3811 metres above sea level. Totora reeds grow around the shores, and the Indians tie bundles of reeds together to make fishing boats. The picture shows the reed shelters they use while they make the boats and go fishing. In the background you can see a mountain rising from the plateau.*

Lake Titicaca is shared between Peru and Bolivia. A steam-powered ferry boat travels the length of the lake.

Why is Lake Titicaca the only stretch of water available for the Bolivian navy? (Check the map!)

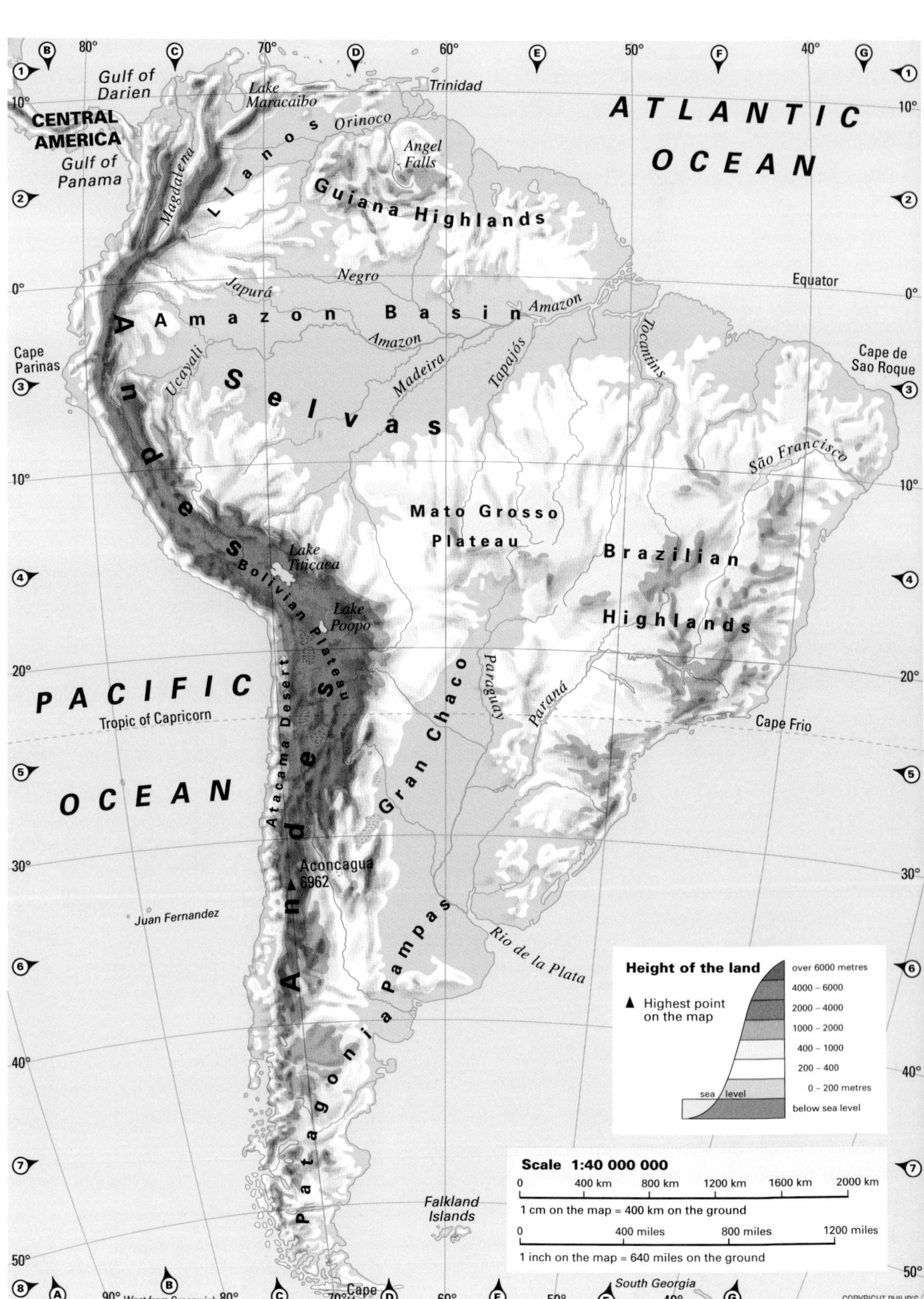

South America stretches further south than any other continent (apart from Antarctica). The cold and stormy tip of South America, Cape Horn, is only 1000 kilometres from Antarctica.

In every South American country, the population is growing fast. Most of the farmland is owned by a few rich people, and many people are desperately poor. Young people are leaving the countryside for the cities, which are growing fast. The city centres have skyscrapers, motorways and superstores, but most newcomers have to settle in the huge shanty towns at the edge of the cities.

ONE country occupies nearly half the total area of South America, and has over half the population of the whole continent: BRAZIL. Look at the map to see which countries touch Brazil. Which two do not?

CENTRAL AMERICA
TRINIDAD & TOBAGO
VENEZUELA
GUYANA
SURINAME
FRENCH GUIANA
COLOMBIA
ECUADOR
PERU
BRAZIL
BOLIVIA
PARAGUAY
CHILE
ARGENTINA
URUGUAY
ATLANTIC OCEAN
PACIFIC OCEAN
Equator
Tropic of Capricorn
Falkland Islands (U.K.)
South Georgia (U.K.)
West from Greenwich

South America in the World
North America
Atlantic Ocean
Africa
Pacific Ocean
Antarctica

Scale 1:40 000 000
0 400 km 800 km 1200 km 1600 km 2000 km
1 cm on the map = 400 km on the ground
0 400 miles 800 miles 1200 miles
1 inch on the map = 640 miles on the ground

▲ ***Carnival in Rio de Janeiro, Brazil.*** *Rio de Janeiro is the second-largest city of Brazil. Every year, it bursts into life and colour at carnival time, in February or March. Huge processions of decorated floats and dancers parade through the streets. Poor people from the shanty towns enjoy it as much as the rich people who pay for seats on the special stands.*

SOUTH AMERICA FACTS

AREA 17,600,000 sq km
HIGHEST POINT Mount Aconcagua (Argentina), 6962 metres
LOWEST POINT Laguna del Carbón (Argentina), 2105 metres
LONGEST RIVER Amazon, 6450 km
LARGEST LAKE Lake Titicaca (Bolivia and Peru), 8300 sq km
BIGGEST COUNTRY Brazil, 8,514,215 sq km
SMALLEST COUNTRY Suriname*, 163,265 sq km
RICHEST COUNTRY Venezuela
POOREST COUNTRY Bolivia
MOST CROWDED COUNTRY Ecuador
LEAST CROWDED COUNTRY Guyana
HIGHEST WATERFALL Angel Falls, 979 metres (a world record)
* French Guiana is smaller, but it is not independent

TROPICAL SOUTH AMERICA

COLOMBIA

AREA 1,138,914 sq km
POPULATION 50,356,000
MONEY Colombian peso

ECUADOR

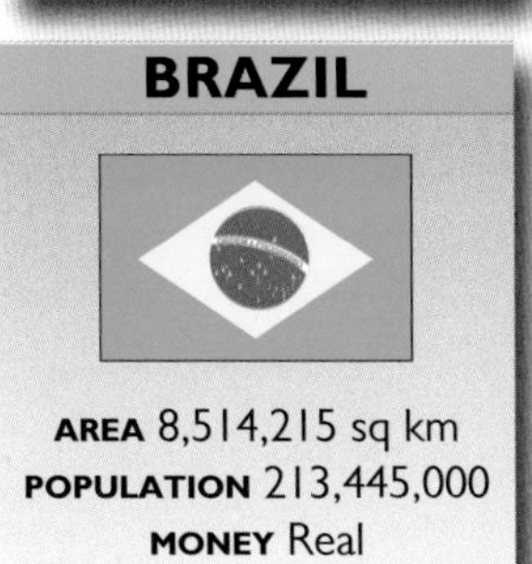

AREA 283,561 sq km
POPULATION 17,093,000
MONEY US dollar

BRAZIL

AREA 8,514,215 sq km
POPULATION 213,445,000
MONEY Real

BRAZIL is by far the biggest country in South America, and has more people (over 204 million) than the rest of South America put together.

Most people still live near the coast. Parts of the Amazon forest are now being settled, but large areas inland are still almost empty. The poorest parts are in the north-east, where the rains often fail, and in the shanty towns around the cities. Modern industry is growing very fast, but there are still too few jobs. **Brazil** has pioneered fuel made from sugar-cane for cars and trucks.

Colombia, **Ecuador**, **Peru** and **Bolivia** are known as the Andean states. Colombia is known for its coffee. Bananas and other tropical crops grow near the coast of Ecuador, but the capital city is high in the mountains. Peru relies on mountain rivers to bring water to the dry coastal area. Tourists come to see ancient Inca cities. Bolivia has the highest capital city in the world. It is the poorest country in South America: farming is difficult and even the tin mines hardly make a profit.

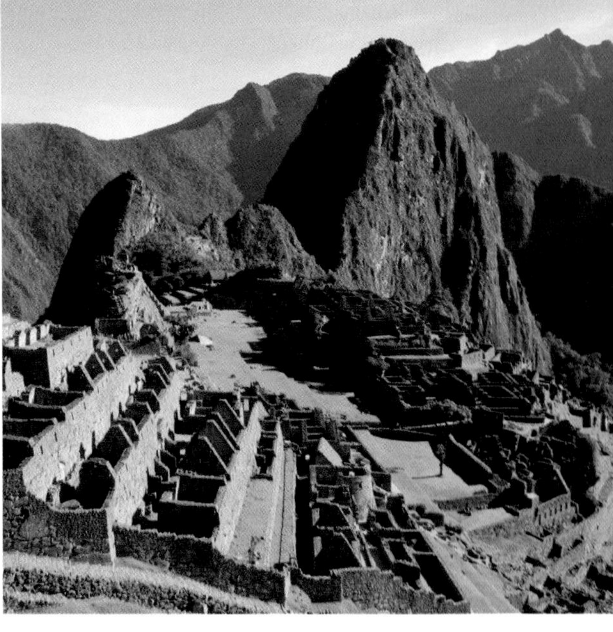

▲ ***Machu Picchu, Peru,*** *the lost city of the Incas, is perched on a mountainside 2400 metres above sea level. The last Inca emperor probably lived here in 1580. The ruins were rediscovered in 1911.*

PERU

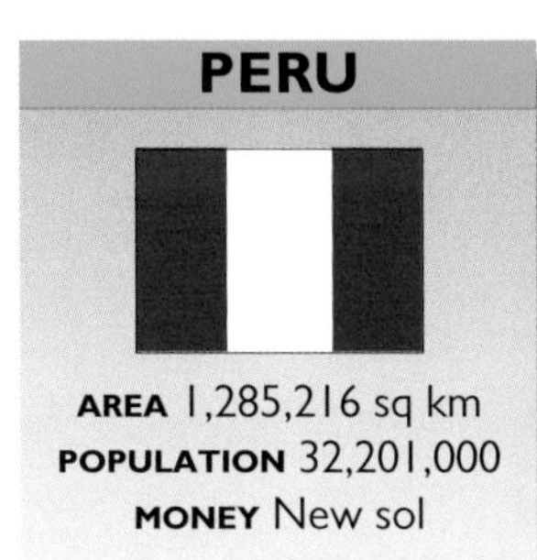

AREA 1,285,216 sq km
POPULATION 32,201,000
MONEY New sol

▲ ***Going to market, Peru.*** *This lady is a descendant of the Incas who lived in Peru before the Spanish arrived. She carries her baby on her back in a fine woven blanket. In most South American countries, the Indians are among the poorest people.*

▲ ***Amazon jungle.*** *The hot, wet jungle covers thousands of kilometres. There is no cool season, and the forest is always green. The trees can be 50 metres high. New roads and villages, mines and dams are being built in the Brazilian jungle, and parts of the forest are being destroyed.*

THE GALAPAGOS ISLANDS

These volcanic islands belong to Ecuador but are 1000 kilometres from the mainland. They have unique plants and animals because they have been isolated for so long.

The giant tortoises are the most famous and spectacular 'residents'.

Venezuela is the richest country in South America because of its mineral wealth. Oil is pumped up from beneath Lake Maracaibo, and iron ore is mined from the plateau south of the River Orinoco. It also has coal, bauxite and gold. The world's highest waterfall, the Angel Falls, is in Venezuela.

In **Guyana** there are important deposits of bauxite, which is used to make aluminium. Guyana was once British Guiana, and **Suriname** was once Dutch Guiana. But **French Guiana** is *still* French.

DID YOU KNOW?

Ecuador means *Equator*: the Equator (0°) crosses the country.

Colombia is named after Christopher Columbus, who sailed from Europe to the Americas in 1492.

Bolivia is named after Simon Bolivar, a hero of the country's war of independence in the 1820s.

La Paz, in Bolivia means *peace*.

▲ ***Cattle and a cowboy in the Mato Grosso,*** *in Brazil. This huge area of dry woodland and grassland is used to graze cattle. Horses are used to round them up.*

Caribbean Sea
NICARAGUA
COSTA RICA
Panama Canal
PANAMA
Gulf of Darien
Gulf of Panama
Barranquilla
Maracaibo
Caracas
Port of Spain
TRINIDAD & TOBAGO
Barquisimeto
Valencia
Orinoco
VENEZUELA
Georgetown
GUYANA
Paramaribo
SURINAME
Cayenne
FRENCH GUIANA
Guiana Highlands
ATLANTIC OCEAN
Medellín
Magdalena
Bogotá
COLOMBIA
Cali
PACIFIC OCEAN
Quito
Galapagos Islands (Ecuador)
ECUADOR
Guayaquil
Gulf of Guayaquil
Japurá
Negro
Amazon
Manaus
Iquitos
Madeira
Tapajós
Tocantins
Belém
Equator 0°
Fortaleza
BRAZIL
Ucayali
Trujillo
Huascarán 6768
ANDES
PERU
Xingu
São Francisco
Recife
Callao
Lima
Machu Picchu
Cuzco
Mato Grosso Plateau
Brazilian Highlands
Salvador
Lake Titicaca
La Paz
BOLIVIA
Arequipa
Lake Poopó
Sucre
Goiânia
Brasília
Belo Horizonte
PARAGUAY
Paraná
Rio de Janeiro
São Paulo
Tropic of Capricorn
Curitiba
CHILE
ARGENTINA
Pôrto Alegre
URUGUAY

Height of the land: over 6000 metres; 4000 – 6000; 2000 – 4000; 1000 – 2000; 400 – 1000; 200 – 400; 0 – 200 metres; sea level; below sea level

▲ Highest point on the map

Country boundaries
Large cities
Capital cities underlined

Scale 1:30 000 000

0 – 300 km – 600 km – 900 km – 1200 km – 1500 km
1 cm on the map = 300 km on the ground
0 – 300 miles – 600 miles – 900 miles
1 inch on the map = 480 miles on the ground

90° West from Greenwich 80° 70° 60° 50° 40°

TEMPERATE SOUTH AMERICA

ARGENTINA

AREA 2,780,400 sq km
POPULATION 45,865,000
MONEY Argentine peso

CHILE

AREA 756,626 sq km
POPULATION 18,308,000
MONEY Chilean peso

URUGUAY

AREA 175,016 sq km
POPULATION 3,398,000
MONEY Uruguayan peso

CHILE is 4300 kilometres long, but it is only about 200 kilometres wide, because it is sandwiched between the Andes and the Pacific.

In the north is the Atacama Desert, the driest in the world. In one place, there was no rain for 400 years! Fortunately, rivers from the Andes permit some irrigation. Chilean nitrates come from this area. Nitrates are salts in dried-up lakes; they are used to make fertilizers and explosives. Copper is mined high in the mountains.

In the centre, the climate is like the Mediterranean area and California, with hot dry summers and warm wet winters with westerly winds. This is a lovely climate, and most Chileans live in this area.

In the south, Chile is wet, windy and cool. Thick forests which include the Chilean pine (monkey-puzzle tree) cover the steep hills. The reason for these contrasts is the wind. It rains when westerly winds blow from the Pacific Ocean. These westerly winds blow all year in the south, but only in winter in the centre, and not at all in the north.

▲ ***Geysers in the Andes, Chile.*** *Hot steam hisses into the cold air, 4000 metres above sea level in the Andes of northern Chile. It shows there is still plenty of volcanic activity in the Andes.*

PARAGUAY

AREA 406,752 sq km
POPULATION 7,273,000
MONEY Guarani

The monkey-puzzle tree comes from Chile. Its proper name is the Chilean pine. The branches are a spiral of very sharp pointed leaves. The cones have tasty seeds. It was called 'monkey-puzzle' tree because to climb it would even puzzle a monkey!

THE ANDES

The Andes are over 7000 kilometres long, so they are the longest mountain range in the world. They stretch from Venezuela (page 85) to southern Chile. The Andes are fold mountains, with a very steep western side, and a gentler eastern side. Mount Aconcagua (6962 metres) is the highest mountain in South America. Many of the highest peaks in the Andes, such as Mount Guallatiri in northern Chile, are active volcanoes.

The higher you climb, the cooler it is. And the further you travel from the Equator, the cooler it is. Therefore, the snowline in southern Chile is much lower than in northern Chile, and in the far south glaciers reach the sea.

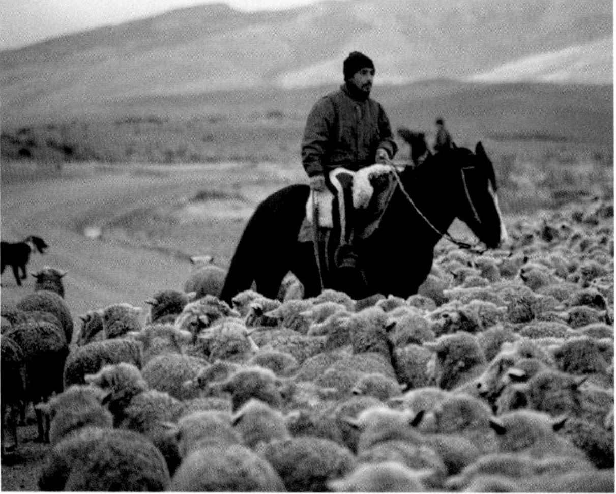

▲ ***Sheep farming in Patagonia, Argentina.*** *Southern Argentina has a cool, dry climate. Very few people live there – but lots of sheep roam the extensive grasslands. There are almost as many sheep in Argentina as there are people.*

Argentina is the world's eighth largest country. Its name means 'silvery' in Spanish: some of the early settlers came here to mine silver. But today, Argentina's most important product is cattle. Cool grasslands called the Pampas (see map below) are ideal for cattle-grazing.

Argentina is a varied country: the north-west is hot and dry, and the south is cold and dry. The frontier with Chile runs high along the top of the Andes.

Buenos Aires, the capital city, is the biggest city in South America; it has 13 million people. The name means 'good air', but petrol fumes have now polluted the air.

Paraguay and **Uruguay** are two countries with small populations: you can find the details near the flags on page 86. Nearly half the population of Uruguay lives in the capital city, Montevideo, which is on the coast. It is an important South American port. In contrast Paraguay is a landlocked country. Find its capital on the map. Animal farming is the most important occupation in both these countries.

All these four countries – Chile, Argentina, Paraguay and Uruguay – have Spanish as their official language. Most of the people have European ancestors, except in Paraguay where there are a lot of South American Indians.

THE FALKLAND ISLANDS

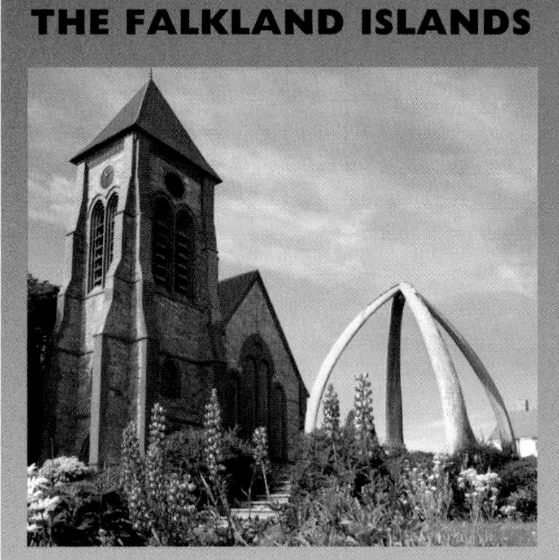

Port Stanley, capital of the Falkland Islands. The monument by the cathedral is a reminder of the whaling industry in the past. Today, fishing and sheep farming are important. These islands are a British colony in the South Atlantic with about 3000 people living there. They are about 480 km east of Argentina, which claims them as the Islas Malvinas.

▲ ***Santiago, capital of Chile,*** *has a beautiful setting between the Andes and the coastal mountains. A third of Chile's people live in Santiago. Its name means 'St James' – the patron saint of Spain, which once ruled Chile.*

THE ARCTIC

THE Arctic is an ocean surrounding the North Pole. It is frozen all through the winter and still has lots of ice in summer. It is surrounded by the northernmost areas of three continents, but Greenland is the only truly Arctic country.

For most of the year the land is snow-covered. For 4 months of summer the sun never sets; only then do temperatures creep above freezing. The snow and frozen topsoil melt, but the deeper soil is still frozen, so the land is very marshy. This treeless landscape is called the *tundra*. Reindeer and caribou can be herded or hunted, but farming is impossible.

In recent years, oil and other rich mineral deposits have been found. Canada, the USA and Russia have military bases near the Arctic Ocean.

From the Atlantic Ocean, there is easy access to the Arctic Ocean. But from the Pacific Ocean, the only route to the Arctic Ocean is the narrow Bering Strait, between Siberia (Russia) and Alaska (USA), which freezes in winter.

ARCTIC FACTS

Fifth largest **ocean** – 14,056,000 sq km;
World record for least sunshine;
Surrounded by cold **land**;
North Pole **first reached** in 1909;
At the North Pole all lines of longitude meet and every direction is **SOUTH**.

▲ *Inuit homes in Godhavn, on the west coast of Greenland.* *This village is called Qeqertarsuaq by the Inuit. In midsummer, most of the snow and ice has melted in this part of Greenland – but there is a big iceberg floating in the sea. These huge blocks of ice break off the ice-sheet that covers Greenland's mountains.*

▲ *Inuit (Eskimo) boy* *fishing for cod through a hole in the ice. Fish are a good source of protein for families in the far north. This boy lives in Nunavik in northern Canada.*

WILDLIFE IN GREENLAND

Land animals have to cope with very long winters. The Arctic fox turns white for camouflage.

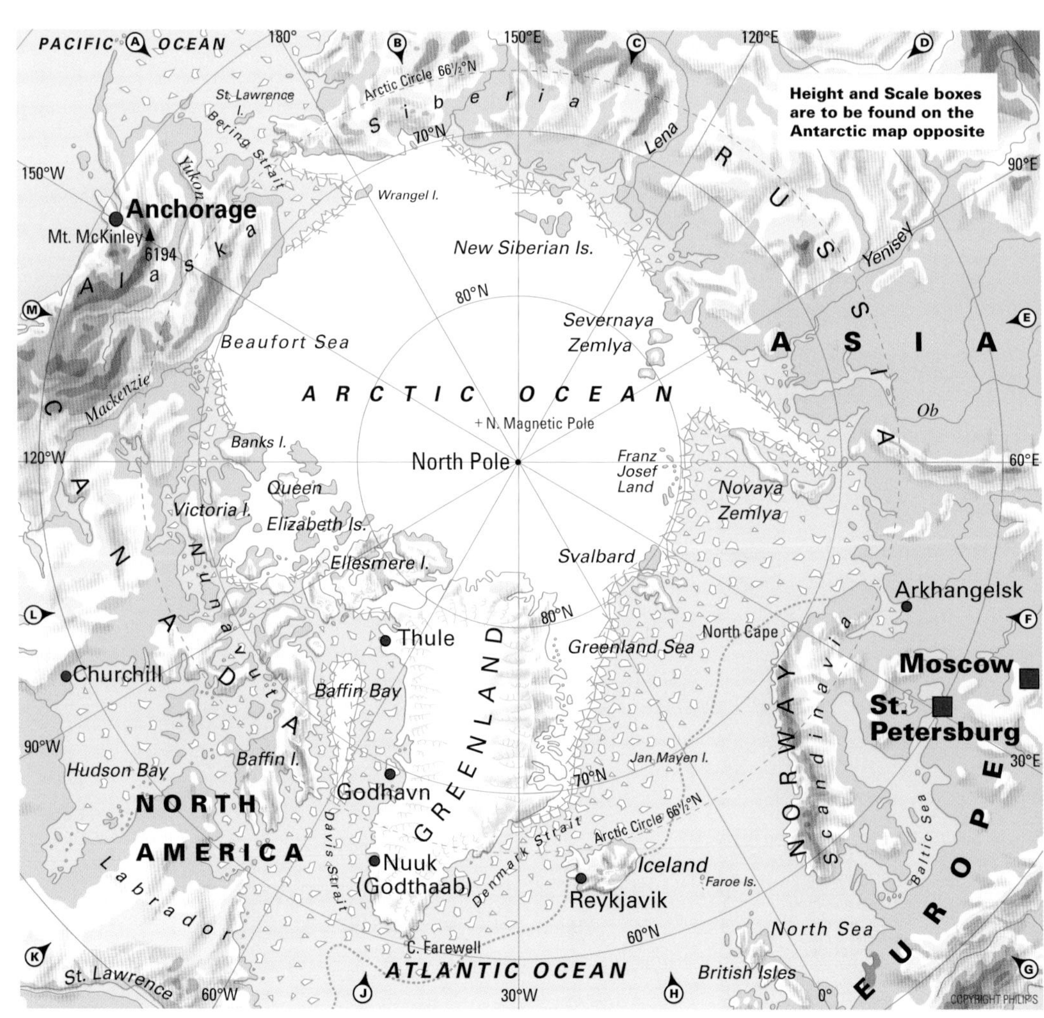

ANTARCTICA

Antarctica is the continent surrounding the South Pole. It is the coldest, windiest and iciest place in the world! It is also very isolated, as the map shows.

No people live in Antarctica permanently. Scientists work in the research stations. Some are studying the effects of our climate warming up. Everything that is needed has to be brought in during the short summer. From November to January, icebreakers can reach the land, but huge icebergs are always a danger. In winter (from May to July) it is always dark, the sea is frozen, and people have to face extreme cold and dangerous blizzards.

No-one 'owns' Antarctica. The Antarctic Treaty ensures that the continent should only be used for scientific research. This means it should remain peaceful for ever. The flags of the 46 nations that have signed the treaty stand in a ring round the South Pole, near the USA's Amundsen-Scott base. Even Antarctica has more and more tourists visiting the area every year.

ANTARCTICA FACTS

Fifth largest **continent** – 14,100,000 sq km;
World record for coldest temperature;
Surrounded by cold **seas**;
South Pole **first reached** in 1911;
At the South Pole all lines of longitude meet and every direction is **NORTH**.

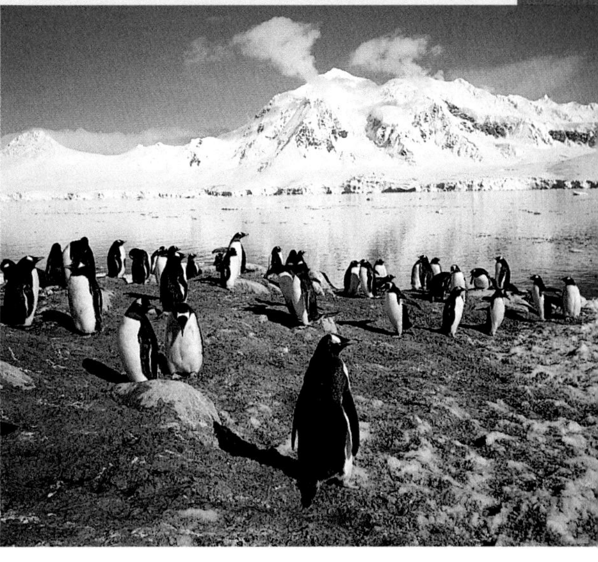

▲ ***Rookery of Gentoo Penguins in Antarctica.*** *Penguins cannot fly, but they can swim very well. The parents use their feet to protect the eggs and chicks from the cold ice! No land animals live in Antarctica, but the ocean is full of fish, which provide food for penguins, seals and whales.*

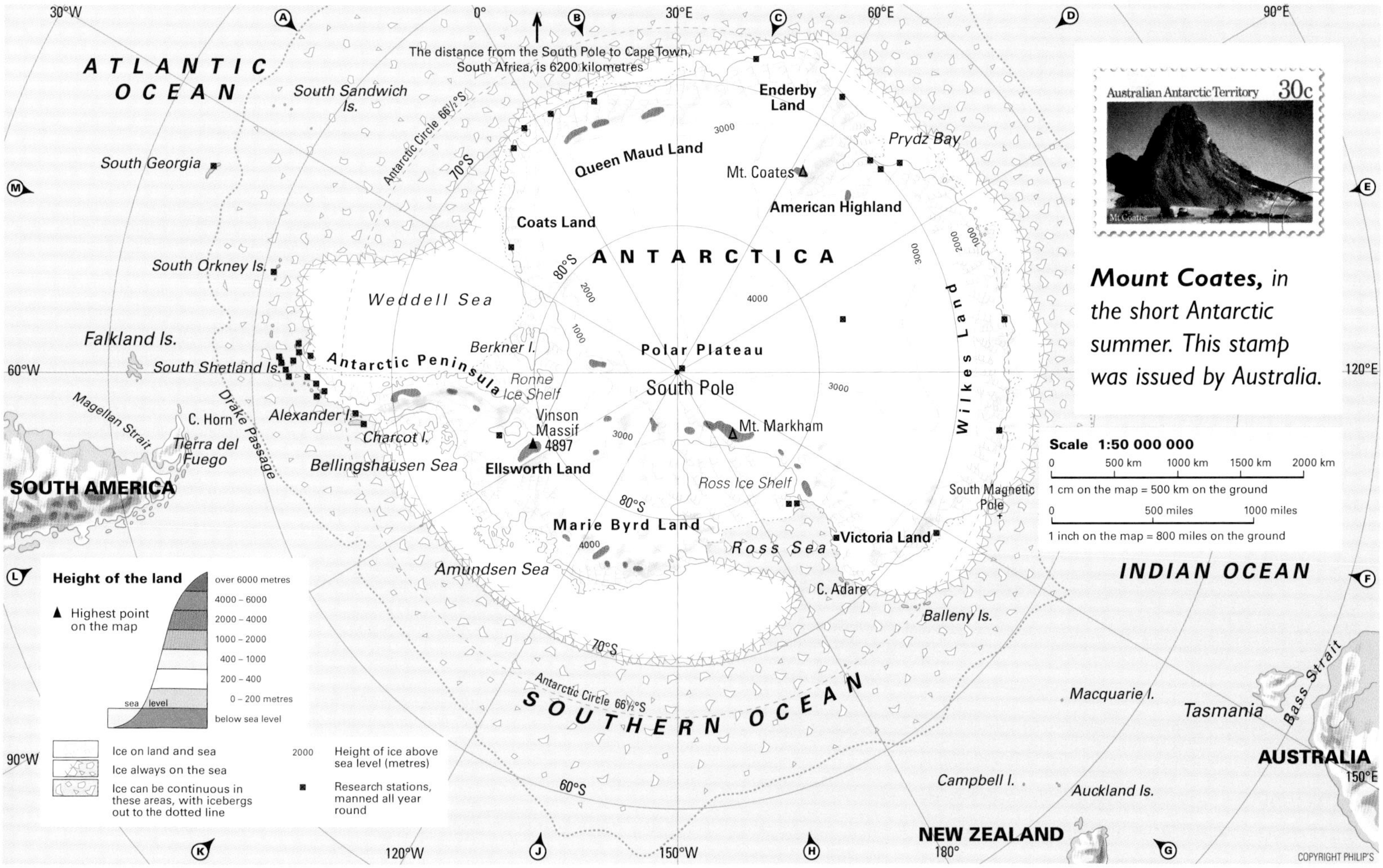

ATLANTIC OCEAN
South Sandwich Is.
South Georgia
South Orkney Is.
Falkland Is.
South Shetland Is.
Magellan Strait
C. Horn
Tierra del Fuego
Drake Passage
SOUTH AMERICA
The distance from the South Pole to Cape Town, South Africa, is 6200 kilometres
Antarctic Circle 66½°S
70°S
Queen Maud Land
Enderby Land
Prydz Bay
Mt. Coates
American Highland
Coats Land
ANTARCTICA
80°S
Weddell Sea
Berkner I.
Polar Plateau
South Pole
Antarctic Peninsula
Ronne Ice Shelf
Alexander I.
Charcot I.
Vinson Massif 4897
Mt. Markham
Bellingshausen Sea
Ellsworth Land
Ross Ice Shelf
Wilkes Land
South Magnetic Pole
Marie Byrd Land
Ross Sea
Victoria Land
Amundsen Sea
C. Adare
Balleny Is.
SOUTHERN OCEAN
INDIAN OCEAN
Macquarie I.
Tasmania
Bass Strait
AUSTRALIA
Campbell I.
Auckland Is.
NEW ZEALAND
30°W 0° 30°E 60°E 90°E 60°W 120°E 90°W 150°E 120°W 150°W 180° 60°S

Australian Antarctic Territory 30c

Mount Coates, *in the short Antarctic summer. This stamp was issued by Australia.*

Scale 1:50 000 000
0 500 km 1000 km 1500 km 2000 km
1 cm on the map = 500 km on the ground
0 500 miles 1000 miles
1 inch on the map = 800 miles on the ground

Height of the land
▲ Highest point on the map
over 6000 metres
4000 – 6000
2000 – 4000
1000 – 2000
400 – 1000
200 – 400
0 – 200 metres
sea level
below sea level

Ice on land and sea
Ice always on the sea
Ice can be continuous in these areas, with icebergs out to the dotted line
2000 Height of ice above sea level (metres)
■ Research stations, manned all year round

QUIZ QUESTIONS

NAME THE COUNTRY

There is a long, thin country in almost every continent. Can you name the countries shown here – and name the continent in which they are found? (If you need help, look at pages 8–9 for a map of the countries of the world.)

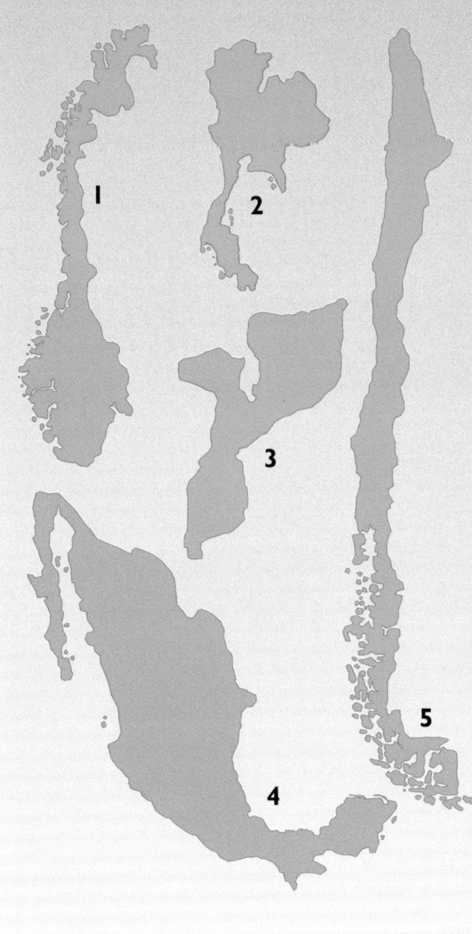

NAME THE ISLAND

The name of the continent where each island is found is marked on each outline. Do you know (a) the name of each island, and (b) to which country each island belongs (or are they island countries)?

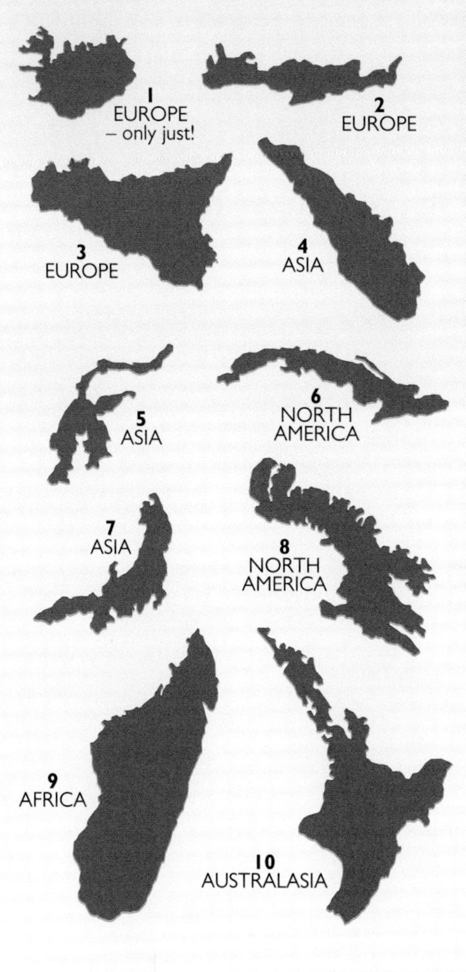

A MYSTERY MESSAGE

Use the map of the countries of the world on pages 8–9 to decode this message. Each missing word is all or part of the name of a country. (For some answers, letters have to be taken out of or added to the name of the country.)

I was _ _ _ _ ~~a~~ _ _ (east of Austria), so I bought a large _ _ _ _ _ _ (east of Greece), some _ _ _ _ _ ~~ns~~ (east of Norway) and a bottle of _ _ _ _ ~~ugal~~ (west of Spain). Finally, I ate an _ _ _ ~~land~~ (west of Norway) -cream. I enjoyed my _ e _ _ ~~i~~ (east of Mauritania), but afterwards I began to _ _ _ _ ~~earia~~ (south of Romania) and I got a bad ~~S~~ _ _ _ _ (south of France). A ~~O~~ _ _ _ (east of Saudi Arabia) told me: 'Just eat ~~Philip~~ _ _ _ _ ~~s~~apples (south of Taiwan) and _ _ ~~gypt~~ (east of Libya), cooked in a ~~Ja~~ _ _ _ (east of Korea). Tomorrow you can eat a ~~Gh~~ban _ _ _ (east of Cote d'Ivoire) and some _ _ _ _ _ _ (east of Peru) nuts. It shouldn't _ _ _ _ ~~a Rica~~ (west of Panama) you too much.' I said: 'You must be _ _ _ ~~agascar~~ (east of Mozambique)! I think I've got _ _ _ _ ~~ysr~~ _ _ (north of Indonesia). I'll have _ _ / _ _ (west of Benin) to a doctor quickly, otherwise I'll soon be _ _ _ _ ~~Sea~~ (lake between Israel and Jordan).'

Happily, the doctor _ _ ~~ba~~red (island country south of USA) me, so I am still ~~M~~ _ _ ~~d~~ _ _ _ ~~s~~ (islands west of Sri Lanka) today!

GREAT RIVERS OF EUROPE

Use pages 18–37 to discover which great river flows through or near each pair of cities.

1 Vienna (Austria) and Budapest (Hungary)
2 Rotterdam (Netherlands) and Bonn (Germany)
3 Avignon (France) and Lyons (France)
4 Worcester (England) and Gloucester (England)
5 Toledo (Spain) and Lisbon (Portugal)

PLACES IN ASIA

Move the letters to find:
Countries RAIN; CHAIN; MOAN; AWAIT N; PLANE
Capital cities ANIMAL; DIARY H; THE TANKS; A BULK; COOL MOB

FIND THE COLOUR

Each answer is a colour. Use the atlas index and the maps to help you. Cover the right-hand column with a piece of paper and try to answer the left-hand column only. Award yourself 2 points for each correct answer to the left-hand column only, or 1 point if you used the clues in both columns.

1	A sea between Egypt and Saudi Arabia . . .	. . . and the river on the border of Oklahoma and Texas, USA.
2	**A big island east of Canada . . .**	**. . . and a bay on the west side of Lake Michigan, USA.**
3	The sea between Turkey and Ukraine . . .	. . . and a forest in Germany.
4	**The sea between Korea and China . . .**	**. . . and a (stony) river in Wyoming, USA.**
5	The sea on which Arkhangelsk lies, in Russia . . .	. . . and the river flowing north from Lake Victoria to Khartoum (Sudan).
6	**A town in southern France which is also a fruit . . .**	**. . . and the river which makes the border between South Africa and Namibia.**
7	The tributary of the River Nile that flows from Ethiopia to Khartoum (Sudan) . . .	. . . and a mountain ridge in eastern USA.

OCEANS AND SEAS

What ocean would you cross on an aeroplane journey . . .

1 From Australia to the USA?
2 From Brazil to South Africa?
3 From Canada to Russia?
4 From Madagascar to Indonesia?
5 From Mexico to Portugal?

What sea would you cross on an aeroplane journey . . .

6 From Saudi Arabia to Egypt?
7 From Korea to Japan?
8 From Denmark to the UK?
9 From Vietnam to the Philippines?
10 From Cuba to Colombia?

THINGS TO DO

COLLECT STAMPS WITH A THEME

A stamp collection soon grows. Try a thematic collection: choose a theme (topic) and collect stamps on that theme. For example, you could collect:
Holidays on stamps – such as the stamps on page 80.
Map stamps – small islands often issue map stamps to show everyone where they are!
Traditional crafts on stamps.

COLLECT YOUR OWN COINS

Ask people who have been abroad for any foreign coins they do not want – you will have an instant collection! If you cannot have the coins to keep, you could make pencil or crayon rubbings on thin paper. The coin box on page 16 is a good starting-point for making sense of the coins in your collection: each coin has a date, a value and a picture.

USA STATES QUIZ

All the answers can be found on the maps on pages 68–69 and 72–77.
* *Do NOT include Alaska and Hawaii.*

1 Which is the *biggest* state?*
2 Which is the *smallest* state?
3 Which state reaches furthest *north*? (Careful!)*
4 Which state reaches furthest *south*?*
5 Which state reaches furthest *west*?*
6 Which state reaches furthest *east*?
7 Which state is split into two by a lake?
8 Which state is split into two by an inlet of the sea?
9 Which two states are perfect rectangles in shape?
10 Which state is shaped like a saucepan?
11 In which state will you be if you visit Lake Huron?
12 In which state will you be if you visit Lake Ontario?
13 In which state will you be if you visit the Great Salt Lake?
14 In which state will you be if you visit the Mississippi delta?
15 Which state in *northern* USA is called South . . . . . ?
16 Which state in *southern* USA is called North . . . . . ?
17 There is only one place in the USA where four states meet: which states?
18 How many states have a border with Mexico?
19 How many states have a coastline on the Pacific?*
20 How many states have a coastline on the Gulf of Mexico?

ANSWERS TO ALL QUIZ QUESTIONS ARE ON PAGE 97

HOW TO USE THIS INDEX

The first number given after each name or topic is the page number; then a letter and another number tell you which square of the map you should look at.

For example, Abidjan is in square B2 on page 57. Find B at the top or the bottom of the map on page 57 and put a finger on it. Put another finger on the number 2 at the side of the map. Move your fingers in from the edge of the map and they will meet in square B2. Abidjan will now be easy to find. It is the capital city of the Ivory Coast, a country in West Africa.

Town names are indexed to the square in which the town symbol falls. However, if the name of a physical feature goes through more than one square, the square given in the index is the one in which the biggest part of the name falls.

Names like Gulf of Mexico and Cape Horn are in the Index as 'Mexico, Gulf of' and 'Horn, Cape'.

A

Aachen 29 B3
Aalborg 21 B4
Aarhus 21 C4
Aberdeen 23 E2
Aberystwyth 23 D4
Abidjan 57 B2
Abu Dhabi 43 E3
Abuja 57 C2
Acapulco 79 B3
Accra 57 B2
Aconcagua 87 C3
Adamawa Highlands 57 D2
Adana 43 C2
Adare, Cape 89 G
Addis Ababa 59 C2
Adelaide 65 G6
Aden 43 D4
Aden, Gulf of 59 D1
Adriatic Sea 33 E3
Aegean Sea 35 C3
Afghanistan 45 B1
Africa 52–53
Agades 55 D3
Agra 45 C2
Ahmadabad 45 C2
Ahvaz 43 D2
Air 55 D3
Aix 27 G5
Ajaccio 33 B4
Akita 51 E3
Akureyri 21 J1
Al Aziziyah 55 E1
Al Jawf 55 F2
Alabama 73
Aland Islands 21 E3
Alaska 73 D2
Alaska Range 73 C2
Alaska, Gulf of 73 D3
Albacete 31 E4
Albania 35 B2
Albany (Australia) 65 C7
Albany (USA) 75 D2
Albert, Lake 59 B2
Alberta 71 G4
Alboran 31 D6
Albuquerque 77 C3
Alderney 27 C2
Aleppo 43 C2
Alesund 21 B3
Aleutian Islands 62 L3
Alexander Island 89 L
Alexandria 55 G1
Algarve 31 A5
Algeria 55 D2
Algiers 55 D1
Alicante 31 E4
Alice Springs 65 F4
Alkmaar 25 C2
Almaty 41 M4
Almeria 31 D5
Alps 33 C1
Alsace 27 H2
Altai Mountains 49 C2
Amarillo 77 C3
Amazon River 85 E3
American Highland 89 D
American Samoa 63 N10
Amersfoort 25 D2
Amiens 27 F2
Amman 43 M9
Amritsar 45 C1
Amsterdam 25 C2
Amundsen Sea 89 K
Amur, River 41 S3
Anadyr Range 41 W2
Anatolia 18 P7
Anchorage 73 D2
Ancona 33 D3
Andalusia 31 C5
Andaman Islands 47 A2
Andes 82 C3
Andorra 31 F2
Angara, River 41 N3
Angers 27 D3
Anglesey 23 D4
Angola 61 A2
Angouleme 27 E4
Anguilla 81 F3
Ankara 43 C2
Annapurna 45 D2
Annecy 27 H4
Annobon 57 C3
Anshan 49 F2
Antananarivo 61 D2
Antarctica 89
Antarctic Peninsula 89 M
Anticosti Island 71 M5
Antigua & Barbuda 81 F3
Antofagasta 87 B2
Antwerp 25 C3
Aomori 51 E2
Aoraki Mount Cook 67 B6
Apeldoorn 25 D2
Apennines 33 D3
Appalachian Mountains 75 C3
Arabia 38 H6
Arabian Sea 38 K7
Arafura Sea 65 F1
Aral Sea 41 K4
Arctic Ocean 88
Ardennes 25 D5
Arequipa 85 C4
Argentina 87 C3
Arizona 73
Arkansas 73
Arkansas River 75 B3
Arkhangelsk 41 H2
Armagh 23 C3
Armenia 41 H5
Arnhem 25 D3
Arnhem Land 65 F2
Arnhem, Cape 65 G2
Arran, Island 23 D3
Aruba 81 D4
Asahigawa 51 E2
Ascension Island 9 M7
Ashgabat 41 J5
Asia 38–39
Asmara 59 C1
Asuncion 87 D2
Aswan 55 G2
Asyut 55 G1
Atacama Desert 87 B2
Athabasca, Lake 71 H4
Athens 35 C3
Athlone 23 C4
Atlanta 75 C3
Atlantic Ocean 18 B3
Atlas Mountains 55 C1
Auckland 67 E3
Auckland Islands 89 G
Augsburg 29 D4
Austin 75 B3
Australia 64–65
Australian Alps 65 J7
Austria 29 E5
Auvergne 27 F4
Avignon 27 G5
Avon, River 23 F4
Axel Heiberg Island 71 K2
Ayers Rock 65 F5
Azerbaijan 41 H4
Azores 55 A1
Azov, Sea of 37 G3

B

Badajoz 31 B4
Baffin Bay 71 M2
Baffin Island 71 L2
Baghdad 43 D2
Bahamas 81 C1
Bahia Blanca 87 C3
Bahrain 43 E3
Baikal, Lake 41 P3
Baku 41 J4
Balearic Islands 31 F4
Bali 47 C4
Balikpapan 47 C4
Balkan Mountains 35 C2
Balkhash, Lake 41 L4
Balleny Islands 89 G
Baltic Sea 21 D4
Baltimore 75 D3
Bamako 55 C3
Banda Sea 47 D4
Bandar Seri Begawan 47 C3
Bandung 47 B4
Bangalore = Bengaluru 45 C3
Bangka 47 B4
Bangkok 47 B2
Bangladesh 45 E2
Bangui 59 A2
Banjarmasin 47 C4
Banjul 57 A1
Banks Island 71 F2
Banks Peninsula 67 D6
Baotou 49 E2
Barbados 81 G4
Barcelona 31 G3
Barcoo, River 65 H4
Barents Sea 41 G1
Bari 33 F4
Barkly Tableland 65 G3
Barranquilla 85 C1
Barrow, Cape 73 C1
Basle 33 A1
Basque Provinces 31 D2
Basra 43 D2
Bass Strait 65 J7
Bastia 33 B3
Bathurst, Cape 71 F2
Baton Rouge 75 B3
Bavaria 29 D4
Bayonne 27 D5
Beaufort Sea 71 D2
Beersheba 43 L9
Beijing 49 E3
Beira 61 C2
Beirut 43 C2
Belarus 37 E2
Belem 85 F3
Belfast 23 D3
Belgium 25 C4
Belgrade 35 C2
Belize 79 D3
Bellingshausen Sea 89 L
Belmopan 79 D3
Belo Horizonte 85 F4
Ben Nevis 23 D2
Benelux 24–25
Bengal, Bay of 38 M7
Bengaluru 45 C3
Benghazi 55 F1
Benin 57 C2
Benin, Bight of 57 C2
Benue, River 57 C2
Bergen 21 B3
Bering Sea 62 L3
Bering Strait 88 A
Berkner Island 89 M
Berlin 29 E2
Bermuda 69 N5
Bern 33 A1
Besancon 27 H3
Bethlehem 43 M9
Bhutan 45 E2
Bida 57 C2
Bielefeld 29 C2
Big Timber 77 B2
Bilbao 31 D2
Billings 77 C2
Bioko 57 C2
Birmingham (UK) 23 F4
Birmingham (USA) 75 C3
Biscay, Bay of 18 G5
Bishkek 41 L4
Bissau 57 A1
Bitola 35 C2
Black Forest 29 C4
Black Hills 77 C2
Black Sea 18 P6
Blanc, Mont 27 H4
Blantyre 61 C2
Blenheim 67 D5
Bloemfontein 61 B3
Blue Nile 55 G3
Bodo 21 C2
Bogota 85 C2
Boise 77 B2
Bolivia 85 D4
Bologna 33 C2
Bolzano 33 C1
Bombay = Mumbai 45 C3
Bonifacio, Strait of 33 B4
Bonin Islands 62 H6
Bonn 29 B3
Boothia, Gulf of 71 K3
Bordeaux 27 D4
Borneo 47 C3
Bornholm 21 D4
Bosnia-Herzegovina 35 B2
Bosporus 35 D2
Boston 75 D2
Bothnia, Gulf of 21 E3
Botswana 61 B3
Bouake 57 B2
Bougainville 62 J9
Boulogne 27 E1
Bourges 27 F3
Bournemouth 23 E5
Bradford 23 F4
Brahmaputra, River 49 C4
Brasilia 85 F4
Brasov 35 D1
Bratislava 37 C3
Brazil 85 E3
Brazilian Highlands 85 F4
Brazzaville 59 A3
Bremen 29 C2
Brescia 33 C2
Brest 27 B2
Bridgetown 81 G4
Brighton 23 F5
Brindisi 33 F4
Brisbane 65 K5
Bristol 23 E5
British Columbia 71 F4
British Isles 23 E4
Brittany 27 C2
Brno 37 C3
Broken Hill 65 H6
Brooks Range 73 C2
Broome 65 D3
Bruges 25 B3
Brunei 47 C3
Brunswick 29 D2
Brussels 25 C4
Bucharest 35 D2
Budapest 37 C3
Buenos Aires 87 C3
Buffalo 75 D2
Bug, River 37 F3
Bujumbura 59 B3
Bukavu 59 B3
Bulawayo 61 B3
Bulgaria 35 C2
Bundaberg 65 K4
Burgas 35 D2
Burgos 31 D2
Burgundy 27 G3
Burkina Faso 57 B1
Burma = Myanmar 47 A1
Burundi 59 C3
Busan 51 B3

C

Cabinda 59 A3
Caceres 31 B4
Cadiz 31 B5
Cadiz, Gulf of 31 B5
Caen 27 D2
Cagliari 33 B5
Cahora Bassa Dam 61 C2
Caicos Islands 81 D2
Cairns 65 J3
Cairo 55 G1
Calais 27 F1
Calcutta = Kolkata 45 D2
Calgary 71 G4
Cali 85 C2
California 73
California, Gulf of 79 A2
Callao 85 C4
Camaguey 81 C2
Cambodia 47 B2
Cambrian Mountains 23 E4
Cambridge 23 G4
Cameroon 57 D2
Cameroon, Mount 57 C2
Campbell Island 89 G
Campeche, Gulf of 79 C3
Canada 71 J4
Canary Islands 55 B2
Canaveral, Cape 75 C4
Canberra 65 J7
Cannes 27 H5
Cantabrian Mountains 31 B2
Canterbury 23 G5
Canterbury Bight 67 D7
Canterbury Plains 67 D6
Canton = Guangzhou 49 E4
Cape Town 61 A4
Cape York Peninsula 65 H2
Caracas 85 D1
Carcassonne 27 F5
Cardiff 23 E5
Caribbean Sea 81 C4
Carletonville 61 B3
Carlisle 23 E3
Caroline Islands 62 J8
Carpathians 37 D3
Carpentaria, Gulf of 65 G2
Cartagena 31 E5
Carthage 55 E1
Casablanca 55 C1
Cascade Range 77 A2
Casper 77 C2
Caspian Sea 38 J4
Castellon 31 F4
Catalonia 31 F3
Catania 33 E6
Caucasus Mountains 41 H4
Cayenne 85 E2
Cebu 47 D2
Celebes 47 D4
Celebes Sea 47 D3
Central African Republic 59 B2
Central America 68 K7
Ceram 47 D4
Ceuta 31 C6
Cevennes 27 F4
Chad 55 E3
Chad, Lake 55 E3
Champagne 27 G2
Chang Jiang, River 49 E3
Changchun 49 F2
Changsha 49 E4
Channel Islands 27 C2
Chari, River 55 E3
Charleroi 25 C4
Charleston 75 C3
Charleville 65 J5
Charlotte 75 C3
Chartres 27 E2
Chatham Islands 62 M13
Chattanooga 75 C3
Chattogram 45 E2
Chelyabinsk 41 K3
Chemnitz 29 E3
Chengdu 49 D3
Chennai 45 D3
Cherbourg 27 D2
Chernobyl 37 F2
Chiang Mai 47 A2
Chicago 75 B2
Chichen Itza 79 D2
Chidley, Cape 71 M3
Chile 87 B3
China 49 C3
Chisinau 37 E3
Chita 41 Q3
Chongjin 51 B2
Chongqing 49 D4
Christchurch 67 D6
Churchill 71 J4
Cincinnati 75 C3
Ciudad Juarez 79 B1
Clermont Ferrand 27 F4
Cleveland 75 C2
Cluj 35 C1
Clutha, River 67 B7
Coast Range 77 A3
Coats Land 89 A
Cod, Cape 75 E2
Coimbatore 45 C3
Coimbra 31 A3
Cologne 29 B3
Colombia 85 C2
Colombo 45 C4
Colorado 73
Colorado River 77 B3
Columbia, River 77 A2
Columbus 75 C3
Comorin, Cape 45 C4
Comoros 61 D2
Conakry 57 A2
Concepcion 87 B3

Congo 59 A3
Congo, Democratic Republic of the 59 B3
Congo, River 59 B2
Connecticut 73
Constance, Lake 29 C5
Constanta 35 D2
Constantine 55 D1
Cook Islands 63 N10
Cook Strait 67 E5
Cook, Mount = Aoraki Mount Cook 67 B6
Copenhagen 21 C4
Coral Sea 65 J3
Cordoba (Argentina) 87 C3
Cordoba (Spain) 31 C5
Corfu 35 B3
Cork 23 B5
Coromandel Peninsula 67 E3
Corsica 33 B3
Cosenza 33 F5
Costa Blanca 31 E4
Costa Brava 31 G3
Costa del Sol 31 C5
Costa Rica 79 D4
Cote d'Ivoire 57 B2
Cotswolds 23 F5
Coventry 23 F4
Craiova 35 C2
Crete 35 D4
Crimea 37 F3
Croatia 35 B1
Crozet Islands 9 R10
Cuando, River 61 B2
Cuba 81 C2
Cubango, River 61 A2
Curaçao 81 E4
Curitiba 85 F5
Cuzco 85 C4
Cyprus 43 J5
Czechia 37 B3

D
Da Nang 47 B2
Daegu 51 B3
Daejeon 51 B3
Dakar 57 A1
Dakhla 55 B2
Dalian 49 F3
Dallas 75 B3
Damascus 43 C2
Dampier 65 C4
Danube, River 35 D2
Dar es Salaam 59 C3
Dardanelles 35 D3
Dargaville 67 D2
Darling Range 65 C6
Darling, River 65 H6
Darwin 65 F2
Davao 47 D3
Davis Strait 71 N3
Dawson 71 E3
Dead Sea 43 M9
Death Valley 77 B3
Deccan 45 C3
Delaware 73
Delhi 45 C2
Den Helder 25 C2
Denali 73 C2
Denmark 21 B4
Denver 77 C3
Derby 23 F4
Derry 23 C3
Detroit 75 C2
Devon Island 71 K2
Dhaka 45 E2
Dieppe 27 E2
Dijon 27 G3
Dili 47 D4
Dinaric Alps 35 B2
District of Columbia 73
Djerid, Lake 55 D1
Djibouti 59 D1
Dnepr, River 37 F3
Dnestr, River 37 E3
Dnipro 37 F3
Dodecanese 35 D3
Dodoma 59 C3
Dominica 81 F3
Dominican Republic 81 E3
Dondra Head 45 C4
Donetsk 37 G3
Dordogne, River 27 E4
Dordrecht 25 C3
Dortmund 29 B3
Douai 27 F1
Douala 57 D2
Douglas 23 D3
Douro, River 31 B3
Dover 23 G5
Dover, Strait of 23 G5
Drake's Passage 89 L
Drakensberg, Mountains 61 B3
Drava, River 35 B1
Dresden 29 E3
Duarte, Pico 81 D3
Dublin 23 C4
Dubrovnik 35 B2
Duero, River 31 D3
Duisburg 29 B3
Duluth 75 B2
Dundee 23 E2
Dunedin 67 C7
Dunkirk 27 F1
Durban 61 C3
Dushanbe 41 K5
Dusseldorf 29 B3
Dzungarian Desert = Junggar Pendi 49 B2

E
East China Sea 49 F4
East London 61 B4
Easter Islands 63 U11
Eastern Ghats 45 C3
Ebro, River 31 E3
Echo Bay 71 G3
Ecuador 85 C3
Edam 25 D2
Edinburgh 23 E3
Edmonton 71 G4
Edward, Lake 59 B3
Egadi Islands 33 D6
Egmont, Cape 67 D4
Egypt 55 F2
Eilat 43 C3
Eindhoven 25 D3
El Aaiun 55 B2
El Fasher 55 F3
El Obeid 55 G3
El Paso 77 C3
El Salvador 79 D3
Elba 33 C3
Elbe, River 29 D2
Elbrus, Mount 41 H4
Elburz Mountains 43 E2
Eleuthera Island 81 C1
Ellesmere Land 71 L2
Ellsworth Land 89 L
Ems, River 29 B2
Enderby Land 89 C
England 23 F4
English Channel 27 D1
Enschede 25 E2
Equatorial Guinea 57 C2
Erfurt 29 D3
Erie, Lake 75 C2
Eritrea 59 C1
Esbjerg 21 B4
Esfahan 43 E2
Espoo 21 E3
Essen 29 B3
Estonia 37 E1
Eswatini 61 C3
Ethiopia 59 D2
Ethiopian Highlands 59 C2
Etna, Mount 33 E6
Etosha Pan 61 A2
Eugene 77 A2
Euphrates, River 43 D2
Europe 18–19
Europort 25 B3
Everest, Mount 49 B4
Everglades 75 C4
Evora 31 B4
Exeter 23 E5
Eyre, Lake 65 G5

F
F'Derik 55 B2
Fairbanks 73 D2
Falkland Islands 87 C5
Farewell, Cape 67 D5
Fargo 75 B2
Faroe Islands 18 F2
Faya-Largeau 55 E3
Fez 55 C1
Fiji 62 L10
Finisterre, Cape 31 A2
Finland 21 F3
Finland, Gulf of 21 F4
Firth of Forth 23 E2
Fitzroy, River 65 D3
Flanders 25 B3
Flensburg 29 C1
Flinders Ranges 65 G6
Florence 33 C3
Flores Sea 47 D4
Florida 73
Foggia 33 E4
Fort McMurray 71 G4
Fort Worth 75 B3
Fortaleza 85 G3
Fouta Djalon 57 A1
Foveaux Strait 67 B8
Foxe Channel 71 L3
France 27 E3
Frankfurt 29 C3
Franz Josef Land 41 N1
Fraser River 71 F4
Freeport 81 C1
Freetown 57 A2
Freiburg 29 B5
French Guiana 85 E2
French Polynesia 63 Q10
Fresno 77 A3
Frisian Islands 25 C1
Fuji, Mount 51 D3
Fukuoka 51 C4
Fukushima 51 E3
Fushun 49 F2
Fuzhou 49 E4

G
Gabon 57 D3
Gaborone 61 B3
Gairdner, Lake 65 G6
Galapagos Islands 85 B3
Galati 35 D1
Galdhopiggen 21 B3
Galilee, Sea of 43 M8
Galway 23 B4
Gambia 57 A1
Ganges, River 45 D2
Gangneung 51 B3
Garda, Lake 33 C2
Garmo Peak 41 K4
Garonne, River 27 D4
Gascony 27 D5
Gävle 21 D3
Gaza Strip 43 L9
Gdansk 37 C2
Geelong 65 H7
Geneva 33 A1
Geneva, Lake 33 A1
Genoa 33 B2
George Town 47 B3
Georgetown 85 E2
Georgia 37 H4
Georgia (USA) 73
Gera 29 E3
Geraldton 65 B5
Germany 29 C3
Ghana 57 B2
Ghent 25 B3
Ghudamis 55 D1
Gibraltar 31 C5
Gibson Desert 65 D4
Gifu 51 D3
Gijon 31 C2
Gisborne 67 F4
Gitega 59 B3
Giza 55 G2
Glama, River 21 C3
Glasgow 23 D3
Gloucester 23 E5
Gobi Desert 49 D2
Godavari, River 45 C3
Godhavn 88 J
Godthaab = Nuuk 88 J
Goiania 85 E4
Good Hope, Cape of 61 A4
Gothenburg 21 C4
Gotland 21 D4
Gottingen 29 C3
Gouda 25 C2
Gozo 33 E6
Gqeberha 61 B4
Grampians 23 E2
Gran Chaco 87 C2
Granada 31 D5
Grand Bahama 81 C1
Grand Canyon 77 B3
Grand Cayman 81 B3
Graz 29 F5
Great Australia Bight 65 E6
Great Barrier Island 67 E3
Great Barrier Reef 65 J3
Great Basin 77 B3
Great Bear Lake 71 F3
Great Britain 18 G4
Great Divide 65 K6
Great Khingan Mountains 49 E2
Great Lakes 69 L4
Great Plains 77 D2
Great Salt Lake 77 B2
Great Sandy Desert 65 D4
Great Slave Lake 71 G3
Great Victoria Desert 65 E5
Great Wall of China 49 D3
Greater Antilles 81 C3
Greece 35 C3
Greenland 88 J
Greenland Sea 88 G
Grenada 81 F4
Grenoble 27 H4
Greymouth 67 C6
Groningen 25 E1
Grossglockner 29 E5
Guadalajara 79 B2
Guadalquivir, River 31 C5
Guadarrama, Sierra de 31 D3
Guadeloupe 81 F3
Guadiana, River 31 B5
Guam 62 H7
Guangzhou 49 E4
Guardafui, Cape 59 E1
Guatemala 79 C3
Guatemala City 79 C3
Guayaquil 85 B3
Guernsey 27 C2
Guilin 49 E4
Guinea 57 A1
Guinea, Gulf of 57 B2
Guinea-Bissau 57 A1
Guiyang 49 D4
Gunsan 51 B3
Guyana 85 E2
Gwangju 51 B3

H
Haarlem 25 C2
Hague, The 25 C2
Haida Gwaii 71 E4
Haifa 43 L8
Hainan 49 E5
Haiphong 47 B1
Haiti 81 D3
Hakodate 51 E2
Halifax 71 M5
Halle 29 E3
Halmahera 47 D3
Hamamatsu 51 D4
Hamburg 29 C2
Hamersley Range 65 C4
Hamhung 51 B3
Hamilton (Canada) 71 L5
Hamilton (NZ) 67 E3
Hanoi 47 B1
Hanover 29 C2
Harare 61 C2
Harbin 49 F2
Hardanger Fjord 21 B3
Harz Mountains 29 D3
Hastings 67 F4
Havana 81 B2
Hawaii 72 G2
Hawaiian Islands 72 F1
Hebrides 23 C2
Heidelberg 29 C4
Helsingborg 21 C4
Helsinki 21 F3
Herat 45 B1
Himalayas 45 D2
Hindu Kush 45 C1
Hiroshima 51 C4
Hispaniola 81 D3
Hitachi 51 E3
Ho Chi Minh City 47 B2
Hobart 65 J8
Hoggar 55 D2
Hokkaido 51 E2
Holyhead 23 D4
Honduras 79 D3
Hong Kong 49 E4
Honolulu 72 F1
Honshu 51 D3
Hook of Holland 25 C2
Horn, Cape 87 C5
Houston 75 B4
Huambo 61 A2
Huang He, River 49 E3
Huascaran 85 C3
Hudson Bay 71 K4
Hudson River 75 D2
Hudson Strait 71 L3
Huelva 31 B5
Hull 23 F4
Hungary 37 C3
Huron, Lake 75 C2
Hwang Ho = Huang He, River 49 E3
Hyderabad (India) 45 C3
Hyderabad (Pakistan) 45 B2
Hyesan 51 B2

I
Iasi 35 D1
Ibadan 57 C2
Iberian Peninsula 18 G6
Ibiza 31 F4
Iceland 21 J2
Idaho 73
Ijssel, Lake 25 D2
Illinois 73
Iloilo 47 D2
Inari, Lake 21 F2
Incheon 51 B3
India 45 C2
Indian Ocean 38 L9
Indiana 73
Indianapolis 75 C2
Indonesia 47 C4
Indore 45 C2
Indus, River 45 B2
Inland Sea 51 C4
Inn, River 29 E4
Innsbruck 29 D5
Interlaken 33 B1
International Date Line 62 L5
Invercargill 67 B8
Inverness 23 E2
Ionian Islands 35 B3
Ionian Sea 35 B3
Iowa 73
Ipswich 23 G4
Iquitos 85 C3
Iraklion 35 D3
Iran 43 E2
Iraq 43 D2
Irbid 43 M8
Ireland 23 C4
Irish Sea 23 D4
Irkutsk 41 P3
Iron Gates 35 C2
Irrawaddy, River 47 A1
Irtysh, River 41 L3
Islamabad 45 C1
Islay 23 C3
Israel 43 M8
Istanbul 43 B1
Italy 33 D3
Izmir 43 B2

J
Jabalpur 45 D2
Jacksonville 75 C3
Jaipur 45 C2
Jakarta 47 B4
Jamaica 81 C3
James Bay 71 K4
Japan 51 D3
Japan, Sea of 51 C3
Java 47 B4
Jedda 43 C3
Jeju-do 51 B4
Jerez 31 B5
Jersey 27 C2
Jerusalem 43 M9
Jinan 49 E3
Johannesburg 61 B3
Jonkoping 21 C4
Jordan 43 C2
Jordan, River 43 M8
Jotunheimen 21 B3
Juan Fernandez Island 63 W12
Juba 55 G4
Jucar, River 31 E4
Juneau 71 E4
Junggar Pendi 49 B2
Jura 27 G3
Jutland 21 B4

K
K2 45 C1
Kabul 45 B1
Kaesong 51 B3
Kagoshima 51 C4
Kaikoura Range 67 D6
Kaimanawa Mountains 67 E4
Kalahari Desert 61 B3
Kalemie 59 B3
Kalgoorlie-Boulder 65 D6
Kamchatka Peninsula 41 U3
Kampala 59 C2
Kananga 59 B3
Kanazawa 51 D3
Kandahar 45 B1
Kangaroo Island 65 G7
Kanggye 51 B2
Kano 57 C1
Kanpur 45 D2
Kansas 73
Kansas City 75 B3
Kaohsiung 49 F4
Karachi 45 B2
Karaganda 41 L4
Karakoram Range 45 C1
Kariba, Lake 61 B2
Karlsruhe 29 C4
Kasai, River 59 B3
Kashmir 45 C1
Kassel 29 C3
Kati Thanda 65 G5
Katmandu 45 D2
Kattegat 21 C4
Kauai 72 E1
Kaunas 37 D1
Kawasaki 51 D3
Kazakhstan 41 K4
Kazan 41 H3
Keflavik 21 H2
Kemi 21 E2
Kemi, River 21 F2
Kentucky 73
Kenya 59 C2
Kerguelen 9 S10
Kermadec Islands 62 L11
Key West 75 C4
Khabarovsk 41 S4
Kharkiv 37 G3
Khartoum 55 G3
Kiel 29 D1
Kiev 37 F2
Kigali 59 C3
Kikwit 59 A3
Kilimanjaro 59 C3
Kimberley (South Africa) 61 B3
Kimberley Plateau (Australia) 65 E3
Kimchaek 51 B2
Kinabalu 47 C3
Kingston 81 C3
Kinshasa 59 A3
Kiribati 62 L9
Kiritimati Island 63 P8
Kirkenes 21 F2
Kirov 41 H3
Kiruna 21 E2
Kisangani 59 B2
Kismayu 59 D3
Kiso, River 51 D3
Kisumu 59 C3
Kitakami, River 51 E3
Kitakyushu 51 B4
Kitwe 61 B2
Klagenfurt 29 F5
Kobe 51 D4
Koblenz 29 B3
Kola Peninsula 41 G2
Kolkata = Calcutta 45 D2
Kolyma Range 41 U2
Korea Strait 51 B4
Kosciuszko, Mount 65 J7
Kosovo 35 C2
Krakatoa 47 B4
Krakow 37 C2
Krasnoyarsk 41 N3
Krishna, River 45 C3
Kristiansand 21 B4
Kuala Lumpur 47 B3
Kucing 47 C3
Kumamoto 51 C4
Kumasi 57 B2
Kunashir 51 F2
Kunlun Shan Mountains 49 B3
Kunming 49 D4
Kuopio 21 F3
Kuria Muria Islands 43 E4
Kuril Islands 62 J4
Kushiro 51 E2
Kuwait 43 D3
Kyoga, Lake 59 C2
Kyoto 51 D3
Kyrgyzstan 41 L4
Kyushu 51 C4

L
La Coruna 31 A2
La Paz 85 D4
La Plata 87 D3
La Rochelle 27 D3
La Spezia 33 B2
Labrador 71 M4
Laccadive Islands 45 C3
Lachlan, River 65 J6

INDEX

Lagos (Nigeria) 57 C2
Lagos (Portugal) 31 A5
Lahore 45 C1
Land's End 23 D5
Languedoc 27 F5
Lanzhou 49 D3
Laos 47 B2
Lapland 21 E2
Las Palmas 55 B2
Las Vegas 77 B3
Latvia 37 D1
Launceston 65 J8
Lausanne 33 A1
Le Havre 27 E2
Le Mans 27 D2
Lebanon 43 C2
Leeds 23 F4
Leeuwarden 25 D1
Leeuwin, Cape 65 B6
Leiden 25 C2
Leipzig 29 E3
Lek, River 25 C3
Lena, River 41 R2
Lens 27 F1
Leon (Mexico) 79 B2
Leon (Spain) 31 C2
Lerida 31 F3
Lesotho 61 B3
Lesser Antilles 81 F4
Lewis, Island 23 C1
Lhasa 49 C4
Liberia 57 B2
Libreville 57 D2
Libya 55 E2
Libyan Desert 55 F2
Liechtenstein 29 C5
Liege 25 D4
Ligurian Sea 33 B3
Likasi 59 B4
Lille 27 F1
Lillehammer 21 C3
Lilongwe 61 C2
Lima 85 C4
Limassol 43 J6
Limerick 23 B4
Limoges 27 E4
Limpopo, River 61 B3
Linares 31 D4
Line Islands 63 P9
Linkoping 21 D4
Linz 29 F4
Lions, Gulf of 27 G5
Lipari Islands 33 E5
Lisbon 31 A4
Lithuania 37 D1
Liverpool 23 E4
Livingstone 61 B2
Ljubljana 35 A1
Llanos 82 C2
Lobito 61 A2
Lodz 37 C2
Lofoten Islands 21 C2
Logan, Mount 71 E3
Loire, River 27 E3
Lome 57 C2
London (Canada) 71 K5
London (UK) 23 G5
Londonderry 23 C3
Lorient 27 C3
Lorraine 27 H2
Los Angeles 77 B3
Louisiana 73
Louisville 75 C3
Lourdes 27 E5
Lower California 79 A2
Lower Hutt 67 E5
Lualaba, River 59 B3
Luanda 61 A1
Lubango 61 A2
Lubeck 29 D2
Lubumbashi 59 B4
Lucknow 45 D2
Lugano 33 B1
Lule, River 21 E2
Lulea 21 E2
Lusaka 61 B2
Luton 23 F5
Luxembourg 25 E5
Luzern 33 B1
Luzon 47 D2
Lviv 37 D3
Lyons 27 G4

M
Maas, River 25 E3
Maastricht 25 D4
Macao 49 E4
Macdonnell Ranges 65 F4
Machu Picchu 85 C4
Mackenzie River 71 F3
Macquarie Island 89 G
Madagascar 61 D3
Madeira 55 B1
Madeira, River 85 D3
Madrid 31 D3
Madras = Chennai 45 D3
Madurai 45 C4
Magadan 41 U3
Magdalena, River 85 C2
Magdeburg 29 D2
Magellan's Strait 87 B5
Mahajanga 61 D2
Maiduguri 57 D1
Main, River 29 D3
Maine 73
Majorca 31 G4
Makasar 47 C4
Makasar Strait 47 C4
Makgadikgadi Salt Pan 61 B3
Malabo 57 C2
Malacca, Straits of 47 B3
Malaga 31 C5
Malawi 61 C2
Malawi, Lake 61 C2
Malay Peninsula 38 P8
Malaysia 47 B3
Maldives 45 C4
Mali 55 C3
Malmo 21 C4
Malta 33 E6
Man, Isle of 23 D3
Manado 47 D3
Managua 79 D3
Manapouri, Lake 67 B7
Manaus 85 D3
Manchester 23 E4
Manchuria 49 F2
Mandalay 47 A1
Manila 47 C2
Manitoba 71 J4
Mannar, Gulf of 45 C4
Mannheim 29 C4
Maputo 61 C3
Maracaibo 85 C1
Margarita 81 F4
Maria van Diemen, Cape 67 C2
Mariana Trench 62 H7
Marie Byrd Land 89 J
Markham, Mount 89 G
Marquesas Islands 63 R9
Marrakesh 55 C1
Marseille 27 G5
Marshall Islands 62 L7
Martinique 81 F4
Maryland 73
Maseru 61 B3
Mashhad 43 E2
Massachusetts 73
Massif Central 27 F4
Matadi 59 A3
Mato Grosso Plateau 85 E4
Matsuyama 51 C4
Maui 72 G1
Mauna Kea 72 G2
Mauna Loa 72 G2
Mauritania 55 B3
Mauritius 53 J7
Mayotte 61 D2
Mbabane 61 C3
Mbandaka 59 A2
Mbeya 59 C3
McKinley, Mount = Denali 73 C2
Mecca 43 C3
Medan 47 A3
Medellin 85 C2
Medicine Hat 71 G5
Medina 43 C3
Mediterranean Sea 19 K7
Mekong, River 47 B2
Melanesia 62 J9
Melbourne 65 J7
Melilla 31 D6
Melville Island (Canada) 71 G2
Melville Islands (Australia) 65 F2
Memphis 75 C3
Mendoza 87 C3
Mentawai Islands 47 A4
Meseta 31 C4
Mesopotamia 43 D2
Messina (Italy) 33 E5
Messina (South Africa) 61 B3
Metz 27 H2
Meuse, River 25 D4
Mexico 79 B2
Mexico City 79 B3
Mexico, Gulf of 79 D2
Miami 75 D4
Michigan 73
Michigan, Lake 75 C2
Micronesia 62 K8
Middlesbrough 23 F3
Midway Island 62 M6
Mikonos 35 D3
Milan 33 B2
Milwaukee 75 B2
Mindanao 47 D3
Minho, River 31 A2
Minneapolis 75 B2
Minnesota 73
Minorca 31 G4
Minsk 37 E2
Mississippi River 75 B3
Mississippi, State 73
Missouri, State 73
Mitchell, Mount 75 C3
Mjosa, Lake 21 C3
Mogadishu 59 D2
Moldova 37 E3
Molokai 72 F1
Molucca Sea 47 D4
Mombasa 59 D3
Monaco 27 H5
Mongolia 49 D2
Mongu 61 B2
Monrovia 57 A2
Mons 25 B4
Montana 73
Montbeliard 27 H3
Montego Bay 81 C3
Montenegro 35 B2
Monterrey 79 B2
Montevideo 87 D3
Montgomery 75 C3
Montpellier 27 F5
Montreal 71 L5
Montserrat 81 F3
Moorea 63 Q10
Morava, River 35 C2
Morena, Sierra 31 C4
Morocco 55 C1
Moscow 41 G3
Moselle, River 27 H2
Moshi 59 C3
Mosul 43 D2
Moulmein 47 A2
Mount Isa 65 G4
Mozambique 61 C2
Mozambique Channel 61 D2
Mulhacen 31 D5
Mulhouse 27 H3
Mull, Island 23 C2
Multan 45 C1
Mumbai 45 C3
Munich 29 D4
Munster 29 B3
Muonio, River 21 E2
Mur, River 29 F5
Murcia 31 E5
Murray, River 65 H6
Murrumbidgee, River 65 J6
Musala 35 C2
Muscat 43 E3
Musgrave Ranges 65 F5
Mutare 61 C2
Mwanza 59 C3
Mweru, Lake 59 B3
Myanmar 47 A1

N
Nafud Desert 43 D3
Nagasaki 51 B4
Nagoya 51 D3
Nagpur 45 D2
Nairobi 59 C3
Namib Desert 61 A3
Namibia 61 A3
Namur 25 C4
Nan Shan Mountains 49 C3
Nanchang 49 E4
Nancy 27 H2
Nanjing 49 E3
Nantes 27 D3
Nao, Cabo de la 31 F4
Napier 67 F4
Naples 33 E4
Nara 51 D4
Narmada, River 45 C2
Narvik 21 D2
Nashville 75 C3
Nassau 81 C1
Nasser, Lake 55 G2
Nauru 62 K9
Naypyidaw 47 A2
Nazare 31 A4
Nazareth 43 M8
Ndjamena 55 E3
Ndola 61 B2
Neagh, Lough 23 C3
Nebraska 73
Negro, River 85 D3
Neisse, River 29 F3
Nelson 67 D5
Nelson, River 71 J4
Nemuro Strait 51 F2
Nepal 45 D2
Netherlands 25 E2
Nevada 73
Nevada, Sierra 31 C5
New Brunswick 71 M5
New Caledonia 62 K11
New Castile 31 C4
New Guinea 62 H9
New Hampshire 73
New Jersey 73
New Mexico 73
New Orleans 75 C4
New Plymouth 67 D4
New Siberian Islands 41 U1
New South Wales 65 J6
New York 75 D2
New York State 73
New Zealand 66–67
Newcastle (Australia) 65 K6
Newcastle-upon-Tyne (UK) 23 F3
Newfoundland 71 N5
Newman 65 C4
Niagara Falls 71 L5
Niamey 55 D3
Nicaragua 79 D3
Nice 27 H5
Nicobar Islands 47 A3
Nicosia 43 J5
Niger 55 D3
Niger, River 57 C1
Nigeria 57 C2
Niigata 51 D3
Nijmegen 25 D3
Nile, River 55 G2
Nimes 27 G5
Nis 35 C2
Nizhniy Novgorod 41 H3
Nome 73 B2
Norfolk 75 D3
Normandy 27 E2
Norrkoping 21 D4
North America 68–69
North Cape 21 E1
North Carolina 73
North Dakota 73
North European Plain 18 L4
North Island, New Zealand 67 E4
North Korea 51 B3
North Macedonia 35 C2
North Magnetic Pole 88 M
North Pole 88
North Sea 18 H3
North West Highlands 23 D2
Northwest Territories 71 H3
Northampton 23 F4
Northern Ireland 23 C3
Northern Territory 65 F3
Norway 21 C3
Norwich 23 G4
Nottingham 23 F4
Nouakchott 55 B3
Nova Scotia 71 M5
Novaya Zemlya 41 J1
Novosibirsk 41 M3
Nullarbor Plain 65 E6
Nunavut 71 K3
Nuremberg 29 D4
Nur-Sultan 41 L3
Nuuk 88 J

O
Oahu 72 E1
Oamaru 67 C7
Ob, River 41 K2
Oban 23 D2
Odense 21 C4
Oder, River 29 F2
Odesa 37 F3
Ogbomosho 57 C2
Ogooue, River 57 D3
Ohio 73
Ohio River 75 C3
Okavango Swamp 61 B2
Okayama 51 C4
Okhotsk, Sea of 41 T3
Oki Islands 51 C3
Oklahoma 73
Oklahoma City 77 D3
Oland 21 D4
Old Castile 31 C3
Oldenburg 29 C2
Omaha 75 B2
Oman 43 E3
Oman, Gulf of 43 E3
Omdurman 55 G3
Omsk 41 L3
Ontario 71 K4
Ontario, Lake 75 D2
Oporto 31 A3
Oran 55 C1
Orange 27 G4
Orange, River 61 A3
Ore Mountains 29 E3
Orebro 21 C4
Oregon 73
Orense 31 B2
Orinoco, River 85 D2
Orizaba, Pico de 79 C3
Orkney Islands 23 E1
Orleans 27 E3
Osaka 51 D4
Oslo 21 B4
Ostend 25 A3
Ostersund 21 D3
Otaru 51 E2
Otranto, Strait of 33 G4
Ottawa 71 L5
Ouagadougou 57 B1
Oulu 21 F3
Oulu, Lake 21 F3
Oviedo 31 C2
Oxford 23 F5

P
Pacific Ocean 62 K6
Padang 47 B4
Padua 33 C2
Pakistan 45 B2
Palau 62 G8
Palawan 47 C2
Palembang 47 B4
Palermo 33 D5
Palm Beach 75 D4
Palma 31 G4
Palmerston North 67 E5
Pampas 87 C3
Pamplona 31 E2
Panama 79 E4
Panama Canal 79 D3
Pantellaria 33 D6
Papua New Guinea 62 H9
Paraguay 87 D2
Paramaribo 85 E2
Parana River 87 D2
Paris 27 F2
Parma 33 C2
Patagonia 87 C4
Patrai 35 C3
Pau 27 D5
Peace River 71 G4
Pegasus Bay 67 D6
Peking = Beijing 49 E2
Pemba 59 C3
Pennines 23 E3
Pennsylvania 73
Penzance 23 D5
Perm 41 J3
Perpignan 27 F6
Persian Gulf, The 43 E3
Perth (Australia) 65 C6
Perth (UK) 23 E2
Peru 85 C4
Perugia 33 D3
Pescara 33 E3
Philadelphia 75 D3
Philippines 47 C2
Phnom Penh 47 B2
Phoenix 77 B3
Phoenix Islands 62 M9
Picardy 27 F2
Pietermaritzberg 61 C3
Pilatus, Mount 33 B1
Pindus Mountains 35 C3
Pisa 33 C3
Pitcairn Island 63 S11
Pittsburgh 75 C2
Plata, Rio de la 87 D3
Plenty, Bay of 67 F3
Ploiesti 35 D2
Plovdiv 35 D2
Plymouth 23 D5
Po, River 33 C2
Podgorica 35 B2
Pohang 51 B3
Pointe-Noire 59 A3
Poitiers 27 E3
Poland 37 C2
Polar Plateau 89 C
Polynesia 63 N8
Pontianak 47 B4
Poopo, Lake 85 D4
Port Harcourt 57 C2
Port of Spain 81 F4
Port Pirie 65 G6
Port Said 55 G1
Port Sudan 55 G3
Port Talbot 23 E5
Port-au-Prince 81 D3
Portland 77 A2
Porto Alegre 85 F5
Porto-Novo 57 C2
Portsmouth 23 F5
Portugal 31 B4
Potsdam 29 E2
Prague 37 B2
Prairies 70
Pretoria 61 B3
Prince Edward Island 71 M5
Prince George 71 F4
Prince Rupert 71 F4
Pripet, River 37 E2
Pristina 35 C2
Provence 27 G5
Providence 75 D2
Prudhoe Bay 73 C2
Prut, River 35 D1
Prydz Bay 89 D
Puebla 79 C3
Pueblo 77 C3
Puerto Rico 81 E3
Pune 45 C3
Punta Arenas 87 B5
Pyongyang 51 B3
Pyrenees 31 F2

Q
Qatar 43 E3
Qingdao 49 F3
Qiqihar 49 F2
Quebec 71 L5
Queen Elizabeth Islands 71 J2
Queen Maud Land 89 B
Queensland 65 H4
Queenstown 67 B7
Quetta 45 B1
Quezon City 47 D2
Quimper 27 B2
Quito 85 C3

R
Rabat 55 C1
Race, Cape 71 N5
Ravenna 33 D2
Rawalpindi 45 C1
Reading 23 F5
Recife 85 G3
Red Sea 43 C3
Red, River (USA) 75 B3
Red, River (Vietnam) 47 B1
Regensburg 29 E4
Reggio 33 E5
Regina 71 H4
Reims 27 G2
Reindeer Lake 71 H4
Rennes 27 D2
Reno 77 B3
Réunion 53 J8
Revilla Gigedo Islands 79 A3
Reykjavik 21 H2
Rhine, River 29 B3
Rhode Island 73
Rhodes 35 D3
Rhodope 35 C2
Rhone, River 27 G4
Richmond 75 D3
Riga 37 D1
Rimini 33 D2
Rio de Janeiro 85 F5
Rio Grande, River 77 D4
Rio Muni 57 D2
Riviera 33 B2
Riyadh 43 D3
Rockhampton 65 K4
Rocky Mountains 68 H4
Romania 35 C1
Rome 33 D4
Ronne Ice Shelf 89 L
Rosa, Monte 33 B2
Rosario 87 C3
Ross Ice Shelf 89 H

Ross Sea 89 H
Rostock 29 E1
Rostov 41 G4
Rotorua 67 F4
Rotterdam 25 C3
Rouen 27 E2
Rub 'al Khali 43 D4
Rugen 29 F1
Ruhr, River 29 B3
Ruse 35 D2
Russia 41 L2
Rwanda 59 C3
Ryukyu Islands 38 R6

S

Saarbrucken 29 B4
Saaremaa 37 D1
Sabah 47 C3
Sable, Cape (Canada) 71 M5
Sable, Cape (USA) 75 C4
Sacramento 77 A3
Sado 51 D3
Sahara 55 D2
Sahel 52 C4
Saimaa, Lake 21 F3
Saint Etienne 27 G4
Saint Gallen 33 B1
Saint George's Channel 23 C5
Saint Gotthard tunnel 33 B1
Saint Helena 52 C7
Saint John 71 M5
Saint John's 71 N5
Saint Kitts & Nevis 81 F3
Saint Lawrence, River 71 M5
Saint Louis 75 B3
Saint Lucia 81 F4
Saint Malo 27 C2
Saint Nazaire 27 C3
Saint Paul 75 B2
Saint Petersburg 41 G3
Saint Pierre & Miquelon 71 N5
Saint Vincent & the Grenadines 81 F4
Sakai 51 D4
Sakhalin 41 T3
Salamanca 31 C3
Salerno 33 E4
Salt Lake City 77 B2
Salvador 85 G4
Salween, River 47 A2
Salzburg 29 E5
Samara 41 J3
Samoa 62 M10
San Antonio 75 B4
San Diego 77 B3
San Francisco 77 A3
San Jose (Costa Rica) 79 D3
San Jose (USA) 77 A3
San Juan 81 E3
San Lucas, Cape 79 A2
San Marino 33 C3
San Salvador 79 C3
San Sebastian 31 E2
San'a 43 D4
Santa Fe 87 D3
Santander 31 D2
Santarem 31 A4
Santiago (Chile) 87 B3
Santiago (Dominican Republic) 81 D3
Santiago de Cuba 81 C3
Santo Domingo 81 E3
Sao Francisco, River 85 F4
Sao Paulo 85 F5
São Tomé & Príncipe 57 C2
Saone, River 27 G3
Sapporo 51 E2
Sarajevo 35 B2
Sarawak 47 C3
Sardinia 33 B4
Sarh 55 E4
Saskatchewan 71 H4
Saskatoon 71 H4
Sassari 33 B4
Saudi Arabia 43 D3
Sault Sainte Marie 71 K5
Sayan Mountains 41 N3
Scandinavia 18 K2
Schelde, River 25 C3
Schwerin 29 D2
Scilly, Isles of 23 C6
Scotland 23 D2
Seattle 77 A2
Segura, River 31 E4
Seine, River 27 F2
Selvas 82 D3
Semarang 47 C4
Sendai 51 E3
Senegal 57 A1
Senegal, River 55 B3
Seoul 51 B3
Serbia 35 C2
Sevastopol 37 F4
Severn, River 23 E4
Severnaya Zemlya 88 D
Seville 31 B5
Sfax 55 E1
Shanghai 49 F3
Shannon, River 23 B4
Sheffield 23 F4
Shenyang 49 F2
Shetland Islands 23 G1
Shibeli, River 59 D2
Shikoku 51 C4
Shiraz 43 E3
Siberia 41 N2
Sicily 33 D6
Sidra, Gulf of 55 E1
Siena 33 C3
Sierra Leone 57 A2
Sierra Madre 79 B2
Sierra Nevada 77 B3
Sikhote Alin Range 41 S4
Sinai 52 G3
Singapore 47 B3
Sinuiju 51 A2
Sioux Falls 75 B2
Siracusa 33 E6
Sjaelland 21 C4
Skagerrak 21 B4
Skopje 35 C2
Skovorodino 41 R3
Skye, Island 23 C2
Slovak Republic 37 C3
Slovenia 35 A1
Snake River 77 B2
Snowdon 23 D4
Society Islands 63 P10
Socotra 43 E4
Sofia 35 C2
Sogne Fjord 21 B3
Solomon Islands 62 K9
Somali Republic 59 D2
Somerset Islands 71 J2
Songhua Jiang, River 49 G2
Sorano 33 C3
South Africa 61 B3
South America 82–83
South Australia 65 G5
South Carolina 73
South China Sea 47 C2
South Dakota 73
South Georgia 89 M
South Island, New Zealand 67 C6
South Korea 51 B3
South Magnetic Pole 89 F
South Orkney Islands 89 M
South Pole 89
South Sandwich Islands 89 A
South Shetland Islands 89 M
South Sudan 55 F4
Southampton 23 F5
Southampton Island 71 K3
Southern Alps 67 C6
Southern Ocean 65 D7
Southern Uplands 23 D3
Spain 31 C4
Spenser Mountains 67 D6
Spiez 33 A1
Split 35 B2
Spokane 77 B2
Sri Lanka 45 D4
Srinagar 45 C1
Stanley 87 D5
Stanovoy Range 41 R3
Stavanger 21 B4
Stewart Island 67 A8
Stockholm 21 D4
Stoke-on-Trent 23 E4
Storsjon 21 C3
Strasbourg 27 H2
Stuttgart 29 C4
Sucre 85 D4
Sudan 55 F3
Sudbury 71 K5
Suez 55 G2
Sulawesi 47 D4
Sulu Islands 47 D3
Sulu Sea 47 D3
Sumatra 47 B4
Sumbawa 47 C4
Sunda Islands 47 C4
Sunderland 23 F3
Sundsvall 21 D3
Superior, Lake 75 C2
Surabaya 47 C4
Surat 45 C2
Suriname 85 E2
Surtsey 21 H2
Svalbard 88 G
Sverdrup Islands 71 H2
Swansea 23 D5
Sweden 21 D3
Switzerland 33 B1
Sydney 65 K6
Syria 43 C2
Syrian Desert 43 C2

T

Ta'izz 43 D4
Tabora 59 C3
Tabriz 43 D2
Tagus, River 31 A4
Tahiti 63 Q10
Tainaron, Cape 35 C3
Taipei 49 F4
Taiwan 49 F4
Taiyuan 49 E3
Tajikistan 41 L5
Takla Makan Mountains 49 B3
Tallinn 37 D1
Tampa 75 C4
Tampere 21 E3
Tana, Lake 59 C1
Tana, River (Kenya) 59 C2
Tana, River (Norway) 21 F2
Tanami Desert 65 F3
Tanega Island 51 C4
Tanga 59 C3
Tanganyika, Lake 59 C3
Tangier 55 C1
Tangshan 49 E3
Tanzania 59 C3
Tapajos, River 85 E3
Taranaki, Mount 67 E4
Taranto 33 F4
Tarim He, River 49 B2
Tarragona 31 F3
Tashkent 41 K4
Tasman Bay 67 D5
Tasmania 65 H8
Tatra Mountains 37 C3
Taupo, Lake 67 E4
Taurus Mountains 43 C2
Taymyr Peninsula 41 P1
Tbilisi 41 H4
Te Anau, Lake 67 B7
Tegucigalpa 79 D3
Tehran 43 E2
Tel Aviv-Jaffa 43 L8
Tema 57 C2
Tennessee 73
Tennessee River 75 C3
Terni 33 D3
Texas 73
Thabana Ntlenyana 61 C3
Thailand 47 B2
Thailand, Gulf of 47 B3
Thames, River 23 F5
Thessaloniki 35 C2
Thimphu 45 D2
Thionville 27 H2
Thule 88 K
Thunder Bay 71 K5
Tian Shan Mountains 49 B2
Tianjin 49 E3
Tiber, River 33 D3
Tibesti 55 E2
Tibet 49 B3
Tierra del Fuego 87 C5
Tigris, River 43 D2
Tijuana 79 A1
Tilburg 25 D3
Timaru 67 C7
Timbuktu 55 C3
Timisoara 35 C1
Timor-Leste 47 D4
Timor Sea 65 D2
Tirane 35 B2
Tirol 29 D6
Titicaca, Lake 85 D4
Togo 57 C2
Tokelau Islands 62 M9
Tokyo 51 D3
Toledo (Spain) 31 D4
Toledo (USA) 75 C2
Toliara 61 D3
Tone, River 51 D3
Tonga 62 M11
Toowoomba 65 K5
Torne, River 21 E2
Toronto 71 L5
Torrens, Lake 65 G6
Torreon 79 B2
Torres Strait 65 H1
Toubkal 55 C1
Toulon 27 G5
Toulouse 27 E5
Tours 27 E3
Townsville 65 J3
Toyama 51 D3
Transylvanian Alps 35 C1
Trent, River 23 F4
Trieste 33 D2
Trinidad & Tobago 81 G4
Tripoli 55 E1
Tromso 21 D2
Trondheim 21 C3
Troyes 27 G2
Trujillo 85 C3
Tsangpo, River 49 B4
Tsugaru, Strait 51 E2
Tsushima 51 B4
Tuamotu Archipelago 63 R10
Tubuai Islands 63 P11
Tucson 77 B3
Tucuman 87 C2
Tulsa 75 B3
Tunis 55 E1
Tunisia 55 D1
Turin 33 B2
Turkana, Lake 59 C2
Turkey 43 C2
Turkmenistan 41 J5
Turks Islands 81 D2
Turku 21 E3
Tuvalu 62 L9
Tyrrhenian Sea 33 D5

U

Ubangi, River 59 A2
Udine 33 D1
Uganda 59 C2
Ukraine 37 F3
Ulan Bator 49 D2
Ulan Ude 41 P3
Ulsan 51 B3
Uluru = Ayers Rock 65 F5
Ume, River 21 D3
United Arab Emirates 43 E3
United Kingdom 23 G4
United States of America 72
Uppsala 21 D4
Ural Mountains 41 J3
Ural, River 41 J4
Urmia, Lake 43 D2
Uruguay 87 D3
Ürümqi 49 B2
Ushant 27 B2
Utah 73
Utrecht 25 D2
Uzbekistan 41 K4

V

Vaal, River 61 B3
Vaasa 21 E3
Valence 27 G4
Valencia 31 E4
Valenciennes 27 F1
Valladolid 31 C3
Valletta 33 E6
Valparaiso 87 B3
Van, Lake 43 D2
Vancouver 71 F5
Vancouver Island 71 F5
Vaner, Lake 21 C4
Vantaa 21 E3
Vanuatu 62 K10
Varanasi 45 D2
Vardo 21 G1
Varna 35 D2
Vasteras 21 D4
Vatican City 33 C4
Vatnajokull 21 J2
Vatter, Lake 21 C4
Venezuela 85 D2
Venice 33 D2
Verkhoyansk Range 41 R2
Vermont 73
Verona 33 C2
Versailles 27 F2
Vesteralen 21 C2
Vesuvius 33 E4
Victoria (Australia) 65 H7
Victoria (Canada) 71 F5
Victoria Falls 61 B2
Victoria Island 71 G2
Victoria Land 89 G
Victoria, Lake 59 C3
Vienna 29 F4
Vientiane 47 B2
Vietnam 47 B2
Vigo 31 A2
Vilnius 37 E2
Virgin Islands 81 F3
Virginia 73
Viscount Melville Sound 71 H2
Vishakhapatnam 45 D3
Vistula, River 37 D2
Vitoria 31 D2
Vladivostok 41 S4
Volga, River 41 H3
Volgograd 41 H4
Volos 35 C3
Volta, Lake 57 B2
Vosges 27 H2

W

Waal, River 25 D3
Wadden Zee 25 D1
Wadi Halfa 55 G2
Waikato, River 67 E4
Waitaki, River 67 C7
Wake Island 62 K7
Wakkanai 51 E1
Walcheren Island 25 B3
Wales 23 E4
Walvis Bay 61 A3
Wanaka, Lake 67 B7
Wanganui 67 E4
Warrego, River 65 J5
Warsaw 37 D2
Wasatch Range 77 B3
Wash, The 23 G4
Washington 75 D3
Washington, State 73
Waterford 23 C4
Weddell Sea 89 M
Weipa 65 H2
Wellington 67 E5
Weser, River 29 C2
West Bank 43 M8
West Indies 80–81
West Virginia 73
Western Australia 65 D5
Western Ghats 45 C3
Western Sahara 55 B2
Westland Bight 67 B6
Wexford 23 C4
Whangarei 67 E2
White Nile 55 G4
White Sea 41 G2
Whitehorse 71 E3
Whitney, Mount 77 B3
Whyalla 65 G6
Wichita 75 B3
Wick 23 E1
Wicklow Mountains 23 C4
Wiesbaden 29 C3
Wight, Isle of 23 F5
Wilkes Land 89 F
Windhoek 61 A3
Windsor 71 K5
Windward Passage 81 D3
Winnipeg 71 J5
Winnipeg, Lake 71 J4
Winterthur 33 B1
Wisconsin 73
Wollongong 65 K6
Wonsan 51 B3
Worcester 23 E4
Wrangel Island 41 W1
Wroclaw 37 C2
Wuhan 49 E3
Wurzburg 29 D4
Wye, River 23 E4
Wyndham 65 E3
Wyoming 73

X

Xi Jiang, River 49 D4
Xian 49 D3

Y

Yakutsk 41 R2
Yamoussoukro 57 B2
Yangon 47 A2
Yangtze = Chang Jiang, River 49 E3
Yaounde 57 D2
Yekaterinburg 41 K3
Yellow Sea 49 F3
Yellowknife 71 G3
Yellowstone, River 77 C2
Yemen 43 D4
Yenisey, River 41 M2
Yerevan 41 H4
Yokohama 51 D3
York 23 F4
York, Cape 65 H2
Yucatan 79 D3
Yukon 71 E3
Yukon, River 73 C2

Z

Zagreb 35 B1
Zagros Mountains 43 E2
Zambezi, River 61 C2
Zambia 61 B2
Zamboanga 47 D3
Zanzibar 59 C3
Zaragoza 31 E3
Zaria 57 C1
Zeebrugge 25 B3
Zhengzhou 49 E3
Zimbabwe 61 B2
Zurich 33 B1
Zwolle 25 E2

GLOSSARY

Arable farming – growing crops.

Border – the line along which two countries meet. Country borders are shown by red lines on all the maps in this atlas (see p. 16).

Canal – a man-made waterway that allows boats to travel from one ocean or place to another (examples on pp. 32, 34, 54, 79).

Canyon – a deep, steep-sided valley, usually cut by a river in a desert area. The most famous is the Grand Canyon (p. 76). A small canyon is called a gorge (examples on pp. 28, 34).

Capital city – the city where the government of a country meets. Every capital city is underlined on the maps in this atlas (explained on p. 16).

Continent – a very large land-mass. Of the 7 continents (pp. 2, 6-7) only Australia and Antarctica are not divided into countries.

Coral – tiny creatures which live in the sea. When they die, their shells join together to make coral reefs (p. 64) and islands (p. 62).

Core – the inner part of the Earth (p. 4).

Crops – plants grown for people or animals. There are many examples in this atlas: fruit and vegetables (pp. 34, 56, 66); rice (pp. 45, 46); wheat (p. 76); tea (pp. 44,50); oil-palm (p. 57).

Crust – the outer layer of the Earth (p. 4).

Delta – an area where mud and sand are dumped at the mouth of some rivers. Deltas occur where the river dumps more sand and mud than currents in the sea or lake can carry away. The River Nile has a large delta (p. 55) and so does the Mississippi (p.75). The name comes from the 4th letter of the Greek alphabet - find its shape on p. 35.

Desert – a large dry area where very little grows (pp. 14-15). The Sahara is the largest desert (pp. 11, 55); the Atacama is the driest (see the map on p.87).

Earthquake – a sudden movement in the Earth's crust causes shock waves which make the Earth's surface shake. Earthquakes are recorded on a seismograph.

Exports – the products of a country which are sold to other countries. They may be crops (p. 66); animals or meat; wood or minerals; or goods produced in factories or workshops.

Fjord – a long, steep-sided inlet of the sea. Once it was a valley eroded by a glacier, but after the glacier melted, the valley was drowned when the sea level rose. There are beautiful fjords in Norway (p. 20), New Zealand and Chile.

Geothermal power – electricity is made from steam which rises from the ground in some volcanic areas (p. 67).

Geyser – a hot spring which throws out a jet of hot water. Geysers are found in volcanic areas where the water is heated underground (pp. 67, 86).

Glacier – a mass of ice which flows downhill very slowly along a valley. As it moves, it makes the valley deeper and straighter. (p. 45 and the satellite image on p. 5).

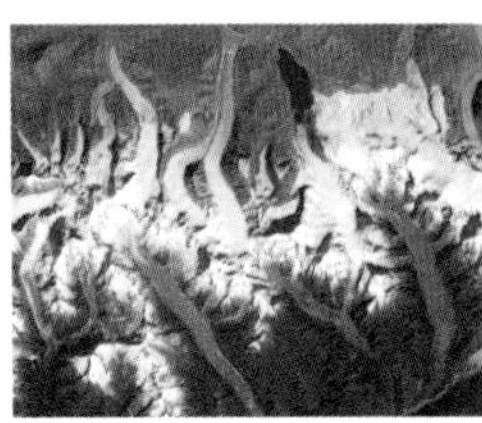

Hurricane – a severe storm with very strong winds (up to 340 km per hour!) which cause a lot of damage (p. 81). Heavy rain and high tides may cause flooding, too. The same kind of storm is also called a cyclone or typhoon.

Hydro-electric power – electricity is made by water rushing through turbines in a power station. The water may come from a waterfall – as at the Niagara Falls (p. 70) – or from behind a man-made dam (p. 22).

Ice Age – a time in the Earth's history when the climate was much colder than today and ice spread over large areas of the world. Rocks we see today may have been shaped by ice during the last Ice Age (p. 23).

Iceberg – lump of floating ice, most of which is underwater. It may be small or really big (pp. 19, 88).

Ice-sheet – a huge, thick area of ice which is slowly moving outwards. The largest ice-sheet covers Antarctica (p. 89).

Irrigation – watering the land to help crops grow when the weather is dry. Often, people dig channels from a lake or river to the edge of fields. When they want to water the field, they make gaps to let the water flow over the land (p. 45).

Jungle, or rainforest – thick forest with large trees in hot, wet parts of the world near the Equator (see map p. 15 and pp. 13, 84).

Lake – an area of water that is surrounded by land. Find examples on pp. 5, 14, 20, 29, 40, 74, 75, 82.

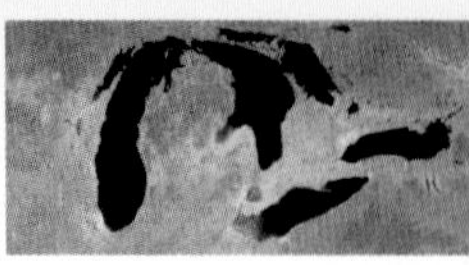

Land-locked countries – countries that do not have any coastline or ports. This makes it more difficult and expensive to send exports or get imports from other countries (pp. 37, 60, 87).

Marshland – land that is wet and soggy because the water on it cannot drain away (pp. 22, 88).

Minerals – rocks which are mined or quarried and used in different kinds of industry. Iron ore, gold and bauxite (for aluminium) are examples.

Monsoon – explained on p. 45.

Oasis – an area in a desert with water at or near the surface. People can live there and use the water from springs or wells to grow crops or keep animals (p. 54).

Ocean – a huge area of sea-water covering a large part of the Earth's surface (p. 6-7). The largest is the Pacific (pp. 62-63).

Pasture – grass grown or used for feeding animals (pp. 19, 66, 85).

Peninsula – an area of land almost completely surrounded by water, but joined to the mainland at one point.

Plain – an area of low land with a fairly level surface, though there may be some low hills. It is (or was) often grassland (pp. 6, 18, 70).

Plantation – a very large farm where only one crop is grown. This is sold for export or to be used in factories. For example, tea (pp. 44, 50) and oil-palm (p. 56).

Plateau – an area of high land with a fairly level surface. Some plateaus are divided by deep valleys (pp. 30, 38, 49, 78).

Polar – to do with the area near the North or South Poles, inside the Arctic or Antarctic Circles (pp. 12, 88–89).

Population – the number of people in a country or city or area of the world (p. 20).

Port – a town or city at or near the sea or on a navigable river where ships can tie up to load or unload goods (pp. 24, 49, 70, 87).

Savanna – tropical grassland, often with some scattered trees. The weather is hot all year but there is a wet season when the tall grass is green and good for the animals to eat, and a dry season when the grass turns brown and dry (pp. 14-15, 58).

Season – a time of the year with distinct weather. People in temperate lands talk about hot and cold seasons (summer and winter). People in many tropical areas talk about wet and dry seasons. The reason for seasons is explained on p. 12.

Semi-desert – an area that is mainly dry, but small amounts of rain allow some plants to grow.

Temperate lands – parts of the world between the tropics and the polar areas which have a cold season (winter) and a hot season (summer) (see p. 12).

Terraces – wide steps cut into a hillside to make flat land for farming (p. 46). They also stop soil erosion.

Tropical areas – parts of the world between the Tropic of Cancer and the Tropic of Capricorn. Here the climate is hot, and the sun is overhead at midday twice each year (explained on pp. 12-13).

Tsunami – a huge wave caused by an earthquake under the bed of the sea (mentioned on pp. 4, 38, 50).

Tundra – an area around the Arctic Circle where it is too cold for trees to grow. Lichens and small plants grow, but deep down the soil is frozen even in summer (pp. 14, 20, 88).

Valley – a low area between mountains or hills which has been made by a river or glacier (pp. 22, 45).

Volcano – a mountain or hill made of lava and ash that has come from inside the Earth's crust. Active volcanoes are still sending out lava, ash and gases (pp. 5, 21, 33, 50, 72). Those that are no longer active are called 'dormant' (meaning 'sleeping') or extinct (p. 59).

Waterfall – the place where a river falls over a layer of hard rocks. Famous waterfalls are the Victoria Falls (p. 60) and the Niagara Falls (p. 70).

ANSWERS TO QUESTIONS

Page 4 Atlantic Ocean; Indian Ocean; South America; Brazil.

Page 6 Vicuña in the Andes of Argentina, South America.

Page 18 Brussels, Belgium: it is the headquarters of the European Union.

Page 22 The London landmarks featured on the stamp are *(from left to right)*: Westminster Abbey; Nelson's Column (in Trafalgar Square); statue of Eros (in Piccadilly Circus); Telecom Tower; clock tower of the Houses of Parliament (containing the bell Big Ben); St Paul's Cathedral; Tower Bridge; White Tower of the Tower of London.

Page 24 Left coin: Belgium (King). Centre: Luxembourg (Grand Duke). Right: Netherlands (Queen Beatrix).

Page 24 The yellow objects are Gouda CHEESES.

Page 33 The brown smoke is from Mount Etna, an active volcano, which you can find on the map.

Pages 38–39 The script reads across the two pages:
1 Australia;
2 Egypt;
3 Hong Kong;
4 United States;
5 Taiwan.

Page 39 The five countries which share the shoreline of the Caspian Sea are Russia, Kazakhstan, Turkmenistan, Iran and Azerbaijan.

Page 40 The 15 'new' countries formed at the break-up of the USSR are (from largest to smallest): Russia, Kazakhstan, Ukraine, Turkmenistan, Uzbekistan, Belarus, Kyrgyzstan, Tajikistan, Azerbaijan, Georgia, Lithuania, Latvia, Estonia, Moldova and Armenia.

Page 41 Khabarovsk is on the River Amur. Moskva (= *Moscow*) to Vladivostok.

Page 44 Clockwise (from the top right-hand corner): samosas, ground coriander, coriander leaves, cumin, pakoras, rice, poppadums, red chilli powder next to yellow turmeric powder, green okra (also called 'ladies fingers'), garlic and bay leaves.

Page 50 These decorations are lanterns, made out of paper.

Page 65 Australia, of course!

Page 68 The north shores of Lakes Superior, Huron, Erie and Ontario are in Canada, and the south shores are in the USA. Lake Michigan is entirely in the USA.

Page 69 El Salvador only has a coastline on the Pacific Ocean. Belize only has a coastline on the Caribbean Sea. (Honduras has a tiny coastline on the Pacific – look closely at the map!) One island has two countries on it: Haiti and the Dominican Republic.

Page 73 Seattle to Miami is 5445 kilometres; New Orleans to Chicago is 1488 kilometres.

Page 76 The Spanish words mean: Amarillo = Yellow; Colorado = Coloured; El Paso = The pass; Los Angeles = The angels; San José = St Joseph; San Francisco = St Francis.

Page 81 Aruba and Curaçao are part of the Netherlands; Turks Is, Caicos I., Grand Cayman, Anguilla and Montserrat are owned by the UK. The islands of Guadeloupe and Martinique are both part of France. Some of the Virgin Islands belong to the UK, and some belong to the USA. The island of Hispaniola is shared by Haiti and the Dominican Republic.

QUIZ ANSWERS *(on pages 90–91)*

NAME THE COUNTRY
1 Norway (Europe)
2 Thailand (Asia)
3 Mozambique (Africa)
4 Mexico (Central America)
5 Chile (South America)

NAME THE ISLAND
1 Iceland
2 Crete (Greece)
3 Sicily (Italy)
4 Sumatra (Indonesia)
5 Sulawesi (Indonesia)
6 Cuba
7 Honshu (Japan)
8 Baffin Island (Canada)
9 Madagascar
10 North Island (New Zealand)

A MYSTERY MESSAGE
I was *hungry*, so I bought a large *turkey*, some *swedes* and a bottle of *port*. Finally, I ate an *ice*-cream. I enjoyed my *meal*, but afterwards I began to *bulge* and I got a bad *pain*. A man told me: 'Just eat *pine*apples and *egg* cooked in a *pan*. Tomorrow you can eat a *banana* and some *Brazil* nuts. It shouldn't *cost* you too much.' I said: 'You must be *mad*! I think I've got *malaria*. I'll have *to go* to a doctor quickly, otherwise I'll soon be *dead*.'

Happily, the doctor *cured* me, so I am still *alive* today!

GREAT RIVERS OF EUROPE
1 Danube; **2** Rhine;
3 Rhône; **4** Severn; **5** Tagus.

PLACES IN ASIA
Countries
Iran; China; Oman; Taiwan; Nepal.
Capital cities
Manila; Riyadh; Tashkent; Kabul; Colombo.

COLOUR QUIZ
1 Red (Red Sea/Red River)
2 Green (Greenland/Green Bay)
3 Black (Black Sea/Black Forest)
4 Yellow (Yellow Sea/Yellowstone River)
5 White (White Sea/White Nile)
6 Orange (Orange/Orange River)
7 Blue (Blue Nile/Blue Ridge)

STATES OF THE USA
1 Texas
2 Rhode Island
3 Minnesota
4 Florida
5 Washington
6 Maine
7 Michigan
8 Maryland
9 Wyoming and Colorado
10 Oklahoma
11 Michigan
12 New York
13 Utah
14 Louisiana
15 South Dakota
16 North Carolina
17 Utah, Colorado, Arizona and New Mexico
18 Four (California, Arizona, New Mexico and Texas)
19 Three (Washington, Oregon and California)
20 Five (Texas, Louisiana, Mississippi, Alabama and Florida)

OCEANS AND SEAS
1 Pacific; **2** Atlantic;
3 Arctic; **4** Indian;
5 Atlantic;
6 Red Sea;
7 Sea of Japan;
8 North Sea;
9 South China Sea;
10 Caribbean Sea.

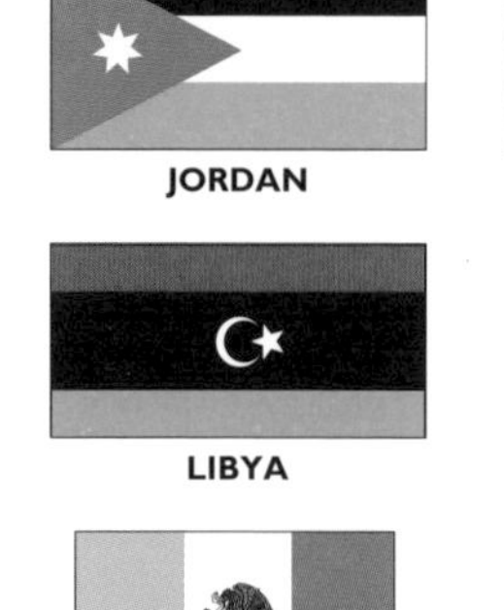

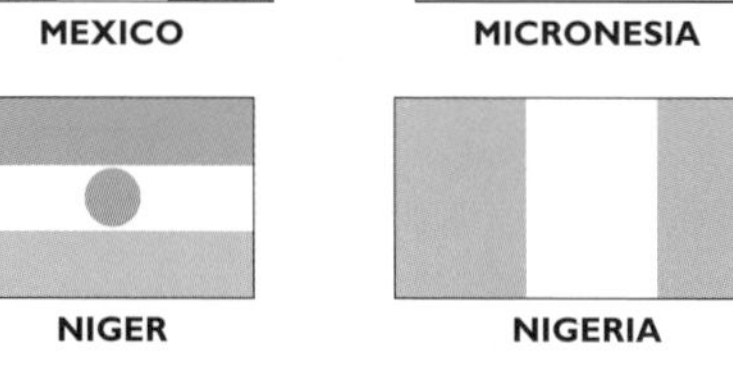
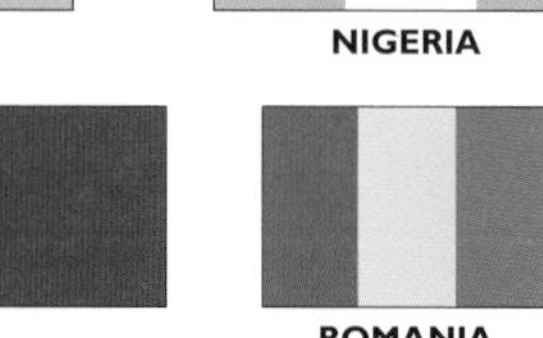

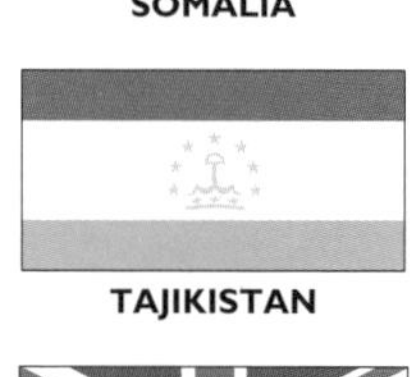

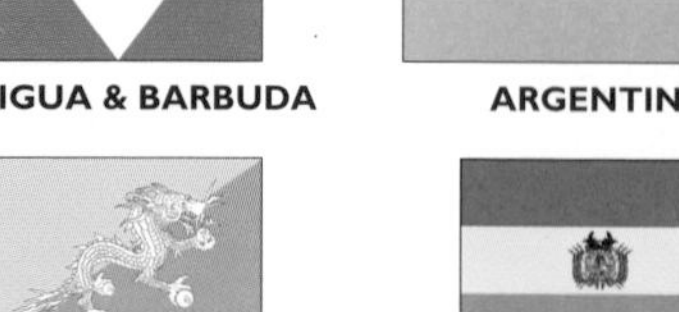
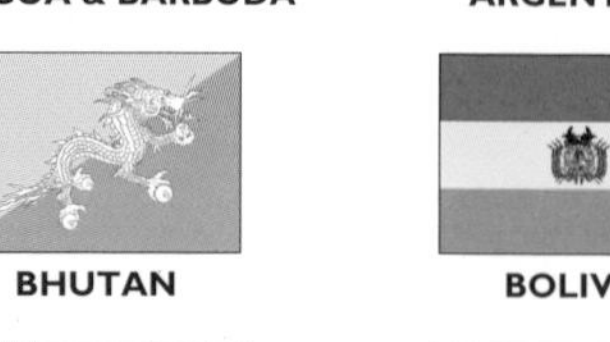
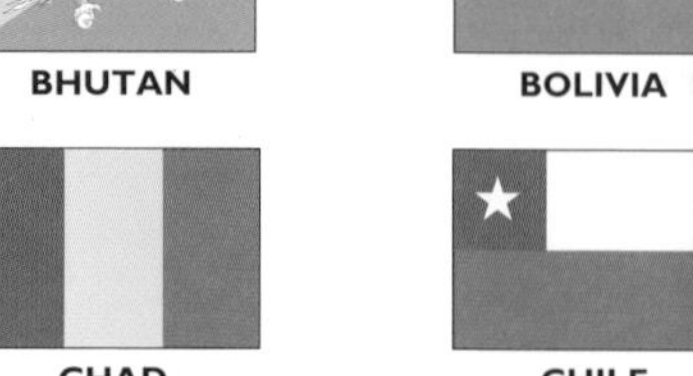
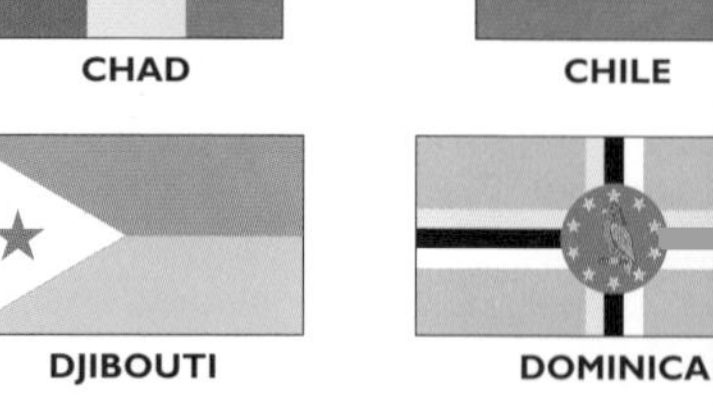
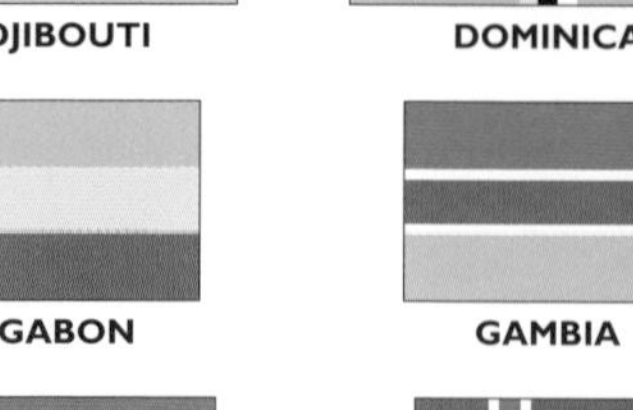
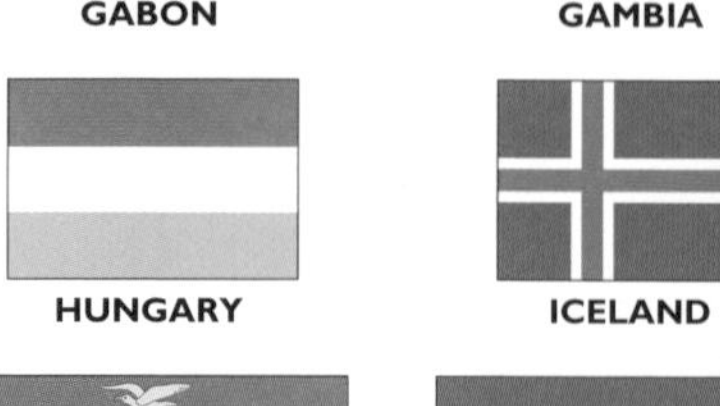

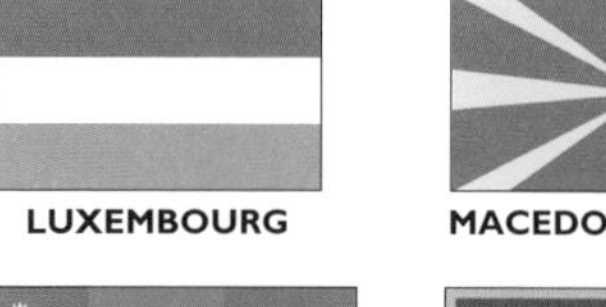
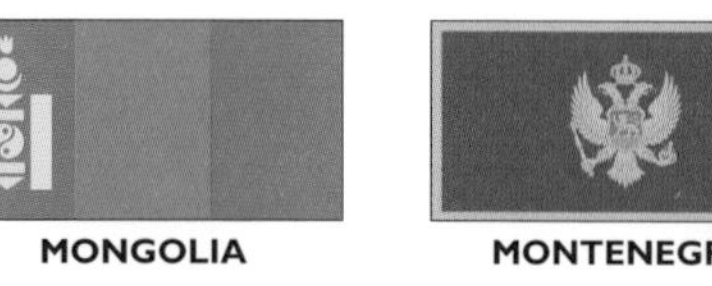
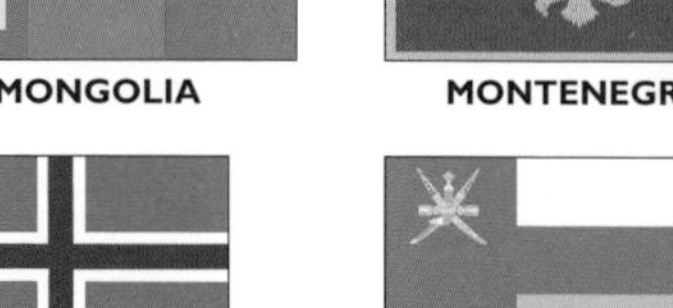
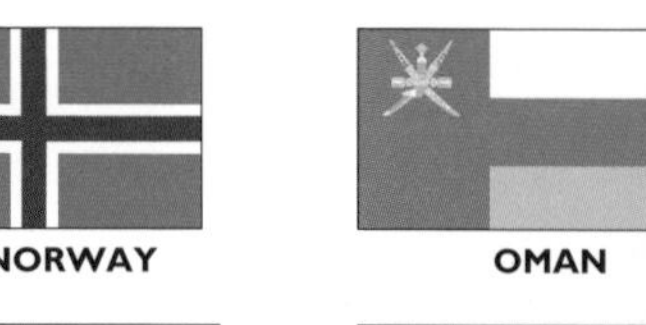

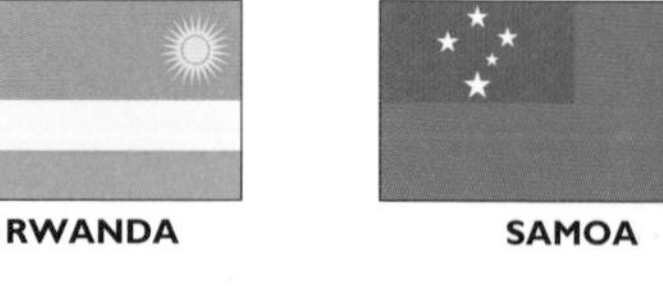
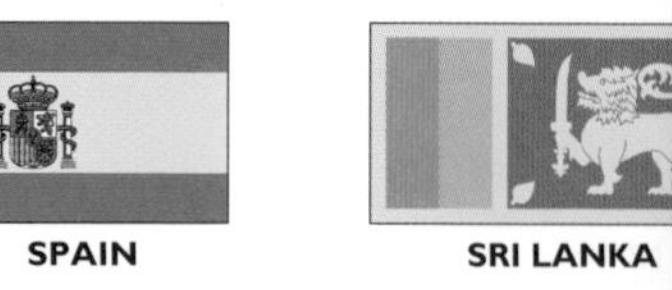
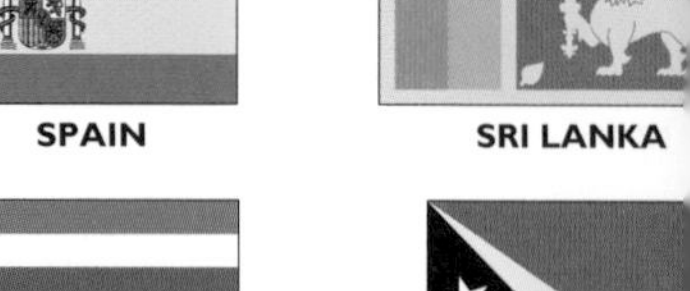
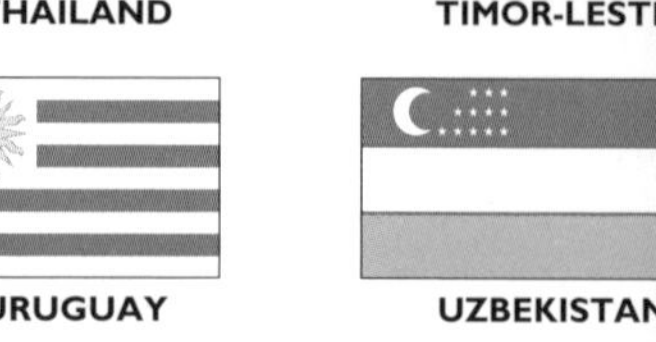

AFGHANISTAN ALBANIA ALGERIA ANDORRA ANGOLA ANTIGUA & BARBUDA ARGENTINA

BARBADOS BELARUS BELGIUM BELIZE BENIN BHUTAN BOLIVIA

CABO VERDE CAMBODIA CAMEROON CANADA CENTRAL AFRICAN REP. CHAD CHILE

CROATIA CUBA CYPRUS CZECHIA DENMARK DJIBOUTI DOMINICA

ESWATINI ETHIOPIA FIJI ISLANDS FINLAND FRANCE GABON GAMBIA

GUINEA GUINEA-BISSAU GUYANA HAITI HONDURAS HUNGARY ICELAND

JAMAICA JAPAN JORDAN KAZAKHSTAN KENYA KIRIBATI KOREA, NORT

LESOTHO LIBERIA LIBYA LIECHTENSTEIN LITHUANIA LUXEMBOURG MACEDONIA, NO

MAURITANIA MAURITIUS MEXICO MICRONESIA MOLDOVA MONGOLIA MONTENEGR

NEW ZEALAND NICARAGUA NIGER NIGERIA NORTHERN MARIANAS NORWAY OMAN

PORTUGAL PUERTO RICO QATAR ROMANIA RUSSIA RWANDA SAMOA

SLOVAKIA SLOVENIA SOLOMON ISLANDS SOMALIA SOUTH AFRICA SPAIN SRI LANKA

SWITZERLAND SYRIA TAIWAN TAJIKISTAN TANZANIA THAILAND TIMOR-LESTE

UGANDA UKRAINE UNITED ARAB EMIRATES UNITED KINGDOM UNITED STATES URUGUAY UZBEKISTAN